SURFING ECONOMICS

SURFING ECONOMICS

Essays for the Inquiring Economist

HUW DAVID DIXON

palgrave

First published 2001 by
PALGRAVE
Houndmills, Basingstoke, Hampshire RG21 6XS and
175 Fifth Avenue, New York, N.Y. 10010
Companies and representatives throughout the world

PALGRAVE is the new global academic imprint of
St. Martin's Press LLC Scholarly and Reference Division and
Palgrave Publisher Ltd (formerly Macmillan Press Ltd).

ISBN 0–333–76061–1 hardback

This book is printed on paper suitable for recycling and
made from fully managed and sustained forest sources.

A catalogue record for this book is available
from the British Library.

Library of Congress Cataloging-in-Publication Data

Dixon, Huw David.
    Surfing economics : essays for the inquiring economist / Huw David
    Dixon
        p. cm.
    Includes bibliographical references and index.
    ISBN 0–333–76061–1
        1. Economics. I. Title.

HB171 .D639 2000
330—dc21   00-052456

Printed in Great Britain by
Antony Rowe Ltd, Chippenham, Wiltshire

This book is dedicated to Carol, Clare and Adam

Contents

Preface

Economics is a social process. Economics is taught in schools and universities; economic research is written, some of it published in books and learned journals; in the public and private sectors economists advise on a variety of issues (sometimes giving good advice, sometimes bad!); economics graduates go on to prosper in a variety of professions, the ideas they have learned influencing the way they think; economic ideas, often in distorted caricatures, circulate around society in newspapers and political debate. Economics is a social phenomenon, it is how society thinks about the economy in which they find themselves. Somewhere within this social process you will find me: lecturing, marking exams, writing research papers, submitting them to journals, refereeing papers submitted by other people, advising government, presenting my research at conferences and seminars. Like any professional or academic economist, I am part of this big show, this evolving monster, sailing through the mist of history to goodness knows where.

We are all part of a process by which human society comes to understand the economy and indeed itself. Much of this 'thinking' goes on behind closed doors between consenting adults. The closed doors are not so much physical, but social. Academic economists write and speak in a special language that is largely incomprehensible to non-economists: it uses lots of specialist jargon and is often mathematical. Indeed, the assumptions made by economists might look bizarre and fantastic to any but the initiated: people live forever, can see into the future with perfect foresight, adopt elaborate statistical methods and live in highly stylised worlds. Indeed, with increasing specialism in economics, there is even a growing gap between what is treated as standard in one part of economics and others.

There is a danger that the world of academic economics will fail to communicate with the rest of society. This would be a real shame: the ideas, concepts and tools of economics deserve a wider audience. It is our duty as economists to convince and engage with others, be they students, government policy-makers or the general public.

The essays in this book are certainly academic in nature: indeed, some have been published in academic journals and learned volumes; and some chapters contain equations and diagrams that may baffle the layperson. However, they are aimed to communicate ideas in a simple and direct way to the student of economics who is interested in thinking a bit more about economics and doing more than just mechanically learning what is in textbooks. I very much hope that this collection will play a small but useful and enjoyable part in the social process of economics.

HUW DAVID DIXON

Acknowledgements

The chapters in this book have been written over a long period. I would like to thank my wife Carol for putting up with me throughout this period: being married to an academic and (even worse) an economist deserves a medal. I would also like to thank the various generations of students at Birkbeck College, Essex and York Universities on whom earlier versions of most of these chapters (or parts thereof) were tried out. Teaching is always a good way to make your own thoughts clear, and I have benefitted from much valuable feedback. Lastly, I would like to thank the publishers for nudging me repeatedly to get the book finished.

I would like to thank the following publishers for giving me permission to reprint the various chapters in this collection, reproduced with minor amendments: Blackwells for permission to reprint 'Equilibrium and Explanation', in J. Creedy (ed.), *The Foundations of Economic Thought*, Blackwell 1990, chapter 13, pp. 356–94. Cambridge University Press for permission to reprint 'Of Coconuts, Decomposition, and a Jackass: A Geneology of the Natural Rate of Unemployment', in R. Cross (ed.), *The Natural Rate 25 Years on*, Cambridge University Press 1995, pp. 57–74. Edward Elgar for permission to reprint 'Some Thoughts on Artificial Intelligence and Economic Theory', in S. Moss and J. Rae (eds), *Artificial Intelligence and Economic Analysis*, Edward Elgar 1992, pp. 131–154; 'Reflections on New Keynesian Economics; the Role of Imperfect Competition', in H. Vane and B. Snowden (eds), *Reflections on Modern Macroeconomics*, Edward Elgar 1998, pp. 158–203. Pearson Group for permission to reprint 'Oligopoly Theory made Simple', in S. Davies *et al.* (eds), *The Economics of Industrial Organisation*, Longmans 1988, chapter 4, pp. 127–63. Taylor & Francis Ltd for permission to reprint 'New Keynesian Economics, Nominal Rigidities and Involuntary Unemployment', *Journal of Economic Methodology*, 1999, vol. 6, pp. 221–38 <*http://www.tandf.co.uk/journals/.htm*>.

Introduction

I remember sitting in my fourth-floor office on a sunny day. I was a young lecturer (assistant Professor in US terms) at Birkbeck College in London, busy teaching and establishing my research career. The phone rang, and I heard the voice of my friend Steve Davies asking me if I would like to write a chapter on oligopoly theory for a book he was writing on Industrial Organisation. Well, yes, this seemed like an excellent opportunity. I was teaching a course on IO for the graduate students at Birkbeck, and it was already apparent to me that there was a real gap in what was going on in IO. On the one hand, the real action was happening in conferences and seminars around the world: researchers were busy talking to each other and developing many new and interesting ideas (the early mid-1980s were an exciting time for IO!). Much of this could be read about, but only in a highly technical and condensed form found in academic journals; not really suitable for students. On the other hand, there were a variety of textbooks that tended to rehash the same old things that other people had done before. However, what I wanted to get over was the truly exciting and fundamental ideas that were being developed, but in a simple form. Well, I only had a few weeks to write the chapter (six weeks I seem to remember), so I just developed my lecture notes. The end result was 'Oligopoly Theory made Simple' (1988). What I tried to achieve was to communicate the fundamental ideas in a rigorous but simple manner, so that people reading the chapter would know what was going on at the frontier of research: maybe not the details of course, it was the spirit that mattered.

I could tell a similar story for most of the chapters in this book. In each case, an invitation by letter or phone (and later still by e-mail) provided me with the opportunity to communicate something I felt passionately about. John Creedy asked me to write about the concept of equilibrium: the end result was 'Equilibrium and Explanation' (1990). This reflects very much my thoughts arising out of various lectures: at Birkbeck College again on general equilibrium theory and introductory micro and macro. Also, my interest in philosophy found an outlet (I had read economics and philosophy as an undergraduate at Balliol College Oxford). Rod Cross asked me to write about the Natural Rate: this was a real joy, because I felt that the textbook treatment was so bad! You can read the end result in 'Of Coconuts, Decomposition, and a Jackass: The Genealogy of the Natural Rate' (1995).

Two of the chapters have arisen from academic conferences. The first was an excellent conference organised by Scott Moss at Manchester on Artificial Intelligence and Economics, with a mixture of computer scientists, economic theorists and management scientists. This conference made a big impact on me. As a student at Balliol, I had always been suspicious of the assumption of optimising behaviour, becoming a great fan of the writings of people like Herbert Simon, Brian Loasby, George Shackle and Axel Leijohufvud (amongst many others!). However, as a doctoral student I set to learning all of the technical stuff and spent more time reading Apostol's *Real Analysis* than worrying about the meaning of it all. However, whilst I went with the flow and adopted the necessary conventions for professional success, I never forgot what I had known. The paper that resulted was 'Some Thoughts on Economic Theory and Artificial Intelligence'. The other conference was organised by Roger Backhouse and Andrea Salanti in the beautiful city of Bergamo. This gave me the chance to write a paper that really got to the bottom of what was wrong with the competitive model of the labour market and why a model of involuntary unemployment was so central to any reasonable macroeconomic theory. 'New Keynesian Economics, Nominal Rigidities and Involuntary Unemployment' is the only chapter in this volume that has been published in an economic journal.

None of the chapters mentioned previously were written explicitly for undergraduate students. Things changed when around 1997 Brian Snowden and Howard Vane invited me to write a chapter on new Keynesian economics for an undergraduate text. In 'The Role of Imperfect Competition in New Keynesian Economics', I took part of my then graduate lectures at York and made them simple, trying to get the basic ideas over without too much technicality. As always, what is important is the conceptual framework, not the equations! Lastly, there are the two chapters written exclusively for this book. In 'The Joy of Economics', I bring out the big picture and explain why we should not think of economics as a dismal science. There are some really interesting issues and questions underlying economics which are often left out as lecturers and examiners tend to concentrate on the equations. Lastly, there is 'Donut World and the Duopoly Archipelago'. This is the result of the process started at the Manchester conference. The 1990s were an exciting time for the issues for bounded rationality and social learning. They had a real renaissance in mainstream economics: particularly game theory, behavioural finance and experimental economics. These ideas deserve to be made much more widely available to undergraduates, to serve as an antidote to the otherwise relentless and rather far-fetched notions of rationality that predominate in undergraduate textbooks. As I argue in 'Some Thoughts on Artificial Intelligence and Economics', whilst the standard model of rationality might be a useful tool and a good approximation in certain cases, it should not be the only model we use to the exclusion of all others.

Lastly, a couple of comments on the style of the book. I have left the chapters largely unchanged except for introducing uniformity in terms of numbering of figures and so on. *This means that the chapters are completely self-contained*: each one can be read in complete isolation from the others. I have added cross references, but these are only very general. One result of this is that there is some repetition. However, the repetition serves a purpose: the same material is approached from different directions, giving it a different perspective each time. Thus, for example, the Cournot model of oligopoly appears in three chapters: in

'Equilibrium and Explanantion' it is explored as an equilibrium concept; in 'Oligopoly Theory Made Simple' it is very much worked out as a practical modelling tool; in 'Donut World and the Duopoly Archipelago' it is treated as a social learning model and linked to evolutionary models. Finally, if you read these chapters you will see the evolution of my English style over the last 16 years! This has changed considerably. Perhaps the main shift has been towards a simpler world English. Over the years, I have become much more sensitive to the knowledge that most people reading my work will not have English as a first language: writing for a native British or American reader is a different exercise from writing for a Chinese or Turkish reader. A large vocabulary or common concepts cannot be expected. However, since my prime concern has always been towards clarity and content rather than style, I do not see this as something bad. Lastly, I am an inveterate and incorrigible infinitive splitter. For those poor souls who are still under the misapprehension that there is anything wrong in this, I would direct you to the excellent discussion in *The Cambridge Encyclopaedia of the English Language* by David Crystal.

It is very much hoped that these essays will be able to accompany a student of economics through his or her studies. The 'level' of the chapters differs in terms of content and technical know-how required and the exact place in an under-graduate programme will differ from country to country and the exact nature of the degree programme. However, as a general rule, I think that the chapters can be divided into two by the earliest point at which they can be most usefully read.

The first group are clearly appropriate for students who are studying interme-diate macro or micro texts: these are all of the chapters *except* Chapters 6 and 7, which are more appropriate for students who have mastered the intermediate micro course and are specialising in microeconomics. Some chapters are a mix-ture: for example, 'Equilibrium and Explanation' in the early sections is suitable for intermediate students, but contains some material (on information and sig-nalling) that is often not dealt with until later. Likewise, whilst 'Donut World' is at an intermediate level, the 'Duopoly Archipelago' is more advanced.

These chapters will, hopefully, have something useful for economists at all levels. I very much hope that you enjoy reading them as much as I did writing them.

Part I
Economics and the Meaning of Life

1 The Joy of Economics

1 INTRODUCTION

To me, economics has always been a fascinating subject. On one level, it deals with the economy and how it works, which is one of the central features of our lives today. On another level, it deals with how we make decisions, or at least should make decisions at the level of the individual, firm or society. These two themes will recur throughout this book in differing guises and are central to economics.

Whether we are looking at TV, surfing the internet, eating or drinking, we are inescapably part of the world economic system, the *global economy*. There are very few if any activities that do not in some way involve the market nowadays. Even going for a walk in the countryside might involve us in using special walking shoes, clothing and transport to the countryside. In this we are different to our ancestors in the distant past: 12 000 years ago gatherer-hunters were largely self-sufficient communities who produced all they needed themselves.[1] Even in western European rural communities in the middle ages, there was a much greater degree of self-sufficiency: many things were made within the household and those few goods and services that were exchanged on the market were largely local. At no time in human history has our global interdependence been so great.

The complexity of this system is beyond human comprehension despite being man-made. The economic system links almost all of humanity and involves the decisions and actions of us all; it interacts with the eco-system and weather. The whale was almost hunted to extinction to supply the demands of consumers for its products (from ladies' lingerie to lamp oil). Global warming is occurring as the production of greenhouse gasses increases with economic growth. Every day each one of us makes many economic decisions (what to buy, what to make, what to do at work, charities to donate to etc.) on the basis of our own preferences and information: the economy is the outcome of all of this myriad of interrelated individual decisions and actions.

2 INFINITY IN A PENCIL

> To see a world in a grain of sand
> And heaven in a wild flower
> To hold infinity in the palm of your hand
> And eternity in one hour.
> (William Blake, *Auguries of Innocence*)

3

There is a very real sense in which the economy represents an interconnected whole, in which every individual element is linked with the whole, the global economy. This integration and complexity can be considered if we take almost any commodity and look at what has gone into making it in terms of goods and services.

Let us take the example of looking at the humble pencil:[2] this is an old technology that has been around for sometime, but which has so many inputs that have gone into its making that a book would be needed to list even the main ingredients. And this is just a simple good, not a refrigerator or VCR. Let us ask the question: what inputs have gone into a pencil, either directly (they were used to make the pencil), or indirectly (they were used to make the things that make the pencil, or to make the things that were used to make things that were used to make the pencil, and so on ...).

First, let us take the factory that makes the pencils. A real-life pencil factory is a big building, employing many people with different machinery and different tasks. Let us simplify things a lot: at the simplest level, the pencil is made by combining wood, paint and lead (and possibly some metal alloy and rubber if it has an eraser at the end: to keep life simple, we will assume not). The pencil factory will buy these three ingredients from suppliers and combine them using a mixture of labour and machinery. Over the history of the pencil, the technology has changed. Today, this process might be almost entirely automated, possibly controlled by computer. The human labour input would be in terms of monitoring and maintaining the machinery, managing the firm and various other tasks (cleaning the floors, carrying boxes, and so on). In the past, there might have been a less-integrated manufacturing process: one machine assembled the lead and wood, another painted it; different workers operated each machine.

We can then go back one level: who and what made the machines; who and what made the wood, lead and paint? What about the human labour: this also has inputs (the things it consumes)? What about the factory: the carpets, doors, building and furniture? To keep the story simple for the moment, let us concentrate on the physical inputs.

The wood comes through a process: trees are chopped down by loggers using axes and electronic saws, the logs are transported by lorry to a wood factory that process it into various forms for use (for example) by the pencil manufacturer. This occurs in parts of the world where there are forests: let us say Norway for example. The wood product will then be taken from Norway to where the pencil is made: this might be a journey by rail, road or sea.

The lead[3] for the pencil is mined: the mining process involves digging a mine with machinery and labour for ore. The lead ore is then smelted, possibly on a nearby site or on a distant site (smelting involves heating up the ore which is energy intensive: in the days before widespread use of electricity, this needed to be done near an energy source, usually coal). The lead is then supplied to the pencil maker probably via intermediaries. The paint is nowadays created using advanced chemical processes in largely automated factories.

We have only talked in a very schematic way about how a pencil is made and told part of the story. I could go into more and more details at each stage, listing the processes involved and the human actions and physical inputs at each stage. There are, however, a few general points I want to emphasise. At each stage, the production of almost any commodity involves some general elements: machine tools, human labour, computers, buildings, electricity, petrol, paper etc. Services are not really an exception here; whilst the output is not physical, many of the inputs are (look at a restaurant or accountancy firm and you see plenty of physical inputs). Through these almost universal inputs, almost any good or service is linked to the world economy 'at one step'. *In the economy, everything is interconnected. We can see the whole world economy in a pencil!*

3   HOW WE UNDERSTAND THE ECONOMY: THE PRINCIPLES THAT GUIDE ECONOMISTS

If the economic system is so vast and so complex, perhaps it is beyond understanding? Indeed, the physicist Max Plank is reputed to have looked into economics, but decided it was too complicated so he decided to study physics instead. Well, as it happens, I think that there are some general principles and insights that economists have developed that give us some understanding of how the market and economy work. The general principles which guide economists can be reduced to a list which includes the following eight items. The list could of course be made much longer and more precise: however, it would be difficult to make it any shorter or more general.

1   *The operation of supply and demand in competitive markets.* Lord Carlisle is reported to have said 'If you train a parrot to say supply and demand: there, you have an economist!' The sort of things we learn in our first undergraduate lectures have proven pretty good as a way of understanding what happens in competitive markets: demand increases tend to raise prices, an increase in supply lowers prices, that sort of thing. Of course, some economists even apply this to non-competitive markets, which is wrong! For example, the notion that minimum wage laws will decrease employment is based on the notion that labour markets are competitive. However, there are strong reasons to believe that labour markets for the unskilled have strong monopsony elements: the employers set the wages. In a monopsony market a minimum wage can *increase* employment. Whilst supply and demand analysis is very useful, we need to think before we apply it: *is this market really consistent with the assumptions of perfect competition?*

2   *The response of agents within the economy to incentives.* If you change the incentives you will alter behaviour. This is something that non-economists often have problems with. In everyday life we do not like to think that people are motivated by money: *mercenary* is a dirty word. Well, of course, whilst

people do have other motives, the budget constraint and its slope is always there whether we like it or not! As the British Prime Minister Sir Robert Walpole said: 'Every man has his price'.[4]

3   *The pursuit of profits and economic rents in imperfectly competitive markets.* Firms are not generally altruistic organisations: they are there to make money. They have done and will continue to do almost anything to make more money. There are many examples in business history of murder, the subversion of governments, war and indeed almost anything if it enables more money to be made.

4   *Arbitrage: the tendency of arbitrage behaviour to equate returns across different activities and assets.* This is the basis of much of the theory of financial markets, from Forex to Wall Street. But it also applies across a wider field of assets: whilst arbitrage may be weak sometimes, we can see its force in many markets.

5   *The effect of imperfect information on markets.* The phenomena of adverse selection, signalling, rationing and limits on contractual agreements came to the fore in the 1970s, associated with names such as Joe Stiglitz, George Akerlof and Michael Spence. The classic application was the market for Lemons. George Akerlof was able to explain the discount on second hand cars in terms off the private information car owners have. People with poor quality cars (Lemons) were more likely to want to sell them than people with good cars. Spence highlighted the role of education as a signal of quality: even if education was irrelevant in terms of skills, a good educational performance could be a reliable guide to subsequent productivity.

6   *The concept of opportunity cost.* Accountants are pretty powerful people: they play a key role in business organisations and in government. They look at the bottom line: how much cash does something make, how much does it cost, where's the profit? Accountants are not economists. The fact that things and activities have values other than their market/monetary values is something economists have long understood, and they have developed ways of coming up with monetary values different from market values. Although the theory of value was developed to understand how markets work, it has created a theory which can be applied almost anywhere and anytime, and which is central to environmental economics, public economics and many other areas. The importance of opportunity cost is greatest when it diverges from the actual cost.

7   *The analysis of strategic behaviour, in particular the idea of the Nash Equilibrium.* Much of economic activity occurs in a *strategic environment*, where individual agents affect each other's welfare and there are not many of them. This sort of context is central to *oligopoly theory*, and has a long history of analysis, from Antoine Augustin Cournot's analysis of mineral water duopoly in 1838 to Francis Edgeworth's analysis of price setting duopoly in 1897 (we will discuss this later in more detail – see Chapter 6). The more recent development of game theory generalised and developed these starting points into a general theory of strategic analysis that can be applied as much to how to run

a war as corporate strategy. Indeed, as we shall see in Chapter 8, game theory has even come to play a central role in evolutionary biology!

8 *The welfare properties of markets.* Adam Smith argued that there was something good about the market, and saw it as guided by an invisible hand to bring about some form of common good. This idea became formalised in the *First Fundamental Theorem of Welfare Economics* which we discuss in more detail later. Under certain assumptions, a competitive market is Pareto-optimal. This has some far reaching implications, some of which we explore in both the macro context in Part II of this book, and in the micro context in Part III. Of course, the fundamental ideas of externalities and public goods are also useful in understanding many market failures. Even when markets are not competitive, the welfare properties of imperfectly competitive markets can be understood in terms of concepts such as consumer and producer surplus. Economics provides us with the tools for understanding the welfare properties of markets which will be a central theme running throughout the book.

This list is not meant to be complete or exhaustive. However, it is interesting to note that most of these ideas were developed pretty early on in the history of economics (50–100 years ago), with the exception of the economics of information and game theory.[5] Furthermore, most of these ideas are dealt with in first-year economic principles courses.

There have of course been many advances in economics in the last century. However, the advances do not often constitute completely new ideas: rather, they develop old ideas in new ways. The advances are often 'technological' in nature: new mathematical or modelling technologies are applied in new settings. Econometrics has benefited from advances in computing. Also, the issues to be addressed have changed with the development of the economy. However, the underlying principles seem to remain the same. These general principles and notions provide the economist with his or her basic framework for analysing a particular problem, issue or phenomenon: the economists 'tool kit'. Different economists will apply them differently, and there is much controversy in economics. It is to this issue that we can now turn our attention: the how and why of controversy in economics.

4   WHAT DO ECONOMISTS ARGUE ABOUT?

Why do economists argue and what do they argue about? Clearly, this is a very big question and raises many issues that are general to any area of human understanding: people disagree and argue about many things and indeed almost anything. However, in the case of economics I believe that we can usefully simplify matters into three major levels or sources of disagreement:

• The extent to which economists adhere to the *laissez-faire*[6] view that the market gets things right (or as right as possible).

- The appropriate model that best describes the economy or market being analysed.
- The relative importance in practice of different factors within a model.

Of course, in any one debate, all three of these sources are often present and interact: for example, take the issue of anti-trust regulation. An economist who is relatively *laissez-faire* in outlook will tend to think that the competitive model is most appropriate and that market imperfections that do exist are not important in magnitude. However, it is useful to divide up these different levels at least conceptually when we read a particular controversy.

4.1   World-Views and Spectacles

If you wear sunglasses, then the world becomes a darker place. Green-tinted glasses make the world look green. Economists have different perspectives or world-views that act like spectacles and shade how they look at any problem. There are traditionally two dominant views on policy: *laissez-faire* and interventionist. I will outline a brief sketch (caricature) of these views.

Laissez-Faire: The Free Market Works!

Economists wearing these spectacles tend to think of the economy as a (more or less) well-functioning competitive free-market economy. The First Fundamental Theorem of Welfare Economics says that such an economy should be 'efficient' in the technical sense of Pareto-optimality. According to this sort of economist, the free market pretty much gets most things right and the role of government is really limited to ensuring that markets can operate freely and perhaps intervening where there are clear and major market failures (due, for example, to externalities or public goods).

   Indeed, in the extreme free-market view government intervention or regulation of markets is seen as a last resort. Far from being the almost divine 'social planner' that can intervene to rectify any problem (however slight) in the functioning of markets, the government is a very imperfect tool. It is itself subject to economic influences (lobbying), the need for re-election (in democracies), whilst regulatory bodies and bureaucracies are difficult to control. Indeed, government intervention in markets often has a lot of unintended side-effects that may be counterproductive. It is the government that has the health warning, whilst the free market is presumed innocent until proven guilty.

Interventionist: The Free Market Works, but ...

The second view has no generic label, but in the macroeconomic field it is certainly linked to the adjective 'Keynesian'. Economists with these spectacles see markets as being inherently imperfect to some significant extent. The free market will often get things wrong if left to its own devices. There is some disagreement over whether the government can do much about it, but the question of regulation or some form of intervention is certainly on the menu as a possibility to be seriously thought about. However, the interventionist has a basic lack of trust about the free market and believes that its outcome can be at best efficient but unjust, and at worst both inefficient and unjust. Even perfectly functioning markets need not get the question of equity and the distribution of income right (it is Pareto-optimal to divide a cake up so that one person has everything and the rest nothing). When there is market power or dominance, imperfect information and other imperfections, the free market can yield highly undesirable outcomes. In this case, the efficient operation of the economy may require some sort of intervention to avoid these imperfect outcomes.

Of course, the extreme *laissez-faire* view is held by few, although free-market ideologues are certainly an important political policy pressure group both sides of the Atlantic and around the world. Likewise, most interventionists would accept that there is no real alternative to the market to achieve the bulk of economic organisation in an economy.

Hence one can say that the real debate is really along a continuum: the question is one of extent. How much should the government intervene and how should this best be done? For example, Mankiw and Romer (1991) state in their collection of *New Keynesian* papers that

> … new Keynesian economists not necessarily believe that active government policy is desirable. Because the theories developed … emphasise market imperfections, they usually imply that the unfettered market reaches inefficient equilibria. Thus these models show that government intervention can potentially improve the allocation of economic resources. Yet whether the government should intervene in practice is a more difficult question that entails political as well as economic judgements. Many of the traditional arguments against active stabilisation policy, such as long and unpredictable lags with which policy works, may remain valid even if one is persuaded by new Keynesian economics.[7]

Thus Mankiw and Romer are very equivocal about intervention despite their belief that market imperfections are central to understanding the economy.

The importance of history in determining which view is more or less popular is clear. The experience of the depression in the 1930s and the success of the highly interventionist postwar reconstruction in Western Europe meant that most economists until the mid-1970s were interventionist in instinct. The revival of *laissez-faire* economics started in the 1970s with the world slow-down in growth. It reached its fulfilment in the 1980s with the two icons of free-market economics in Britain and the USA, Prime Minister Thatcher and President Reagan. Privatisation and deregulation became the buzz words of the 1980s, whilst international bodies such as the IMF and World Bank tried to foist these reforms on otherwise unwilling countries. Others simply imitated what seemed like a successful policy, if only as a political strategy to reduce taxes.

This seemed to have reached its zenith in 1990 when the Soviet Union collapsed: for many this symbolised the triumph of the free market over the state as an economic organiser. However, the pendulum is perhaps swinging back. Privatisation has never really worked well, creating many unforeseen problems: regulating a privatised monopoly is not an easy thing to achieve, particularly as in most countries there is little tradition in anti-trust law and regulation. Indeed, the USA is the exception: in a wave of anti-big-business populist sentiment, the Sherman Act was passed in 1890. Hence the USA has a century-old tradition of anti-trust litigation and an army of lawyers who make money out of conducting cases under this legislation. In contrast, most of the rest of the world actively encouraged cartels and restrictive practices until the 1960s. Most countries (including the UK) still lack effective anti-trust legislation. Whilst hordes of western consultants and advisers to the ex-Soviet sphere encouraged the instant dismantling of the planning system, this has had disastrous consequences in the short run. At the time of writing (2000) the transition is still to yield growth in the former Soviet Union. One can only compare this to the great success of China, which has instead gone for a gradualist and highly regulated transition, being possibly the most successful economy in the 1990s. Most of Europe is in recession whilst the Far East has faced financial collapse. This will no doubt foster a return to more Keynesian macroeconomics and interventionist policies: we will have to wait and see.

4.2 Evidence

Even though economists might agree on the basic framework, they might disagree on the practical importance of different forces at work. For example, economic theory says that demand curves can slope up or down: in the case of an inferior good, the *income effect* of a price rise is positive and may outweigh the *substitution effect*. It is an empirical question of whether this happens often and for significant classes of goods. I think that most economists would agree that Giffen goods are a rarity. However, let us take a more controversial case: do labour supply curves slope up or down? In this case, even for normal goods, the income and substitution effects of a wage increase work in different directions. It is simply an empirical question of which will dominate. However, it has important consequences: for example, will people work harder if income taxes are cut (the susbstitution effect dominates), or less (the income effect dominates)?

Many disagreements are about the relative importance of different factors in a particular phenomenon. For example, financial liberalisation has many effects: some good and some bad for growth. The key issue is which of these tends to predominate in practice. To answer this we need to look at some evidence. If you do not take the extreme *laissez-faire* view, then really it comes down to what you think in practice the important elements are. For example, whilst the world might not be perfectly competitive, is the imperfect competition that is present a *significant* deviation from perfect competition or not?

Unfortunately, the evidence is rarely conclusive. To test a hypothesis it is necessary to choose a data set, to formulate a statistical model and framework to estimate the economic model. There are different statistical/econometric methodologies about how to go about this. At a first stage there is the testing of the model against the data: is it acceptable as a Null hypothesis? A second stage is to test competing models: this is often not undertaken, and is often inconclusive. At each stage decisions need to be made that are open to debate. The results of empirical evaluation and testing are often not decisive in convincing people that they are wrong in what they believe (indeed, it is very difficult to convince some people that they are wrong using *any* evidence, let alone econometric evidence). For many economists the process of empirical testing is so imperfect that they prefer to rely on theory alone to inform their views. Certainly, there are few examples of economic theories that have been abandoned solely because of the evidence:[8] evidence plays a role in shifting opinion in the profession, but only a very selective role. If only economists could test their theories in laboratories![9]

4.3 Arguing and the Advance of Economics

It is important that economists argue about things. Of course, an economist should be forced to develop his or her views and if possible to find evidence to back it up. However, this sort of process is fairly weak. When we develop a theory, we tend to use it to interpret the world (it is a bit like sunglasses): we tend to focus upon evidence that confirms our beliefs and we ignore or play down evidence to the contrary. Nobody likes to be wrong or to have to change their fundamental beliefs (on the economic consequences of cognitive dissonance[10] see Akerlof and Dickens[11]). Argumentation forces an economist to confront and answer to other economists. Other economists will often represent different theories, put emphasis on different evidence or interpret existing evidence differently. The need to persuade others places constraints on what can become generally accepted. Of course, an individual may continue to believe something despite what others believe: however, a belief can only become *widespread* in the economics profession if it has some sort of reasonable foundation. The interplay of debate ensures that there is a constant process of going through arguments, sifting evidence, looking at new ideas and new evidence. Over time, we can but hope the ideas that become widespread amongst economists are reasonable and appropriate. The process of argumentation ensures that this is the case.

The fact that many controversies remain unresolved does not necessarily mean that there is no progress. Rather, it is like a tug-of-war. The truth lies in between the two teams (points of view): the process of debate determines some sort of equilibrium that reflects a mid-point. As outlined earlier, few people adopt the most extreme views: to some extent we are all eclectic and middle of the road. However, we come at problems from different directions and try to pull other people towards us. Different types of evidence become salient or important at different times and so lead to shifts of emphasis. For example, with a few hyper-inflationary exceptions, significant inflation was a rarity in peace-time before 1970: economists had tended to ignore it. During the 1970s and 1980s inflation was significant in many OECD countries and inflation and inflationary expectations became a major concern of economists. By the late 1990s, inflation was already looking like a phenomenon of the past: the 1970s and 1980s as much a Dark Age aberration for inflation as the 1950s and 1960s were a Golden Age of high employment in Europe.

5   THE LIMITS OF ECONOMICS: ARE ECONOMISTS STUPID?

Weathermen are often blamed for the bad weather; the messenger that brings bad news is shot.

Economists are unable to fully understand the economy. Does this mean that economists are stupid or in some way lacking in common sense? No, as we have already seen, the economy is an incredibly complex system. There are many processes at work, billions of people all over the surface of the earth linked in a web of ceaseless interaction. As the case of the pencil illustrates, almost every activity we undertake connects us with the wholeness of the world economy. There are many reasons that economics is not easy!

We need to understand the limits of economists' understanding as well as its strengths. We should understand right from the start that we will never have an understanding of the economy that is comparable to classical mechanics (physics) and its understanding of (for example) the behaviour of the planets. In particular, we will never be able to predict the future course of the economy over anything but the short term. Secondly, we must understand that economists must always use simplified models which leave many and indeed most things out. There is a limit to the complexity of economic models imposed by our ability to think about and use them (although this frontier is being pushed back by advances in computing).

Whilst we may well understand the things that we have put in the model, the things we leave out might be important sometimes. Inflation is an interesting example, as we have already noted. In many macroeconomic models of the 1950s and early 1960s, the notion of inflation was largely absent reflecting the fact that inflation was not a problem and was so low it could largely be ignored. When inflation became very important in many economies in the 1970s and 1980s, it became necessary to include inflation as a central feature of macroeconomic models (for example, using the expectations-augmented Phillips curve).

The comparison is often made between economics and modelling the weather system. Although we understand most of the underlying physical processes generating the weather, the presence of threshold effects and non-linearities in general give rise to chaotic behaviour. This means that initial conditions matter: small changes in the state of the weather system can have dramatic effects once we move beyond the immediate future. A butterfly can flutter its wings in Kentucky and it leads to snow in Oslo. Furthermore, our knowledge of the state of the economic system is partial and inaccurate: economic statistics are costly to gather and by their nature often ambiguous, incomplete and inaccurate. National income statistics are a minefield of unresolved problems: whether we are talking of measurements of unemployment or gross national product, there are many contentious issues that are not solved except by accounting convention.

However, the basic processes in economics involve humans: humans acting in organisations and in society. We certainly do not fully understand individual human behaviour: the detailed behaviour of an individual is often unpredictable and incomprehensible to anyone but the person concerned. When groups of individuals get together and interact within groups and organisations, the results can be very strange indeed. Economics is an attempt to understand this in terms of certain organising principles, within the notion of rational choice and equilibrium as discussed in Chapter 2. Economists tend to talk of economic agents: these would be the household or the firm, which assume act as if they were individual rational agents. However, this is not the case! There is no better place to start than by examining Condorcet's paradox.

5.1 Condorcet's Paradox

The French mathematician and man of letters Marie-Jean-Antoine-Nicolas de Caritat, Marquis de Condorcet was born in 1743 and died in 1794. In 1785 he wrote his *Essay on the Application of Analysis to the Probability of Majority Decisions*. He showed how collective decision-making could be inconsistent (intransitive) even if the individual preferences were consistent (transitive). Let us have a look at how this works.

Let us assume that the Condorcet family has three members – Pierre, Jacques and Martine – and they decide to go out for a meal. There are three types of restaurant: French (F), Vietnamese (V) and Arab (A). Their preference rankings are

	1st choice	2nd choice	3rd choice
Pierre	F	V	A
Jacques	V	A	F
Martine	A	F	V

They take a democratic vote. 'Shall we go French or Vietnamese' says Pierre; Pierre and Martine prefer French. OK, so French beats Vietnamese. 'So, shall we go to French or Arab?': now, both Jacques and Martine like the Algerian sweets, so Arab beats French. So it looks like Arab food. But Pierre is not so happy with this, so he says, 'Let's have a last think: Do we really prefer Arab to Vietnamese? I don't'. 'Me neither' says Jacques. Now Martine is unhappy: 'Well, we agreed that a French was better than a Vietnamese, so ... ' . There are many different endings to this story! The point is that anything can happen if they have these preferences, since there is a *preference cycle* if the household uses majority voting as its decision rule. It does not make sense to represent it as a single rational agent.

Now, this is a simple organisation with a simple decision: what about a firm, university or union? Well, sometimes it is almost impossible to understand how some crazy decision has been taken from a common-sense point of view. However, when you look at an organisation and how it works it becomes much clearer: every individual can be behaving rationally, but the organisation is set up so that it takes wrong decisions. *When we think of higher levels of organisation and interaction, things rapidly become very complex.*

Economists base their analysis on a hope: in general, firms and households behave as if they were individual rational agents. Now, this may be an *a priori* hope, an act of faith which is a core belief which remains unquestioned. Alternatively, it might be a belief that idiosyncrasies do not matter that much. However, one possible answer that may apply at least to commercial organisations is that the economic process provides a process of natural selection which forces organisations to be efficient and so, presumably, act as a consistent goal-oriented entity (at least most of the time). We will look at this argument in the next section and in more detail in Chapter 8.

Whilst the Condorcet paradox shows us how economic agents which consist of several individuals may be difficult to understand, how about the actual individual. How does economic motivation fit in with the wider human condition? For most of us, the economic aspect of our lives is secondary: what matters to us is family, children, friends, arts, sport, hobbies, religion or spirituality, politics and ideology. However, whilst we may not focus on the economic aspects, they surround and pervade most things that we do. First there is the need to earn a living: most people are doing work they would rather not do. If given the choice, who would get up at 7 a.m. and rush into work on a crowded bus or train, undertake work they would rather not do, and rush home at 6 p.m.? Since most of us spend 40–50 hours a week working and travelling to work, it is the dominant feature of our lives.

Second, there is the need to have money to pursue our other ends: we need money to house and clothe ourselves and our families; we need money to go out to a restaurant or to go on holiday. There is a budget constraint linking all of our different activities: in some sense out expenditure must not exceed our income. As Charles Dicken's Mr Micawber said:

> Annual income twenty pounds, annual expenditure nineteen six, result happiness. Annual income twenty pounds, annual expenditure twenty pounds ought and six, result misery. (*David Copperfield*)

Whilst economics might not be an explicit or conscious element in many of our activities, it has its effect anyway. We might object to its presence when it intrudes, but like Mr Micawber we cannot ignore it except at our peril!

6   THE ECONOMY IS INTELLIGENT

How is all of the economic activity organised? Well, clearly, no person or group of people organises this activity directly – there have been centrally planned economies, but that is another story. If we think back to the ancient world, the trade in spices and silk, the countries trading with each other had no idea what the world looked like, and probably little idea of each other's existence in any detail.

The answer is that the economy is an intelligent system which organises economic activity: it is a *self-ordering system*. This might sound a little odd. What is the economy: I can see people, cars, houses, products: I can even 'see' firms and corporations (at least I understand and can identify them). Surely, the idea of an 'intelligent economy' is a useful fiction, as in 'the economy behaves as if was organised by something'? No, I mean that *the economy itself is an intelligent self-ordering system*.

The idea that the pursuit of self-interest by economic agents could lead to an good outcome has been around for a long time. Perhaps the first person to write about this was Bernard Mandeville (1670-1730) in his famous book, *The Fable of the Bees: or Private Vices and Publick Benefits*. Mandeville believed that the 'private vice' of self-interest led to the public good. Adam Smith (1723–90) also famously wrote:

> It is not from the benevolence of the butcher, the brewer or the baker that we expect our dinner, but from their regard to their own self interest. We address ourselves not to their humanity but to their self love … Nobody but a beggar chooses to depend chiefly on the benevolence of his fellow-citizens. (Smith, 1776)

Adam Smith saw the whole universe, including the economic system, as operating to maximise the welfare of all beings: the divine Being's 'benevolence and wisdom have, from all eternity, contrived and conducted the immense machine of the universe, so as at all times to produce the greatest possible quanitity of happiness' (Smith, 1759). Thus when we read Adam Smith's statements about an *invisible hand* guiding the market, he had in mind the invisible hand of a divine entity. The universe was a machine designed by god, the economy a part of this vast machine.[12] This sort of view perhaps made good sense in the eighteenth century, when most people believed in an active God, but nowadays most thinkers do not see the economy as having a divine order imposed on it.

Older views of the intelligent market were very much linked to the *laissez-faire* view discussed earlier. Indeed, at times, this view seems to be very much in tune with the inimitable Dr Pangloss. As Voltaire's good Doctor said to his patron the Baron:

> 'It is demonstrable,' said he, 'that things cannot be otherwise than as they are; for as all things have been created for some end, they must necessarily be created for the best end. Observe, for instance, the nose is formed for spectacles, therefore we wear spectacles. The legs are visibly designed for stockings, accordingly we wear stockings. Stones were made to be hewn and to construct castles, therefore My Lord has a magnificent castle; for the greatest baron in the province ought to be the best lodged. Swine were intended to be eaten, therefore we eat pork all the year round: and they, who assert that everything is right, do not express themselves correctly; they should say that everything is best.' (Voltaire, 1759)

Modern views of the intelligence of markets are not based on the idea of a divinely-imposed order, but rather the view that the order of the economy emerges: like life itself the economy is a *self-ordering* system. To understand this we need to think of other intelligent self-ordering systems. Biological systems are one obvious example (we will be looking into this a bit more in Chapter 8). Since Darwin, we have understood how a principle of natural selection can operate to create an orderly eco-system: species adapt to themselves, other species and the environment. No one plans this: it is the way nature works that order can arise out of chaos (to steal Ilya Prigogine's book title). It we look at an ecosystem, we see the end result of this process: a delicately balanced system where everything seems to hang together in a finely choreographed dance of life. Natural selection is based on one fundamental principle: those features that enhance replication (the generation of progeny) are favoured. Genes are passed on from generation to generation of all life on earth: which genes prosper and develop depends on how successful they are in making copies of themselves. The genes interact with themselves and the environment giving rise to the natural world of living things.

The ordering principle in economics is almost as simple: activities that generate profits are favoured; activities that do not generate profits are discouraged. In order for some sort of activity to be sustained over time it requires some sort of profit to be made. In order for something to be profitable, it needs to generate revenue: this means that people with money are willing to pay for the activity either directly or indirectly. The costs of an activity need to be less than the revenue, at least in the long run. This idea should not be taken to an extreme: it is not the case that all activities that can make a profit happen all of the time; it also the case that activities that do not make a profit can happen in the short run. There are other motivations driving humans to do things.

If an activity does not earn profits, it can only survive if there is some other such motivation for it. For example, charities and religious organisations rely on a non-economic motivation, relying on people giving time and resources. They are able to undertake and sustain activities which no strictly commercial organisation would undertake. However, you can reinterpret the religious organisation as supplying a product or service (e.g. salvation, entertainment), but the transactions are largely non-market – whilst the activities and services can be valued implicitly, they do not have a market value. However, there is one school of thought that sees churches as commercial organisations (Ekelund *et al.*, 1996).

Replication happens in economics: those activities that earn profits are sustained through time and become more common. Profitable firms grow and take over others; less profitable firms wither or go bust. Firms and consumers imitate successful firms and consumers. A good example here is crime: despite attempts to stamp it out for centuries, the fact that there is money to be made by crime means that it survives and seems to prosper across almost all times and societies.

So, economic order emerges *spontaneously* from the process of selection and replication. The question then arises, is this a good order from the point of view of *homo sapiens*? Diseases and earthquakes are natural phenomena, but even Dr Pangloss had trouble convincing Candide that such outcomes were the best of all possible outcomes. If we view the order as set up by a benevolent deity, then it seems pretty plausible that the economy would be set up to operate 'for good'. If the order is not set up in this way, then we may have a problem. Disease occurs through natural processes of selection and replication, yet most people believe that we need to intervene and treat or prevent disease in a variety of ways.

Is the order which emerges from the economic system in any sense *optimal* or even just *pretty good*? Or is it sometimes or most of the time pretty bad or very bad? Well, here we come back to the fundamental dichotomy. *Laissez-faire* free marketers believe that the market is pretty much as good as you can get. Others disagree.

In order to understand the intelligence of the economy, recall the Fundamental Theorem of Welfare Economics. This says that under certain circumstances, which we can summarise as being that markets operate perfectly, the market outcome will be Pareto-optimal. Pareto-optimality means that the economy yields an outcome such that you cannot make one agent better off without making someone else worse off. If for simplicity we imagined an economy where everyone was identical in terms of their abilities, preferences and initial wealth, Pareto-optimality implies that the welfare of the representative household will be maximised. In unequal economies, Pareto-optimality is not so attractive: a Pareto-optimal outcome might involve very unequal outcomes for different people.

The exact reasoning behind this outcome is beyond this introductory chapter; however, we learn from introductory economic principles courses how resources are allocated by the price mechanism (at least when markets operate competitively). No-one needs to know the big picture: each individual agent just gets on with his or her own business, earns money, spends it and lives their life. The market in some fundamental sense 'works', prices are established often without the need for complex institutions or planning by anyone. In the ancient world spices travelled from China and India to Europe, and people in Europe did not even know that China or India existed! It is pretty amazing how all this can happen, but it does and has done so since the beginning of civilisation.

The basic mechanism underlying the optimality of competitive markets is that voluntary exchange makes both parties better off. If all opportunities for exchange are taken up, then all opportunities for making people better off will be exploited. So, why do people think that the market might get things wrong? Well, we discussed this earlier, and there are fundamentally two reasons. First, the fact that not all exchange is voluntary. This is not the way it is usually expressed, but I think that it captures the notion of externalities and public goods pretty well. An externality happens when I am affected by an action taken by someone else which is not mediated through the market (by which I mean properly functioning competitive markets). In a competitive world, prices reflect opportunity costs. Individuals take actions which reflect these costs; all agents are doing as well as they can given the prices they face. When an externality occurs, this is not the case. Of course, agents continue to do as well as they can, but the prices no longer reflect the true cost. This means that you are able to undertake an action which makes me worse off, which is in effect an involuntary exchange. If a property developer buys some land next to my back door and builds a house there, he makes me worse off. The land price does not include the value of the open view/ quietness to me. Likewise, if a car or factory pollutes the neighbourhood, the people polluted are forced to consume the pollution. The market does not work: the outcome is not Pareto-optimal. The welfare of all could improve in principle.

The second reason why the Fundamental Theorem breaks down is that there is *imperfect competition* in the economy. This theme occurs in several of the following chapters. Perhaps the best way to illustrate this is with the Prisoner's Dilemma, a model that we will meet several more times in this volume. This model is very important in the social sciences: it is seen as capturing the idea that *when agents pursue their own interest an inefficient social outcome results*. This stands directly in opposition to the perspective of Barnard Mandeville and Adam Smith. The model is important because it can be seen as standing for the equilibrium viewpoint of game theory, which has become almost as central to economics today as the competitive model.

The basic idea is that there are two players (Alice and Bill) and two strategies: cooperate C, and defect D. If both players cooperate, they get a payoff (money, utility) of 2 each; if they both defect, they get 1 each. Now, if one (Alice) defects whilst the other cooperates, the defector gets 3 and the cooperator (Bill) 0. Now, the social optimum can be seen as the outcome when both cooperate: they each get 2. They are both better of than when they both defect and get 1. However, note that when Alice defects whilst Bill cooperates, she does very well (3) whilst he does badly (0). Whilst Alice might be pretty happy with this outcome, Bill would certainly not be. From an objective outside view, we would prefer both to cooperate unless we put Alice's welfare first. Now, what will happen in this situation? Well, there has been a lot of debate about this if the game is repeated, but most people agree that if it is only played once, then the equilibrium is with both people playing defect, D. Why is this? Well, all that either player needs to note is that defect earns the highest payoff *whatever the other player does*. If one player chooses cooperate, the other earns 3 by defecting and only 2 by cooperating. If one chooses defect, the other earns nothing if by cooperating and 1 by defecting. So, the argument goes, both would choose defect. But this is not Pareto-optimal. Alice and Bill would both be better off if they could cooperate.

In general, we can see the inefficiency arising quite simply: each person acts to maximise his or her own utility or payoff, but ignores the effects of his actions on others. In this case, if Bill is cooperating, Alice acts to maximise her own well-being and ignores the fact that by defecting her own gain (from 2 to 3) is outweighed by Bill's loss (from 3 to 0). This fundamental feature happens whenever there is imperfect competition. Imperfect competition occurs in any market where agents have market power. It is thus a very important model if we do not live in an economy characterised by perfectly competitive markets.

We will explore these themes in much more detail in this volume, but for now we have the conclusion that although the economic system might be intelligent, it does not have to be socially optimal. We live in a pretty clever social system, the global economy. However, there are winners and losers. Indeed, we all may end up as losers. Take the greenhouse effect on climatic change: it results from the emission of greenhouse gases all over the world cumulated year by year. If there is drastic climatic change in the next century, we may all be the losers. There is no particular reason to think that the market will get this right: the people who will be suffering are not born yet and are unable to express their demands. The market will not work here: it requires governments to have the vision to look into the future and do something now. Some hope!

So here we have the main dichotomy amongst economists. On the one hand we have those who believe that the spontaneous order generated by the economic process is in some sense optimal, based on the model of perfectly competitive markets without imperfections. On the other we have those that believe that the spontaneous order may be far from optimal, based on the idea of imperfect markets. As we have remarked earlier, this split explains the origin of most debates amongst economists. This is as much an ideological difference as a scientific one, and, as such, it is unlikely to be resolved by evidence unless historical experience provides unambiguous evidence either way.

Perhaps I must come clean here. As you will discover from reading the following chapters, I am myself very much in the second camp: whilst markets work, they are far from perfect. My PhD at Oxford was on the subject of oligopoly theory, markets which are by their very nature non-competitive. Since then, all of my research has explored the implications of imperfect competition, whether it be in labour or output markets, at the micro or the macro level. To me perfect competition is at best an interesting special case, a first attempt to understand the economy. However, to stop there is to miss out on the real journey of discovery, to understand how agents interact with each other. This journey may not be easy and it may have many difficulties, but it has to be done if economics is to be taken seriously and develop as a science of human society.

7   CONCLUSION

Well, I hope I have given you some idea of the issues and perspectives on economics that excite me. Economics often becomes a dull subject for students and others, the dismal science. This happens because economists tend to get caught up in their own world and miss the big picture. With increasing specialisation and technical demands on researchers, they have little time left over once they have done their teaching and research. This is a real shame. The issues and the ideas of economics are fascinating: they can and should be explained to a wide audience in a non-technical manner. The essays in this book have been written not for the general public, but for economics students. However, I have tried to make the ideas as simple and clear as possible whilst keeping their essential message. I very much hope that you find the chapters stimulating and that they convey some of the pleasure and excitement that being an economist has given to me.

Notes

1   However, there is still evidence of trading networks even in Stone Age communities: high quality flint was quarried and mined and then traded over wide areas (Rudgely, 1998, p. 173).
2   This idea is based on a story originally written in 1958 and recounted by Milton Friedman in his book *Free to Choose*, written in 1980.
3   In fact, various alloys are used nowadays, but let us stick to good old fashioned (if poisonous) lead.
4   In fact, he said 'All those men have their price', referring to fellow members of parliament.
5   Although, as we discuss in Chapter 8, the concept of the Nash Equilibrium originates in Cournot's 1838 book.
6   The term *laissez-faire* is traditionally associated with free trade: there should be no restrictions to free trade in the form of tariff or non-tariff barriers. However, I use it in a wider context of a general belief that the market is best left to its own devices in most or all areas. *Laissez-faire* is a French term which literally means 'let make!', which is best translated as 'leave alone'.
7   Mankiw and Romer (1991), p. 3.
8   It is always possible to recast a theory ('generalise' it) so that it can conform more closely to the facts. A theory is only abandoned when this process of generalisation results in a ramshackle theory and a simpler alternative comes along.
9   Some people have interpreted certain decisive historical events as almost experiments: for example, the Thatcher Years or the Vietnam War. However, the essence of experimental methodology is that experiments can be repeated and the design developed over time. Thatcher and Vietnam only happened once, so our ability to evaluate their effects is limited and inconclusive.
10 Cognitive dissonance occurs when there is a conflict between what you believe and what you see. For example, at various times Messianic groups have predicted the imminent end of the world: a classic case of cognitive dissonance occurs when the end of the world fails to materialise at the appointed time. It is amazing how many people prefer to stick to their beliefs come what may: 'do not adjust your mind, reality is at fault'.
11 Akerlof and Dickens (1982), pp. 307–19.
12 For a full argument supporting this view of Smith, see Denis (1997).

2 Equilibrium and Explanation

This chapter presents my personal views on the method of equilibrium in economics. The problem posed by this topic is that there is no general *concept* of equilibrium: rather, there is a *method* of equilibrium analysis that is employed in most of economics. Thus, the subject of enquiry is as diverse as economics itself. The chapter is therefore a compromise between a discussion of the general method of equilibrium itself, and an examination of its various manifestations in particular economic models. A resolution of this tension is sought by a detailed examination of the models that seem to form the core of standard undergraduate and graduate courses. This is a useful exercise since the 'concept' of equilibrium is born early on in a student's career – indeed, in the opening lectures of an introductory course. Once it has been introduced, it is rarely discussed in detail again.

Since there are so many different types of economic models with diverse preoccupations, the selection reflects personal whim and current fashion. Ten or 20 years ago,* these factors would have indicated different topics: most notably capital theory and the associated issues raised by growth theory would have been central to any discussion of equilibrium. Consideration of these has been omitted mainly because they were well aired at the time.

In this chapter, attempts have also been made to steer clear of technicalities, which, although sometimes enabling a more precise expression, all too often embroil us in details so that we lose the more general perspective. More importantly, the technicalities often add little or nothing to the basic equilibrium concept employed. Lastly, I have sought to avoid long-winded caveats and qualifiers, leading to some sweeping generalizations. The arguments should be seen as expressing a point of view, and it is certainly accepted that there are many other possible interpretations of particular models.

At its most general, we can say that 'equilibrium' is a method of solving economic models. At a superficial level, an equilibrium is simply a solution to a set of equations; however, there is more to it than that. Whilst economists rarely argue over how to solve equations, they do argue over whether a particular solution represents a 'real' equilibrium or not. What is at stake is the economist's view of economic agents and the market.

The equilibrium method has come to play a central role in explanation in economics, and in this it differs from other sciences where disequilibrium states are also the object of explanation. What then is the role of equilibrium in the process

---

* Editor: this chapter was written in 1990.

of explanation in economics: how do economists explain? The remarks in this chapter are restricted to theoretical economics. Very generally, economic explanation consists of two levels. At the first level, the *microstructure*, the economist posits the behaviour of the elements of the model. In most microeconomics, the basic elements of the model consist of agents (e.g. firms and households), whose behaviour is explained and understood as some form of constrained optimization. The agent maximizes some objective function (utility, profit) subject to some constraint (budget, technology). This constrained maximisation is in effect the model of individual economic rationality. In other cases, the microstructure might simply take the form of directly postulating a behavioural relationship – as for example in Keynes's consumption function. At the second level, the *macrostructure*, the individual elements of the model are put together. (The method of equilibrium consists precisely in putting together the elements in a consistent manner in solving the model.)

This dual level of explanation is best exemplified by the most common equilibrium employed in economics: the competitive equilibrium. The microstructure consists of households who maximise utility subject to a budget constraint, and firms that maximise profits subject to a technology. The microstructure is summarised by demand and supply curves. At the macro level, we put these elements together using an equilibrium concept: in the case of competitive equilibrium, we have trade occurring at the price which equates demand with supply. Actual trades equal desired trades, and demand equals supply. The theory of the competitive market (price theory) can then be used to explain prices by relating them to individual behaviour through the market equilibrium. Thus, for example, changes in the cost of inputs can be seen as altering firms' supply decisions, and hence shifting the supply curve. This will then lead to an alteration in the equilibrium price.

Equilibrium thus plays a central role in the enterprise of explanation. Parts of the model are put together and, through the application of a particular equilibrium concept, the model comes to life. Once alive, economists see what it looks like, examining the model for properties of interest (is it Pareto-optimal? how does it compare with other models?). Sometimes the models are made to 'dance' through the method of comparative statics, twitching from one position to another. The economist has real or imagined properties he wishes to explain: if the model displays them, he exhibits the model as an explanation. The crux of the explanation is: 'everyone is doing as well as they can (microstructure): when everyone is doing as well as they can, X happens (equilibrium or macrostructure).'

This is seen as explaining phenomenon X. It is rather as if an inventor has an idea, constructs a machine and proudly exhibits its performance. For the economist, however, the machine remains an idea on paper. (A notable exception is Phillip's water model of the Keynesian income-expenditure model. This, however, is still a representation.)

Given the role of equilibrium in the process of explanation, what can be said of it in general? Perhaps the main discussion of 'equilibrium' occurs for most

Table 2.1   *Equilibrium properties*

	Demand–supply	Income–expenditure
P1	Demand equals supply	Income equals expenditure
P2	Actual trades equal desired trades	Planned expenditure equals actual expenditure
P3	*Tâtonnement*	Multiplier

economists in introductory textbooks and lectures. This tends to be geared to the demand–supply model and/or the Keynesian income–expenditure model. We shall discuss these in detail in the next section. However, three basic properties of equilibrium in general are proposed:

P1   The behaviour of agents is consistent;
P2   No agent has an incentive to change his behaviour;
P3   Equilibrium is the outcome of some dynamic process (stability).

These properties are illustrated for the demand–supply and income–expenditure models in Table 2.1. The importance of these properties is by no means equal or uniform. In particular, the stability property P3 is often played down, since it is almost impossible to provide a coherent account of stability in economics. P2 is the key to constructing convincing economic equilibria: if a rival economist can point out that some agent can do better than he does, then the equilibrium model presented is cast into doubt. It is thus necessary to look more closely at how equilibrium consists in agents' having no incentive to alter their behaviour. In the following section the three basic equilibria employed in economics are examined; and particular issues are discussed in subsequent sections: disequilibrium analysis, information and time.

1   THE THREE CROSSES

Here we examine three different equilibria which are central and paradigmatic to economic analysis. First, we explore the competitive equilibrium which forms the foundation of price theory and dominates the syllabus of most undergraduate economics courses. Second, we consider the income–expenditure equilibrium which forms the foundation of macroeconomic analysis, giving as it does the notion of the multiplier. Third, we consider the Cournot–Nash equilibrium: this is the standard model of oligopoly and is chosen to represent the game-theoretic approach to equilibrium. Each of these equilibria has a central role in the teaching of economics: each is represented by a simple two-dimensional diagram in which the equilibrium is represented by the intersection of two functions (invariably drawn as straight lines in textbooks). Hence, each is a cross: borne by the student and

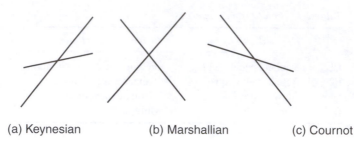

(a) Keynesian   (b) Marshallian   (c) Cournot

Figure 2.1   *The three crosses*

named after its creator (or some approximation thereto). The competitive equilibrium has two lines, one sloping up and one down, sometimes called the
Marshallian cross; the income–expenditure equilibrium has two upward-sloping
lines and is sometimes called the Keynesian cross: the Cournot– Nash equilibrium has two downward-sloping lines and for consistency is called here the
Cournot cross. The three crosses are depicted in Figure 2.1.

   As we shall see, although these three equilibria lie at the centre of the discipline of economics, they are very different, and in some sense contradictory, or
at least incommensurable.

1.1   The Marshallian Cross

> I saw the best minds of my generation destroyed by madness,
> starving hysterical naked,
> dragging themselves through the ... streets at dawn looking for
> an angry fix,
> angelheaded hipsters burning for the ancient heavenly connection
> to the starry dynamo in the machinery of night ...
>
> (Allen Ginsburg, *Howl*)

The idea of competitive equilibrium stems from the vision of the market acting
as an invisible hand, the price mechanism bringing into balance the two sides of
the market – demand and supply. As a formal idea it surfaces in its modern form
in Marshall's *Principles* (1890). The equilibrium is represented in Figure 2.2. The
demand curve D slopes down; it represents the amount that households would
like to buy at a given price. Thus at price P' demand is X'. The demand curve is
derived under the assumption that households are *price-takers*: they treat prices
as exogenous, unaffected by the action of any individual household. Under the
assumption of price-taking behaviour, households have a linear budget constraint
from which they 'choose' the utility-maximising combination of goods. The
demand curve in a particular market represents the utility-maximising quantity of

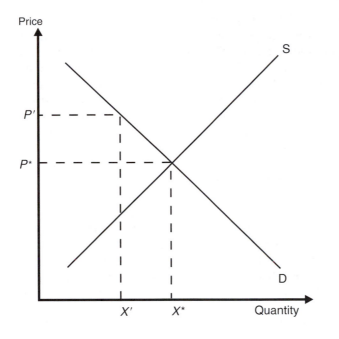

Figure 2.2 *Supply and demand*

the goods as the price varies (holding other prices etc. constant under the *ceteris paribus* assumption).

The supply curve S is also derived under the assumption of price-taking behaviour: it represents the quantity that firms wish to supply at each price. Profit-maximising firms will choose the output which equates marginal cost with price; hence the supply function is simply the summed marginal cost functions of firms in the market, and is upward-sloping due to the assumption of diminishing marginal productivity of labour or diminishing returns to scale. The demand and supply curves represent the microstructure of the market.

In Figure 2.2 the supply and demand functions appear together, and the competitive equilibrium occurs at the intersection of the two lines, with resultant price and quantity (P^*, X^*). Why is this seen as an equilibrium? The argument was outlined above in terms of the three properties P1–P3. At the competitive equilibrium the amount demanded equals the amount supplied (P1); desired trades equal actual trades (P2); at any non-equilibrium price there will be excess supply or demand which will tend to lead to a movement in price towards equilibrium – the *tâtonnement* process (P3).

Let us focus on P2, the notion that agents have no incentive to change their actions in equilibrium. What exactly do firms and households 'do' in a competitive equilibrium, and how might they do something else? In one sense the answer is obvious: firms and households exchange and trade; firms produce output which households consume. So it might be thought that, in evaluating the competitive equilibrium, we might consider whether firms or households might want to alter their production or consumption. For example, suppose that a firm reduces its output so that, in terms of Figure 2.2, supply reduces from equilibrium $X*$ to X'. What will happen? This raises the general problem of specifying non-equilibrium behaviour in any model. There are at least two possibilities: first, that the price remains at $P*$, and a reduction in supply simply leads to excess demand $X* - X'$; second, that the reduction in supply leads to a rise in price to P'. In the first case, the firm's behaviour simply leads it to produce at a point where price no longer equals marginal cost, thus reducing its profits. Hence the firm has no incentive to deviate from its competitive output. However, in the second case there will in general be an increase in profits: the reduction in output will increase price (even if only by a very small amount), which may result in an increase in profits (and certainly will result in an increase in profits if the reduction in output is small). In this case, then, the competitive outcome is not an equilibrium from the point of view of P2. This illustrates the strength of the price-taking assumption: not only is it vital to define the competitive outcome (in the sense that it defines the demand and supply functions), but it is also crucial to the notion that a competitive outcome in an *equilibrium* in the sense of P2, since it ties down out-of-equilibrium outcomes.

If we turn to P3, the competitive outcome is also seen as the outcome of the *tâtonnement* price adjustment process. There is a central paradox underlying the notion of price adjustment. How can we explain changes in price in a model in which all agents treat prices as given? One approach is to invent a third type of agent in the economy: the auctioneer. Walras based his idea of the auctioneer on the 'market-makers' of the French Bourse. The auctioneer is the visible, if imaginary, embodiment of the invisible hand. He has no economic involvement in the market: no mention is made of his objectives or constraints. He just adjusts prices in response to excess supply and demand. The story is very simple; the auctioneer calls out some arbitrary prices, agents report their desired demands and supplies, and the auctioneer raises prices where there is excess demand and lowers them where there is excess supply. If and when prices attain the competitive prices and there is no excess demand, the auctioneer waves his flag (or blows his whistle) and everyone then goes ahead and trades at the competitive price: households consume and firms produce. No trade or consumption is allowed before the competitive price is reached. Hahn and Negishi (1962) suggest an alternative 'non-*tâtonnement*' process which allows for *trading* at disequilibrium prices, but not consumption. Otherwise, the story is similar. The competitive outcome can then be seen as the outcome of this dynamic process of price adjustment by the auctioneer. However, it is not clear what has been gained by inventing a fictional price adjustment process to justify the competitive outcome. Perhaps all this means is that, if prices respond to excess demands and supplies, then price will eventually settle down at the competitive level. But it does not tell us *why* prices respond to excess demand or supply.

Textbooks adopt a slightly different approach. Competitive equilibrium is usually introduced and explained to students in an introductory economics course. Whilst the competitive model is later developed and extended, there is often little or no thought as to what it all means. The textbook writers therefore require an intuitive, plausible and convincing story. They argue that if price exceeds $P*$ then there will be excess supply (as in Figure 2.2 at P'): therefore firms will want to cut prices. Below $P*$, there is excess demand and prices will be bid up by consumers or raised by firms. When supply equals demand, everyone can buy or sell what they want to at $P*$, and so no-one will want to change price. This story may be convincing, but it is certainly not correct. Whilst it is true that prices may well change in the desired direction in response to excess demands and supplies, it is not generally true that prices will come to rest at the competitive level. Take the case where firms set prices. If the market price exceeds the competitive price there will be excess supply: firms would like to sell more, and will be rationed by some mechanism to sell less than their profit-maximising trade at that price. By undercutting the other firms by a little, any one firm can therefore attract customers from its competitors and expand sales to its desired supply at only a slightly lower price. Similarly, if there is excess demand, although the firms are able to sell as much as they want, they can increase profits by raising prices. Thus, one might expect a situation where a non-competitive price would move towards the competitive price. There is a serious conceptual issue here: in the case of undercutting, the 'price-war' will never get anywhere – since price is usually modelled as a real variable, the undercut may be arbitrarily small (see Dixon, 1993).

However, the real issue is whether or not the competitive price itself is an 'equilibrium': will firms wish to continue setting the competitive price when and if they have arrived there? In general, the answer is no (see Shubik, 1958; Dixon, 1987). Firms will want to raise prices at the competitive equilibrium (see Dixon, 1987, theorem 1). The reason is simple. At the competitive price, firms are on their supply function: price equals marginal cost. This can only be optimal for the firm if the demand curve it faces is actually horizontal. But if the firm raises its price (a little), it will not lose all its customers since, although consumers would like to buy from firms still setting the competitive price, those firms will not be willing to expand output to meet demand (their competitive output maximises profits at the competitive price). Those customers turned away will be available to buy at a higher price. Thus if a firm raises its price above the competitive price, it will not lose all its customers but only some of them, and so it will face the downward-sloping residual demand curve depicted in Figure 2.3. Since it faces a downward-sloping demand curve, marginal revenue is less than price: hence at the competitive price and output (point a), marginal cost exceeds marginal revenue and the firm can increase profits by raising price (to P' in Figure 2.3). This argument rests on an upward-sloping (and smooth) marginal cost (MC) function; in the standard Bertrand case of constant marginal cost, of course, it is in the interest of firms to continue setting the competitive price. However, the Bertrand

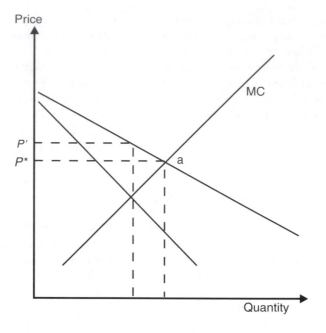

Figure 2.3 *The non-existence of competitive equilibrium*

case is not at all robust, since a slight deviation from constant marginal cost destroys the competitive equilibrium.

The standard textbook story of competitive price adjustment just does not stand up to closer scrutiny. The basic problem is the contradiction between an equilibrium concept based on price-taking and the notion of agents (firms or households) setting prices. Indeed, it has proven very difficult to provide a coherent account of competitive equilibrium which allows for individual agents to do anything other than choose demands or supplies at given prices. This does not mean that many minds have not put their ingenuity to solving this puzzle (see Dubey, 1982; Simon, 1984). However, one can but marvel at the baroque intricacies needed to provide suitable clothing for the classical simplicity of the original competitive edifice.

What are we left with? We shall return again to the Marshallian cross. However, at this stage one is tempted to say that the competitive outcome does not represent an 'equilibrium' at all. This is in a sense surprising since, for most undergraduates, competitive equilibrium is 'the' equilibrium. Certainly, for a couple of generations of academic researchers, the Arrow–Debreu incarnation of the Marshallian cross held an almost ineluctable fixation.

Debreu's *Theory of Value* was published in 1959, and the best minds of a few generations travelled the more arcane regions of 'general competitive analysis'. It is the fate of each generation's passion to seem unnatural to its successors. Perhaps the seduction lay in the panoply of technique needed to analyse the

model: it was, after all, Debreu who established real analysis as the preferred language of economists. On the conceptual level, however, whether one looks at the
competitive outcome as the fixed point of some mapping, or the intersection of
supply and demand, makes little or no difference. Nonetheless, if we look closely
at the Marshallian cross it seems difficult to give a coherent account of equilibrium in terms of either P2 or P3. The central contradiction is that, whilst price
plays a central role in competitive analysis, no agent (excepting the fictitious) has
any direct control over the price. Thus it makes little sense to say either that no-
one has any incentive to deviate from the competitive outcome, or that the price
will adjust towards the competitive price.

This does not mean that the competitive outcome is not useful, despite not
being an equilibrium. It can be seen either as an ideal type, a (possibly unattain-
able) benchmark, or an approximation to a non-competitive market. For example,
since a competitive market has the desirable efficiency property of Pareto-
optimality, governments may wish to make non-competitive markets behave
more like competitive markets (e.g. as in the regulation of natural monopolists).
Or again, under certain circumstances a non-competitive market may behave
almost like a competitive market: for example, under certain assumptions the
Cournot equilibrium 'tends' to the competitive outcome (see below) as the number of firms becomes large. This means that a Cournot market with many firms
can be approximated by its 'limiting case', the competitive outcome. However,
that being said, it seems wrong to view the competitive outcome as an equilibrium at all (except perhaps under certain well-specified cases).

1.2   The Keynesian Cross

The Keynesian cross represents the equilibrium of the income–expenditure relationship developed by Keynes (1936) and is represented in textbooks by the 45°
line diagram developed by Samuelson (1948). The microstructure here consists
of simple behavioural relationships. First, expenditures are divided into
'autonomous' (i.e. uninfluenced by income) and 'induced' (i.e. influenced by
income) expenditures. Investment and government expenditure are usually seen
as autonomous, consumption as induced. A basic behavioural postulate is made
about the relationship between income and consumption expenditure: higher
income leads to higher expenditure, and furthermore the proportion of income
spend falls with consumer income. The macrostructure of the model consists of
putting together these two types of expenditure (autonomous and induced) and
allowing income to adjust to ensure 'consistency' between income and planned
expenditure. In Figure 2.4, income Y is on the horizontal axis and expenditure is
on the vertical axis. Total planned expenditure is consumption plus investment
$I+C(Y)$. The 45° line represents the locus of equality between income and
expenditure. At Y^* in Figure 2.4, planned expenditure equals planned income,
since $I+C(Y^*)$ intersects the 45° line.

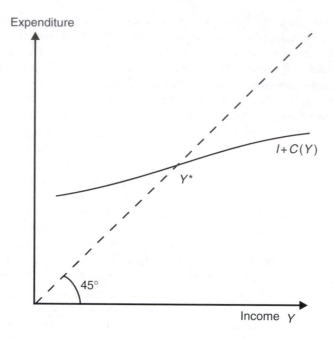

Figure 2.4   *Income–expenditure equilibrium*

   Why is Y^* seen as the equilibrium outcome? Again, look to introductory text-books for the answer; since at Y^* planned expenditure equals income and, in terms of equilibrium property P2, agents have no incentive to change behaviour. At incomes other than Y^*, there will either be an excess of planned expenditure over income $(Y > Y^*)$ or the opposite $(Y < Y^*)$. Given the income–expenditure identity, something has to give (this is variously explained in terms of forced saving by consumers or undesired inventory charges by firms). It needs to be noted that there is no derivation of the consumption function from some constrained maximization, and so no 'explanation' of planned consumption, which is itself a datum of explanation. Furthermore it is an *aggregate* consumption function. It is not clear how we can make sense of behaviour changes by any individual, or consumers in general, and how we might judge the effects of any change. Thus P2 is very weak here.

   However, the 'stability' equilibrium property P3 plays a much larger role in our understanding of the income–expenditure equilibrium. The driving force behind the equilibrium, the pump propelling the circular flow of income, is the multiplier process, which reflects the combination of a behavioural assumption (income generates expenditure through the consumption function) and an identity (income equals expenditure). One can view the equilibrium outcome Y^* as being generated by the following story. In the beginning there is just autonomous expenditure (for simplicity, say investment I). This generates income, in the sense that the act of 'expending' involves a transfer of money from the spender to the vendor (this is the income–expenditure identity). This income then generates consumption through the behavioural assumption that planned consumption depends upon income. As all economics students know, the end result of this infinite income–expenditure series is precisely income Y^*. This stability story is easily adjusted to allow for any 'initial' income.

If we consider the multiplier story underlying the Keynesian cross, we can see it is much more convincing and credible than the *tâtonnement* story. In one sense the multiplier process can never happen: it would take forever for the infinite geometric series to occur in real time and the process would run into serious problems of the indivisibility of currency. However, it is a process that we can observe, and the logic of geometric series implies that even a few iterations will move income close to Y^*. For example, when a foreign firm invests in a depressed region, it hires workers who spend money, shops open to serve them and so on. The *tâtonnement* is not observed. Whilst we see prices changing, there is no direct reason to believe that they come to rest at competitive levels. It is very important to note the contrast in emphasis on P2 and P3. Because the income–expenditure model has little microstructure to flesh out the issue of incentives to alter production or consumption, the explanatory emphasis shifts to the stability issue as embodied in the dynamic multiplier process underlying the equilibrium.

As a final comment, I do not believe that the Keynesian cross model is something of only archaeological interest in the history of macroeconomic thought. It underlies most macroeconomic models in the determination of nominal income. The behaviour of real income is of course a different matter, which depends (usually) upon what happens in the labour market.

1.3   The Cournot Cross

The fact that Cournot published his *Recherches sur la Théorie Mathématique de la Richesse* in 1838 is remarkable. It predates neoclassical economics by at least some 40 years, providing an analysis of duopoly that forms the basic model used in industrial organisation, and is introduced as the oligopoly model in micro texts. More remarkable still, it introduced the basic equilibrium concept of modern game theory: the Nash equilibrium. For these reasons it is perhaps the archetypal model underlying current-day economics, just as Walras reincarnated as Debreu underlay the economic theory of a previous generation.

The basic idea of the Cournot–Nash equilibrium is very simple. Firms choose outputs, and the market clears given those outputs. The key step here is to invert the market demand function: rather than treating household demand as a function of price, price is seen as a function of firms' outputs. This mathematical inversion has significant economic implications. In the standard homogeneous good case, it imposes a single market price on the good. Thus there is not a separate price for each firm's output, but a common market price which each firm can influence by altering its output (see Chapter 6 for a more detailed analysis).

If we stick to the homogeneous goods case, let there be n firms $I = 1, \ldots n$, with individual outputs X_i, summing to total output X. Market price P is then a function of X:

$$P = P(X) \qquad (2.1)$$

We can write each firm's profits U_i as a function of the outputs $\mathbf{X}$ chosen by each firm (where $\mathbf{X}$ is the n-vector of each firm's outputs).

$$U_i(\mathbf{X}) = X_i P(X) - c(X_i) \qquad (2.2)$$

where $c(X_i)$ is the firm's cost function. A Cournot–Nash equilibrium is defined as a vector of outputs $\mathbf{X}^*$, where each firm's output X_i^* yields higher profits than any other output X_i given the outputs of other firms X_{-i}^* (where X_{-i}^* is the $(n-1)$ vector of outputs of firms other than i). Formally, at equilibrium X^*,

$$U_i(X_i^*, X_{-i}) \geqslant U_i(X_i, X_{-i}) \qquad (2.3)$$

for all feasible outputs X_{-i} (usually any positive $X_i \geqslant 0$). There may of course be multiple equilibria or no equilibria: however, we shall proceed as if there is a single Cournot–Nash equilibrium.

The Cournot–Nash equilibrium is therefore almost completely defined in terms of equilibrium property P2. At equilibrium, no firm has an incentive to change its behaviour *given* the behaviour of others. Unlike in the competitive or Keynesian cross equilibria, what happens if one agent deviates from equilibrium is precisely defined. In the Cournot case, there is a function relating the outputs chosen by each firm to their profits (equation (2.2) above). In general game-theoretic terminology firms choose strategies (output) to maximize their pay-offs (profits), given the strategies of other firms. The Nash equilibrium is central to non-cooperative game theory, and its use is spreading through economics as it evolves beyond more traditional competitive or macroeconomic frameworks. The attraction of the Cournot equilibrium is that it is self-enforcing, since no one has an incentive to defect from it. Furthermore, if everyone expects a Nash equilibrium to occur, they will play their Nash strategy.

This is illustrated by the Cournot cross. The Cournot–Nash equilibrium is usually taught using the concept of a 'reaction function' (or, as others prefer, a 'best-response' function). Each firm's reaction function gives its profit-maximising output given the outputs of the other firms. In the case of duopoly, firm 1's reaction function $X_1 = r_1(X_2)$ is derived by solving

$$\max_{X_1} P[(X_1 + X_2) - c(X_1)] \qquad (2.4)$$

This tells us firm 1's best response to any output that firm 2 might choose. Similarly, for firm 2, $X_2 = r_2(X_1)$. Under standard assumptions, each reaction function is downward sloping with an (absolute) slope less than unity. In plain English, if firm 1 were to increase its output by one unit, the other firm's best response

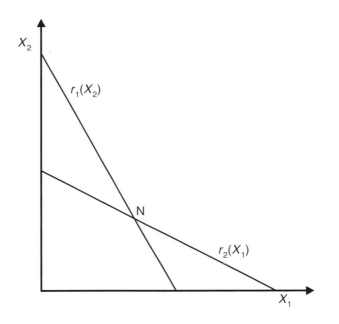

Figure 2.5 *Cournot oligopoly*

would be to reduce its output, but by less than the initial increase in firm 1's output. The Cournot cross is depicted in Figure 2.5. The Cournot–Nash equilibrium occurs at point N, where the two reaction functions cross. Only at N are both firms choosing their profit-maximising output given the output of the other firm.

What of the issue of stability in the Cournot model? The usual textbook story is that, starting from some disequilibrium position, the firms take turns to choose outputs. At each step, the firm chooses its output to maximise its profits given the output of the other firm (i.e. it moves onto its reaction function). In terms of Figure 2.6, starting from point 'a' we follow the arrows: firm 1 moves first to its reaction function, firm 2 moves to its reaction function and so on. This process will 'converge' to the equilibrium at N: although the firms will never reach N, they will get closer and closer (in mathematical terminology, the outputs converge uniformly to N but do not converge pointwise). An alternative adjustment process that is harder to depict is simply to have the firms simultaneously adjust to each other's output for the previous period. Assuming that technical 'stability' restrictions are met by the reaction functions, the Cournot–Nash equilibrium can be seen as the outcome of some dynamic process (P3).

However, rather like the *tâtonnement*, the Cournot adjustment process lacks credibility. The crucial weakness is that, at each step, the firms behave myopically: they choose their output to maximise their current profits given the output of the other firm, but ignore the fact that the process specifies that the other firm will adjust its output as given at the Nash equilibrium N. Suppose that firm 1 alters its output to X' in Figure 2.7. What would firm 2's best response be? One

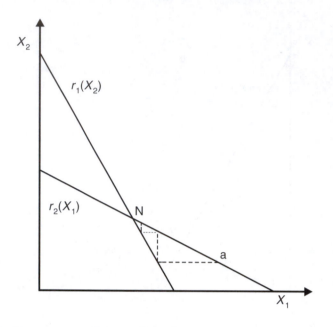

Figure 2.6 *Convergence to Cournot oligopoly*

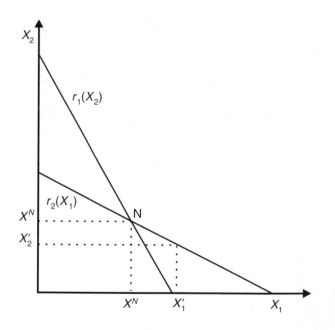

Figure 2.7 *Deviations from equilibrium*

is tempted to say that firm 2 would move along its 'reaction function' to X_2'. However, this will not be so in general if firm 2 envisages firm 1 making a subsequent response (since X_2' is the best response treating X' as given). Thus the issue of how firms respond to each other is rather convoluted: each firm's response depends on how the other firm will respond to it, which depends on what the other firm thinks that the first firm thought ...

However, if we alter the firm's conjectures, we not only alter the process of adjustment, but also the equilibrium itself. The reason for this is that in taking output decisions firms will take into account the other firm's response, rather than treating the other firm's output as given as in the Cournot–Nash equilibrium.

The nature of conjectures can be very general, allowing for the initial position and the size of the change. For example, firm 1's conjecture about firm 2's output could give X_2 as a function K of X_1 and the initial situation (X_{10}, X_{20}):

$$X_2 = K(X_1, X_{10}, X_{20})$$

A much simpler (and more common) form of conjecture is to restrict firms to a specific form of conjecture – namely a proportional response which is invariant to initial position. This restricts firms to constant conjectures z about dX_j/dX_i, called 'conjectural variations'. In a symmetric equilibrium with two firms and a homogenous product this results in the price–cost equation

$$\frac{P - c'}{P} = -\frac{1 + z}{ne}$$

where z is the conjectural variation, c' is marginal cost and e is industry elasticity of demand. If $z = -1$, each firm believes that industry output is constant, since the other firm reduces its output to offset an increase in firm 1's output exactly. In this case $P = c'$ – price equals marginal cost – and we have the competitive outcome. If $z = 0$ we have the Cournot outcome (firms believe the other's output is constant). If $z = +1$ then the price–cost margin equals $-1/e$, which is the collusive or joint profit-maximising outcome. Industrial economists often use the conjectural variation model of Cournot oligopoly because just a single parameter (conjectural variation z) can capture the whole range of competitive behaviour from perfect competition ($z = -1$) to collusion ($z = +1$). The crucial point to note is that the nature of the equilibrium depends crucially on the conjectures firms have about out-of-equilibrium behaviour.

Thus the issue of whether or not firms have an incentive to deviate from equilibrium or not (P2) depends on how they conceive of disequilibrium. This causes problems for stability analysis in the Cournot model: if we allow firms to be aware of the fact that they will respond to each other out of equilibrium, then in general there is no reason for them to treat each other's output as given in equilibrium. The 'myopia' of the adjustment process is crucial for its convergence to the Cournot–Nash equilibrium at N rather than at some other point.

Current sentiment, taking its cue from game theory, does not view the conjectural variations approach with esteem. There are perhaps two main reasons for this. First, the Nash equilibrium is seen as the only sensible equilibrium concept to employ. There is no question of being 'out of equilibrium': rational players would never play any but the Nash equilibrium strategies. Any other choice of strategies would involve one firm or the other being off its best-response function and hence able to do better. No players who recognised each other as rational would play anything but the Nash strategy. Second, on the issue of adjustment, it is currently popular to argue that the conjectural approach attempts to capture dynamics in a static 'one-off' model. If we want to understand the responses of firms to one another over time, we need to have a fully specified dynamic model in which time is explicitly present. In game-theoretic terms, this means dealing with (finitely or infinitely) repeated games, which allow firms to react to (and anticipate) each other. In the conjectural approach, the firm simply considers a range of simultaneous possibilities (different values of its own output with the corresponding conjectures about the other's output).

Under the influence of modern game theory, many economists would reject the importance of traditional 'stability' analysis, and with it equilibrium property P3. Equilibrium is to be purely defined in the form of consistency (P1) and in terms of the incentive to play equilibrium strategies given the other player's strategies (P2). There is a price to be paid for this approach of course, that is, the notion that we must at all times be in equilibrium. This creates some problems, particularly in repeated games which we shall discuss later (p. 48 ff. below).

Comparing the Marshallian and Cournot crosses, we can see that, whereas the Marshallian cross is ill-conceived and defined as an equilibrium, the Cournot cross is well-defined in the sense that it is clear on what firms do and how the incentive to deviate from equilibrium is specified. This has led many economists to see the Cournot–Nash approach as a way of rationalising the Walrasian approach. The basic idea is to see the Walrasian equilibrium as the limit of the Cournot–Nash equilibrium as the number of firms in the industry becomes infinite or – more precisely – as the market share of each firm tends to zero. In this sense, the Walrasian outcome can be seen as an approximation to the 'true' Cournot–Nash equilibrium if there are many firms. The argument here is simple. The Walrasian equilibrium is based on the notion of price-taking behaviour, which means that firms treat marginal revenue as equal to price. Under Cournot competition marginal revenue is less than price since, as the firm increases output, the price falls. The extent to which the firm's marginal revenue is less than price depends upon the firm's elasticity of demand e_i which in turn depends upon its market share s_i and the industry elasticity e:

$$\varepsilon = \frac{P}{X_i} \frac{dP}{dX}$$

$$= \frac{X}{X_i} \frac{P}{X} \frac{dP}{dX}$$

$$= \frac{1}{s_i} e$$

$$= ne$$

If the market share s_i is very small, then we would expect the firm's elasticity e_i to become very large. If the firm's elasticity becomes very large, then marginal revenue becomes closer to price (recall that price taking is often described as having a 'perfectly elastic' or horizontal demand curve). Thus the behaviour of a Cournot–Nash equilibrium with many firms will be close to that of a Walrasian equilibrium.

1.4   An Evaluation

We have explored three different equilibria which lie at the heart of economics. To what extent do they embody a common equilibrium methodology? At the most superficial level, they do. We identified the three equilibrium properties P1–P3 that are often put forward and which seem to encapsulate the general view of equilibrium. All the equilibria possess these three properties in some sense. However, when we look at the equilibria closely, we can see that there are tensions and inconsistencies between both the equilibrium properties themselves (more specifically P2 and P3) and the equilibria. The inconsistency between P2 and P3 arises because of the nature of economic explanation. The tension between different types of equilibria arises because of substantive differences in their vision of how the economic world is conceived.

Let us first address the tension between P2 and P3, a problem that arises in both the competitive and Cournot equilibria. At the heart of this tension lies the problem of explanation. The behavioural model of agents in the microstructure gives rise to the state of the macrostructure. In equilibrium, these two are consistent. Out of equilibrium, they are not. Thus the behavioural model which defines the equilibrium may not be suitable out of equilibrium. Most importantly, it may lead agents to behave suboptimally out of equilibrium, which makes explanation of such behaviour difficult for economists. This problem occurs when we consider P2 and P3: both involve some consideration of both equilibrium and disequilibrium states. In evaluating P2, we consider what happens when agents deviate from equilibrium behaviour, so moving away from equilibrium; in stability we analyse the equilibrium state as the outcome of a sequence of disequilibrium states ('outcome' in the sense of limit, end-point or destination).

The tension between P2 and P3 arises because the equilibrium behaviour used to define equilibrium under P2 seems inappropriate for analysing stability P3. The argument can be put briefly as follows:

1   Equilibrium is defined (partly) by behavioural postulates X.
2   In analysing stability (P3), the reason that the economic system moves towards equilibrium is that agents adjust their behaviour. Thus the driving force of the move towards equilibrium is the response of agents to their mistakes.
3   If agents adapted their behaviour to the disequilibrium situation, the motion of the economic system would differ and, most importantly, it might lead to a

different equilibrium. In particular, behaviour Y which is appropriate in dis-equilibrium may not be consistent with the equilibrium defined by behaviour X.

This tension is present in both the Marshallian and Cournot cross equilibria. In the competitive cases, the equilibrium behaviour employed under P2 is price-taking behaviour. This makes reasonable sense in equilibrium (agents are indeed able to buy and sell as much as they wish), but, in analysing stability, P3, the assumption of price-taking behaviour becomes silly – prices change in response to excess demand, and agents are unable to realise their desired trades. The presence of excess demands drives the *tâtonnement* process, and the presence of excess demands reflects the fact that agents are making mistakes in some sense. Were they to adapt their behaviour to disequilibrium, the resultant end-point might be different from the competitive equilibrium. In the Cournot case we illustrated this argument using conjectural variations.

To turn to the second issue, each of the equilibria embodies a different vision of the economic world. In the competitive world we have individual agents responding to price signals which they receive from an impersonal market. They do not see their own actions influencing anything or anyone but themselves. In the Cournot game-theoretic world, although agents act independently, they see that their own pay-offs (profits, utility) depend upon the other agents' actions as well as their own (and that their own actions influence others). There is no 'invisible hand' or price mechanism to coordinate activity across the economy. Rather, each agent acts in his own self-interest, ignoring the effect of his actions on others. In the Keynesian cross model, there are no individuals as such. Attention is focused on impersonal aggregates which are driven by their own laws rather than through any very specific modelling of individual action.

2   DISEQUILIBRIUM AND EQUILIBRIUM

The analysis of disequilibrium poses great problems for economic explanation. Whilst it is not plausible to maintain that every market and agent is at all times in equilibrium, economists have very little to say about what happens out of equilibrium; this is because equilibrium itself lies at the heart of economic explanation. There is a sense in which economists cannot explain out-of-equilibrium phenomena. If we recall the structure of explanation in economics, it rests on two levels: microstructure, where agents' behaviour is specified (usually as the outcome of constrained optimisations); and macrostructure, where the parts are put together into a whole by the use of an equilibrium concept. Putting these two levels together, we can explain: 'everyone is doing as well as they can (microstructure); if everyone is doing as well as they can, then this happens (macrostructure)'. The equilibrium concept thus relates the properties of the whole (be it macroeconomy, general equilibrium system, market or firm) to behaviour and motivation of the individual agents or parts.

The problem of disequilibrium analysis is that it is not an equilibrium, so that by definition the desired behaviour of agents is not consistent and in some sense their actions are not the best they could take. In essence, explanation of disequilibrium involves the explanation of a mistake. In a theory basis on formal rationality (as opposed to procedural rationality), it is difficult to explain mistakes. With a procedural model of rationality, the explanation of a mistake can consist in showing that (in a particular instance) the procedure generating choices and actions is wrong. With a formal notion of rationality, there is no reference to the procedure: the decision is linked directly to the basic conditions of the problem, and there is no room for explaining the mistake. This difference is perhaps best illustrated by the contrast between adaptive and rational expectations in the context of the Lucas supply curve. With adaptive expectations, there is a procedure generating the expectations of agents in the economy; it may be a good or bad procedure depending on the behaviour of inflation. Whether it is a good or bad procedure, it can explain why agents may make systematic mistakes under certain circumstances (e.g. if inflation accelerates). With rational expectations, however, there can in principle be no explanation of how people make systematic mistakes. Indeed, that people make systematic mistakes would in itself be a refutation of the rational-expectations hypothesis. Thus the formal notion of rationality employed by most economists is rather ill-equipped to deal with disequilibrium.

This point is perhaps best illustrated by looking at disequilibrium in a competitive market. Although more of an allegory than a serious explanation of what happens, we can consider the *tâtonnement* process. Suppose that the price is above the competitive price. Supply exceeds demand, so that desired trades are 'inconsistent' (equilibrium property P1 is not satisfied); the price is falling, so 'price taking' is not appropriate. As to the issue of whether or not agents are doing as well as they can, that depends on how what goes out of equilibrium is specified. The traditional *tâtonnement* story gets around this by saying that there is no trade: in effect nothing happens. In the Hahn–Negishi (1962) story, trade occurs out of equilibrium: the Hahn–Negishi condition states that all agents have the excess demand of same sign. This means that only one side of the market is unable to meet its desired (or 'target') trades at the disequilibrium price. In terms of Figure 2.2, this means that at P' those demanding the good are able to obtain their desired trades, whilst suppliers will in some sense be 'rationed' (more about this later). Thus actual trades will be given by X_0. The rationale for the Hahn–Negishi condition is that markets are 'efficient': if there is someone who wants to buy and someone who wants to sell, they will find each other. If the Hahn–Negishi condition were violated, then there could be agents on both sides of the market unable to trade. Clearly, there must be a sense in which those unable to realise their desired trade could do better. In terms of Figure 2.2, the rationed suppliers could cut their price: again, the price-taking assumption is not appropriate out of competitive equilibrium. The basic assumptions about the behaviour of economic agents (demands and supplies are derived by treating prices as given, and there are no constraints on trades) are not consistent unless they are assumptions of competitive equilibrium. Or, to put it another way, agents display no 'disequilibrium awareness' in Fischer's (1981) terminology; they behave as if they were in equilibrium even when they are not.

One response to this is to extend the model to allow agents to behave in a fundamentally different and appropriate manner out of equilibrium. For the case of competitive price adjustment, Fischer (1981) has attempted the non-*tâtonnement* process in this way. The resultant model is extremely complex and unwieldy. Fischer contemplated submitting an equation in his model to the *Guinness Book of Records* for the longest ever Lagrangean (1981, p. 290n)! This is not the place to discuss whether or not this attempt was successful. However, even if successful, it would simply come close to defining a new equilibrium for when prices are adjusting to the competitive equilibrium rather than studying disequilibrium itself.

This illustrates the fundamental problem posed by disequilibrium: the explanation is either unsatisfactory or it leads to the definition of a new equilibrium. The best illustration of this is the literature on fix-price 'disequilibrium' models.

In the 1960s, workers on the reinterpretation of Keynes (Clower, 1965; Leijonhufvud, 1968) argued that Keynesian macroeconomics was incompatible with Walrasian equilibrium, and that phenomena such as rationing and the income–expenditure process arose from 'false trading' at non-competitive prices. Unless prices were seen as adjusting instantaneously to their Walrasian values, microeconomics would need to be revised to take account of trading 'in disequilibrium'. The response of economists in the 1970s was to pursue the study of *disequilibrium* by defining a new sort of *equilibrium*, fixed-price equilibrium, the main contributions being by Barro and Grossman (1971), Benassy (1975) and Malinvaud (1977). The study of fixed-price equilibria adopted the basic notion of price-taking from the Walrasian approach, but made prices *exogenous* (rather than trying them down to the market-clearing level). The basic task was to provide a consistent and coherent account of trade at 'disequilibrium prices'. In Walrasian microeconomics, agents believe that they can buy or sell as much as they wish at the given price. Out of competitive equilibrium this is inappropriate, and so a new economic variable was introduced – the quantity or rationing constraint. The notion of *effective demand* was specified as the demand which (in the household's case) maximises utility *given* the quantity constraints that it faces in other markets. Thus if a worker is unable to sell his labour (there is an excess supply of labour), this will restrict his demand for consumption goods. Similarly, if a firm cannot sell all it would like to at the current price, then its demand for labour will be influenced. This is the essence of the 'spillover' effect: if an agent is unable to realise his trades in one market, it may affect his demand or supply in other markets. In the eyes of the 'reinterpretation of Keynes' school, this was the very essence of the multiplier process and the income–expenditure feedback, which meant that quantities (rather than just prices, as in the Walrasian case) entered into demand functions.

By introducing a rationing regime into the market process, and allowing rationing constraints to influence individual agents' decisions, the fixed-price approach was able to reconcile the microstructure of the model with the macrostructure. In essence, at non-Walrasian prices, demands and supplies do not equalise; agents are unable to realise their desired trades (macrostructure). Recognising the constraints on trade, agents revise their desired trades to take these into account (microstructure).

Thus the analysis of competitive 'disequilibrium' led to the invention of a new type of 'non-Walrasian' equilibrium. The analysis of 'disequilibrium' did not lead to a genuine disequilibrium analysis; rather, the logic of economic explanation led to the generation of another equilibrium concept. In this case, fix-price equilibria are a *generalisation* of Walrasian equilibria: a Walrasian equilibrium is merely a fix-price equilibrium where agents face no (binding) rationing constraints.

Given the real disequilibrium analysis is to some extent incompatible with standard economic explanation and rationality, to what extent is economics possible without equilibrium? To see what economics looks like without equilibrium, it is salutary to look at one of the few economic models to reach textbook popularity which did not employ the equilibrium method. The example I have chosen is Kaldor's growth model (see Jones, 1975, pp. 146–9, for a concise exposition of Kaldor, 1975). The central issue in Harrod's growth model was the possible divergence of the 'warranted' growth rate (which equates planned saving and planned investment) from the 'natural' growth rate (determined by demography, technological progress etc.). Kaldor's microstructure consisted of the differential savings propensities out of wage and profit income. Thus savings were influenced by the distribution of income between wages and profits. Rather than employ an equilibrium concept in his model, Kaldor used a 'stylised fact': namely that there had been full employment in postwar European economies. Kaldor argued that the distribution of income between wages and profits would adjust to maintain consistency between the warranted and natural growth rates. Thus, a feature of the macrostructure was employed to tie down the distribution of income (to 'close the model'), rather than an equilibrium concept. This explanation is viewed as odd because it works backwards: rather than deducing macro properties from individual and market behaviour, it deduces the distribution of income across wages and profits from the macrostructure. Indeed, Modigliani and Samuelson went so far as to say 'If you can believe this, you can believe anything' (1966, p. 234). The equilibrium methodology is so ingrained in economists' minds that they will not be convinced by non-equilibrium explanations.

3 INFORMATION AND EQUILIBRIUM

Until now we have been considering only 'full-information' models, where agents have a given information set including all the relevant information for them to take decisions. In the 1970s there was a blossoming of interest in exploring the implications of imperfect information for economic behaviour and equilibrium. Perhaps the earliest interest was in the 'search' models of unemployment in the late 1960s. In these models, agents have imperfect information about prices (wages), for example what prices (wages) a particular firm is offering. Search models of unemployment modelled the response of the unemployed to this problem: do they take the next job offered to them at a particular wage, or will they continue to search and incur the cost of further unemployment? The general solution to this problem was the 'reservation wage' rule: the unemployed continue searching until they are offered at least their 'reservation wage'. However, these were not *equilibrium* models, since there was no explanation of the initial distribution of wage offers. Why should firms offer different wages to the same worker or type of worker? However, the model was nonetheless very influential, not least in its influence on Friedman's formulation of the natural rate hypothesis (Friedman, 1968). We shall take Spence's (1974) signalling model as our archetypal imperfect information model. This had a tremendous impact at the time, and introduced the fundamental concept of a *signalling equilibrium* and the crucial distinction between *separating* and *pooling* equilibria which has proved to be so important in subsequent years.

The standard approach to imperfect information is to presume that if agents do not know the true value of X_1 they have some subjective probability density function for X, $f(X)$, in effect treating X as a random variable. Spence took the case of worker productivity, where there was asymmetric information so that, whilst workers knew their own productivity, firms did not. For example, let worker productivity X take discrete values, being either low or high (X_L, X_H respectively). Suppose that it is not possible to test directly for productivity. Whilst the employer might not know the actual productivity of an individual worker, it might have a subjective belief about the probability that the worker is high productivity (q) or low productivity ($1-q$). Assuming that firms are risk-neutral and minimise costs, they will be willing to offer workers their expected productivity $E[X]$:

$$W = E[X] = qX_H + (1-q)X_L \qquad (2.5)$$

The wage offer depends upon both the subjective probability q and the values (X_L, X_H). If we take the latter as given, what is the 'equilibrium' value of W and q?

This raises an issue about beliefs in economic models. Given that beliefs are not 'tied down' by the truth (there is not full information), how do we explain agents' beliefs? We shall consider this issue in this sections and the next. However, there now enters the notion of *epistemological* rationality. The agent is presumed to have (in some sense) the 'best' beliefs given the information available. 'Best' here usually means statistically optimal. An agent's beliefs are then explained by saying that they are (in some sense) statistically optimal. 'Best' in this context means something completely different from the notion of 'best' in the theory of rational choice, where it means the choice which yields maximum utility given the constraints faced. Different notions of rationality are employed in explaining beliefs and explaining consumption or production decisions. The key point is that beliefs are not chosen to maximise utility. It may increase my utility if I believe that I am Napoleon: however, that is not a 'rational' belief. Let us first define economic rationality: it is an *instrumental* rationality in which choices are made merely as a means to an end (utility or profit). If we were to extend economic rationality to beliefs, people would choose beliefs so as to maximise their utility. The belief that I am Napoleon might then be perfectly rational (indeed, not to believe I am Napoleon might be to involve some suboptimality). When beliefs clearly do matter in that they directly affect well-being (in some sense), economic rationality can be used to explain beliefs. However, in most economic models, beliefs do not enter the utility function of households directly. Debreu's households might be deist, pantheist or atheist: they might believe in general relativity or be creationists.

When explaining beliefs, however, a different notion of rationality is employed by economists. Let us take the example above of the firm hiring workers of unknown productivity. In equilibrium, is there any restriction to be placed on the firm's subjective probability q? The usual constraint suggested is that *in equilibrium* the belief is 'confirmed'. In the case sketched above, suppose that the objective (i.e. population) proportion of high-productivity workers is q^*. Then we require that $q = q^*$: the subjective probability equals the objective probability. Assuming that the firm employs a large number of workers, the average productivity of workers the firm employs is

$$\overline{X} = q^* X_H + (1 - q^*) X_L \tag{2.6}$$

for the firm's beliefs are only 'confirmed' if

$$E[X] = \overline{X}$$

requiring that $q = q^*$. If the firm's subjective probability differs from the population proportion, then the average productivity of the workforce differs from what the firm expects.

If $q^* > q$, workers would (on average) be more productive, and vice versa. In the statistical sense, the firm would have an 'incentive' to revise its beliefs If X deviated from $E[X]$. 'Incentive' here is used not in its standard economic sense but in a statistical sense that the optimal estimation of the population parameter would be different. Economists often tend to confuse the language and concepts of economic and statistical rationality, which is probably because both can be expressed mathematically as an optimisation. However, the fact that in one case it is utility (or profit) to be maximised and in the other it is the likelihood (or some such statistical criterion) to be maximised makes the two rationalities completely separate and incommensurable.

In most economic models, this incommensurability does not give rise to any incompatibility. However, I will give an example of when economic and epistemological rationality are incompatible. Let us return to the example of Cournot–Nash equilibrium which we explored above. In Figure 2.8, the Cournot–Nash equilibrium occurs at N: firm 1 is choosing its profit-maximising output given the other firm's output X^N. In effect, firm 1 believes (or expects)

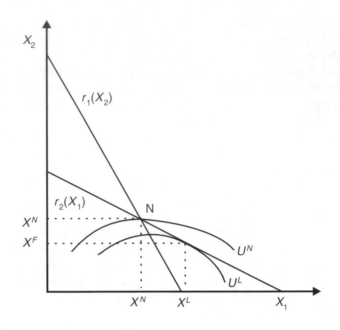

Figure 2.8   *Deviations from equilibrium*

firm 2 to play X^N, and chooses its best response. Furthermore, in equilibrium this belief is confirmed: if firm 1 produces X^N, it is firm 2's best response to produce X^N.

However, suppose that firm 1 believed that firm 2 was producing 0: its best response would be X^L. If firm 1 stuck to this belief, firm 2 would (eventually) produce X^F, its best response to X^L. This is the standard 'Stackelberg' or 'leader-follower' equilibrium with firm 1 the 'leader' producing X^L, and firm 2 the follower producing X^F. Is this an equilibrium? In one sense it is: firm 2 is choosing its best response to X^L; firm 1 is choosing its best response to the output it believes firm 2 to be producing, namely 0. The problem is that firm 1's beliefs are not correct: X^F does not equal 0. If we require firm 1's beliefs to be correct, in addition to both firms' choosing their best response, there is only one possible outcome – the Nash equilibrium at N. In terms of its pay-off (economic rationality), the firm does better to have incorrect beliefs at (X^L, X^F): it loses no profits by the fact that its beliefs about the other firm's output are incorrect (0 differs from X^F), but clearly it gains profits by being the Stackelberg leader as a result $(u^L > u^N)$. However, most economists would not maintain that this was an equilibrium: the firm would have an 'incentive' (in the sense of epistemic rationality) to revise its beliefs about the other firm's output. Thus the firm (it is argued) will change its beliefs about X_2, so that the Stackelberg point (X^L, X^F) is not an 'equilibrium'. Thus despite the reduction in profits caused by the change of belief, epistemological rationality dictates that the belief cannot be maintained in equilibrium. There is thus a clash of rationalities, which are in this instance incompatible.

In this clash of incommensurable rationalities, economists let epistemological rationality overrule economic rationality. Even though the Stackelberg leader's delusion is profitable, he is not allowed to maintain his belief in the presence of clear evidence to the contrary. Thus we can add a fourth equilibrium property to our list:

P4   In equilibrium, agents have no incentive to alter their beliefs

where 'incentive' is interpreted in the strictly epistemological sense, not the economic sense of P2. In the case of the simple example of firms hiring workers, P4 requires that subjective beliefs are 'confirmed', i.e. that $q^* = q$. In more complicated models, where X is a continuous variable, the beliefs might be subjective probability distributions, and P4 might require beliefs about mean, variance and possibly higher moments to be correct.

Having explored the new notion of rationality introduced to tie down beliefs in equilibrium with imperfect information, we can move on to examine perhaps the most important type of such equilibria – signalling equilibria (as introduced by Spence, 1974).

Suppose that we take the case where the firm hires workers of unknown quality, taking the model introduced earlier in this section. In equilibrium, we argued that the wage offer would equal the average productivity X of workers. This is called a pooling equilibrium, because both low- and high-productivity workers are pooled together (i.e. they are treated the same, and receive the same wages). In the full-information case, high-productivity workers would obtain their full marginal product X_H, low-productivity workers would obtain X_L. Thus the high-productivity workers do worse in the pooled equilibrium than in the full-information case, and low-productivity workers do better. There is thus an incentive for high-productivity workers to 'signal' their ability to their prospective employer. Very simply, a high-productivity worker can signal his ability if he can do something which a low-ability worker is unwilling or unable to do. This signalling activity need have no direct causal relationship with the workers' productivity. All that matters is that the high-productivity workers have lower costs of undertaking the activity. It has long been recognised that education is used as a 'screening' device by employers to sift applicants.

Whilst education may sometimes have little direct or vocational content, it can be seen as enhancing the general ability of the educated. However, Spence (1974) abstracts from this, and focuses purely on the signalling element. The essence of a signalling equilibrium is a circular relationship between the beliefs of agents and their behaviour, in that the beliefs induce behaviour which confirms these beliefs. Thus, in the context of Spence's model, employers have a belief about the relationship between education and productivity (higher education is related to higher productivity); this causes firms to offer higher wages to more educated workers; this sets up the incentives workers face to obtain educational qualifications; and

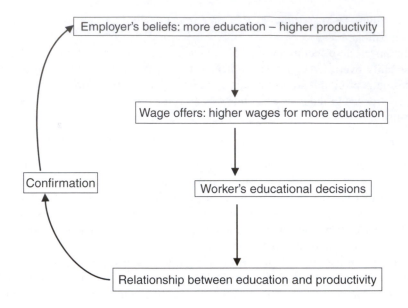

Figure 2.9 *A signalling equilibrium*

workers' decisions about education determine the *actual* relationship (if any) between education and productivity. There is an equilibrium if the employer's beliefs are confirmed (P4 is satisfied). Figure 2.9 is a schematic representation.

The crucial feature of the equilibrium is that the *costs* of signalling (being educated) differ with productivity. More specifically, higher-productivity workers must have lower 'signalling' costs – in this case they must have lower costs of achieving a given level of education. The reason for this is that otherwise (given that the firm's wages are related to education) the low-productivity workers would also find it in their interest to obtain higher educational qualifications, so that the firm would offer them higher wages (in the belief that they were high-productivity workers). This is often called the 'incentive compatibility' constraint. The idea is that, in equilibrium, each different type of worker has the appropriate incentive to behave appropriately to its type. Thus, in the above case, the two types of worker differ by productivity. Suppose that the employer believes that low-productivity workers have no education, whilst those with y^* units of education (a BA degree for example) are high productivity. This wage offer might therefore be

$$W = \begin{cases} X_H & y \geq y^* \\ X_L & y < y^* \end{cases}$$

Assuming that there is no intrinsic value to education, workers will either choose no education ($y = 0$), or $y = y^*$ to get the higher wages. Workers will undertake the education if and only if the cost is less than the extra wages obtained. 'Incentive compatibility' requires that it is in the interest of high-productivity workers to obtain their BA (for them, the cost of attaining y^* is less than $X_H - X_L$); low-productivity workers, on the other hand, would find it too costly to obtain a BA (the cost of attaining y^* is greater than $X_H - X_L$). In the signalling equilibrium (if it exists), the two types of workers are *separated*: the incentives are such that they reveal their true type through their behaviour. When this occurs, there is said to be a *separating* equilibrium. If the employers beliefs were different, there could be a *pooling* equilibrium: if the employer believed that there was no relationship between education and productivity, he would offer the same wage regardless of education; no one would become educated, and thus the employer's beliefs would be confirmed.

In this type of equilibrium with asymmetric information and signalling, there is a very intimate relationship between economic incentives (P2) and the confirmation of beliefs (P4). However, it must be noted that in Spence's model the treatment of beliefs is very rudimentary, which results in multiple equilibria. The possibility of multiple signalling equilibria is easily illustrated using the educational signalling model. Following Spence, suppose that high-productivity workers have a cost $y/2$ of achieving education level y, whereas low-productivity workers have a cost y:

$$X_H - \frac{y}{2} \geqslant X_L \qquad \text{(a)}$$

$$X_H - y < X_L \qquad \text{(b)}$$

Condition (a) states that, given y, it pays the high-productivity worker to invest in education (cost $y/2$), to obtain extra income $X_H - X_L$; condition (b) states that this is not so for the low-productivity worker, who has to invest more effort and resources to obtain y. Both (a) and (b) will be satisfied if

$$X_H - X_L \leqslant y^* \leqslant 2(X_H - X_L) \qquad \text{(c)}$$

Thus, if the employer's beliefs about the 'critical' level of education y^* are in the interval (c), then there will be a separating equilibrium with workers' activity so as to confirm the employer's belief. There is thus a continuum of equilibria. Is there any sense in which one can sensibly rank the equilibria?

Suppose that the employer and workers are economists and understand Spence's model. Then the employer will understand the incentive constraints (a) and (b). He will deduce that anyone undertaking a level of education greater than $X_H - X_L$ must be a high-productivity worker: there is no way that a low-productivity worker would conceivably want to undertake a course of education that would cost more than the possible extra earnings. Thus, if we consider the equilibria with $y^* > X_H - X_L$, they involve unnecessary cost in the form of education in excess of the minimum required. It has been argued (Cho, 1987) that these equilibria will not be 'stable'. A high-productivity worker can educate below y^* but above $X_H - X_L$ and still single himself out as being high-productivity. Thus with 'sophisticated' knowledge about the way the model works, the equilibrium with the minimum amount of signalling necessary to separate types is the most plausible (in the above case, $y^* = X_H - X_L$).

4 TIME AND EQUILIBRIUM

The passing of time is a central feature of human experience. It plays a central role in much economic activity, since production takes time and consumers have to decide how to spread their consumption and labour supply over their (uncertain) lifetime. Yet, all three equilibria studied above were in a fundamental sense static equilibria. They were equilibria in a timeless world, or at most equilibria at a point in time unconnected to the past or future. How does our conception and evaluation of equilibria alter when we allow for time?

First, consider the Walrasian equilibrium. If we introduce time into the picture, there are two fundamentally different ways of conceiving of equilibrium. First is the Arrow–Debreu model, which sees the earth as a large marketplace and world history as the working out of contingent contracts. Second is the notion of temporary equilibrium, which sees history as a *sequence* of transitory equilibria. We shall deal with these two ideas in turn.

Competitive general equilibrium theory explores the issue of the existence and characterisation of competitive equilibrium in an economy with an arbitrary number of markets. For example, these might be seen as corresponding to n basic commodity types (bananas, nuts etc.). As such, the model is timeless. We can then ask how time can be brought into a timeless model. This can be done by a logical exercise of dating commodities. Suppose that the world lasts T periods $t = 1, \ldots T$. We can call a banana at time t a particular commodity, to be different from a banana at time s (where s is not equal to t). Rather than having n markets, we will now have nT markets, corresponding to the n basic commodity types over T periods. This is depicted in Figure 2.10 where time proceeds downwards, each column representing a commodity type.

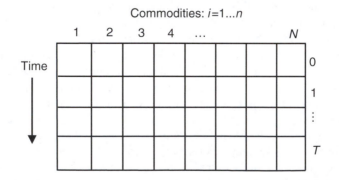

Figure 2.10   *The Arrow–Debreu economy*

A particular square represents the market for a particular commodity *i* at a specific date *t*. Each market has a price P_{it}. Consumers will derive utility from the consumption of all *nT* dated commodities, which they will maximise subject to a budget constraint reflecting relative prices. Thus a household can as much sell an umbrella in the year 2000 for a corset in the year 1901 as it can exchange a banana for a nut in 1990.

In a certain sense, then, introducing dated commodities and their corresponding markets and prices into the abstract notion of competitive general equilibrium enables time to be included in the model. This is really just a purely logical exercise, however. To see why, just think what the Arrow–Debreu world would be like to live in! Competitive general equilibrium occurs at a list of prices – one for each market – at which demand equals supply in each market (or, more generally, there is no excess demand).

The key feature is that there is *simultaneous* equilibrium across markets. In the full Arrow–Debreu world, prices across history need to be 'simultaneously' determined together 'outside' the historical process itself. Following the great religious texts, we can place that which is beyond time at some notional beginning of time. Thus we can imagine that at the beginning of time the souls of all the world's population-to-be assemble in a large building (let us say the Albert Hall). The auctioneer would cry out a long vector of prices covering each commodity over world history. A *tâtonnement* process would occur until every market was in equilibrium, whether for second-hand animal skins in 2000 BC or microwave ovens in AD 2000. Once equilibrium had been reached, the final prices would be struck. The souls of the future world would then dissolve from the Albert Hall to return to the unmanifest, each with a contract. This contract would tell them the prices of each commodity at every time, and their trades. Time would then begin, and souls would become manifest as people and live their allotted lives. History would simply be the working out of the original contract: each day economic man would look at his contract, and carry out his pre-ordained trades (as would economic woman). Economists have competing views as to whether this world would last forever ('infinite horizon' with *T* infinite), or whether the world would end after some period *T*. In the latter case, others have argued that perhaps, the world having ended, the whole process would begin again: perhaps the same souls involved in the infinite repetition of the same history, or different souls subject to the same laws. Alas, econometrics remains powerless to adjudicate on this issue. Clearly, the Arrow–Debreu world has little in common with our own world.

A more realistic vision of world history is given by the *temporary equilibrium* approach. This has the advantage that price formation is historically situated. It also has the advantage that each day that economic man wakes up he does not know what is going to happen. The basic vision in its simplest form is to *truncate* the Arrow–Debreu model. At time *t*, we can differentiate between *spot* markets, which are for goods to be traded in the current period *t*, and futures markets at which deal with trades to be made in the future, in dates *s* following *t*, $s = t \ldots \infty$.

An extreme form of temporary equilibrium is to assume that the economy is rather like an adolescent punk – *all spots and no future*. Thus at any time there would be a market for each basic commodity, but no markets for future commodities. Suppose an infinitely-lived household wishes to sell its 2000 BC sheepskin to buy an AD 1990 microwave. Whereas in the Arrow–Debreu world this can be done directly at the Albert Hall in year 0, in a temporary equilibrium sequence economy the transaction is more difficult. The sheepskin would have to be sold in 2000 BC and exchanged for money (or some other store of value). The money could then be held as an asset until AD 1990 arrives, when it is handed over for the microwave. The reverse transaction is rather more difficult: without a futures market for microwaves, our household would have to persuade the then equivalent of a bank manager to provide it with a bridging loan until the microwave sale in AD 1990. This should prove no problem with perfect information and perfect foresight. However, if money balances are constrained to be positive (i.e. no borrowing), then the absence of this futures market might prevent the purchase of the sheepskin in 2000 BC.

'All spots and no future' is an extreme form of temporary equilibrium. There might be some futures markets allowed (e.g. in financial assets or chosen commodities), and in the above example our household could then trade in these futures markets to finance the sheepskin purchase – for example by selling future money for current (i.e. 2000 BC) money. This is in effect borrowing the money to buy the sheepskin.

World history, here, is a sequence of temporary equilibria. Unlike the Arrow–Debreu world, markets unfold sequentially rather than all at once. From the household's point of view, rather than there being one big intertemporal budget covering all of time at once, there is a sequence of budget constraints, one for each point in time (or, with uncertainty, for each state of nature at each point in time). At any one time, all the consumer 'observes' are current prices in the markets in which the consumer trades. Whilst the consumer will of course base his current consumption decisions on what he thinks may happen in the future, the absence of futures markets gives him little or no indication of what future prices might be. This contrasts with the Arrow–Debreu story, where all prices for all time are known in the Albert Hall. This of course raises problems of intertemporal coordination. Taking our previous example, if the ancient Briton wishes to exchange his sheepskins for a future microwave, he will have to save (i.e. hold money). This act of saving transmits no direct signal to the microwave manufacturer to invest in order to provide for the eventual demand. This contrasts with the Arrow–Debreu story, where this is all sorted out in the Albert Hall. The absence of futures markets thus poses a decisive problem for coordinating economic activity over time, a problem first highlighted by Keynes (1936) and also by his subsequent reinterpreters (e.g. Shackle, 1974; Liejunhufvud, 1968; *inter alia*). The first 'fundamental theorem' of welfare economics – which states that any competitive equilibrium is Pareto-optimal – is only generally valid in the Arrow–Debreu world: in a temporary equilibrium sequence economy the problem of intertemporal coordination is almost insuperable.

Although the Arrow–Debreu and temporary equilibrium approaches seem so different, economic theorists have taken pains to demonstrate that their outcomes need not be so different. With perfect foresight, for example, the history of the world (in terms of prices, consumption and so on) will look the same as if history had started in the Albert Hall. Whilst it might be reasonable to assume that infinitely-lived households have perfect foresight, it is less appealing in the case of mortal households. The assumption of perfect foresight assumes that each and every agent can work out the equilibrium prices over time. This destroys the appealing notion of 'decentralisation' by the price mechanism. Rather than each agent simply responding to prices on the basis of his own information, in a perfect-foresight-sequence economy each agent is required to have full information about the whole economy. In effect, each agent in the economy becomes the auction-eer. Indeed, each agent knows more than Walras's auctioneer, since he merely groped blindly to equilibrium, whereas our prescient agents calculate the path of prices over history. Of more interest, perhaps, are results which show that a full set of futures markets is not needed to replicate the Arrow–Debreu world: see Marimon (1987) for a survey and discussion of some of the important results.

We have seen the implications of time for Walrasian equilibrium. What of Cournot? The Cournot–Nash equilibrium is best conceived of as a one-shot game. What happens if firms compete over time? We shall examine the issues raised by competition over time to explore the concept of *subgame-perfect* equilibrium; for a fuller exposition, see Chapter 6. The basic idea of a subgame-perfect equilibrium is that at each point in time agents choose their best responses to each other, given that in each subsequent period they will continue to do so. The main use of this equilibrium concept has been to rule out non-credible threats, by which it is meant threats that it is not in the interest of the threatener to carry out (put another way, if the threatened agent called the bluff of the threat-ener, the threatener would not carry out the threat). The logic of subgame-perfect equilibrium rules out such non-credible threats by requiring agents to act in their best interest for each and subsequent periods. For example, I could threaten to kill you in a most unpleasant manner if you did not send me a £5 postal order. This is not a credible threat since, were you not to comply, it would not be in my inter-est to kill you (certain readers excepted). Suppose that the Cournot scenario is repeated for T periods. The 'subgame' for each period $t = 1, \ldots T$ is simply the remainder of the game from period t through to T (for example, in period 5 of a ten-year game, the subgame consists of periods 5 through to 10). At each point in time t, we can imagine each Cournot duopolist choosing his outputs for the remaining periods (i.e. choosing outputs to produce in each period $s = t$, $t + 1, \ldots T$). If the outputs chosen over the remaining periods by each firm are the best response to the other firm's choice, there is a Nash equilibrium in the period to subgame. Subgame perfection requires that the firms' strategies are a Nash equilibrium in each and every subgame. This rules out non-credible threats, since in effect it requires the firm to choose its strategy optimally at each stage of the game. When we arrive at the period when the non-credible threat needs to be carried out, the firm will not do this because it is not in its interest to do so.

In order to solve for a perfect equilibrium, agents need to 'work backwards'. In order to know what they will do in period $T-1$, they need to work out what they will do in period T to evaluate the consequences of their choice of strategy in $T-1$. They then proceed to work out what will happen in period $T-1$ conditional on the choice of strategies in $T-2$ and so on. In a perfect equilibrium, agents in effect become super-rational game theorists: in evaluating the consequences of their actions, each agent takes into account that future responses by all agents will be chosen optimally.

This equilibrium notion has been very popular in the last decade. However, it has a serious methodological paradox at its heart. If the players of the game are super-rational and solve the game, then the equilibrium will occur. However, in evaluating the equilibrium, the agents considered the possibility of taking non-equilibrium actions (i.e. actions off the equilibrium path) but, if agents were rational, then they would never take actions off the equilibrium path. If an agent were to move off the equilibrium path, then he could not be 'rational' in the sense required by the equilibrium concept. Indeed, what would his fellow players think of the player who deviated from the equilibrium path? It is as if the rationality of the players binds and constrains them to a certain course of action. Thus the equilibrium property P2 which defines equilibrium is in conflict with the notion of rationality underlying the equilibrium. Equilibrium is defined by comparison with a hypothetical deviation from equilibrium: yet no such deviation is consistent with the rationality of players.

There are of course ways of attempting to resolve this paradox: the players may be rational, but may make mistakes in choosing their actions (their hands might 'tremble'). However, the paradox remains and stems from the same source as the general problem with disequilibrium analysis that we noted above (p. 38 ff). If agents deviate from equilibrium, then in some sense they could do better: they have made a mistake. A formal notion of economic rationality cannot explain such mistakes: as economists we cannot understand such mistakes.

To close this section on time and equilibrium, it is worth noting that in the case of an intertemporal equilibrium (e.g. the Arrow–Debreu world or a perfect equilibrium) the stability property P3 is redundant. In an intertemporal equilibrium, actions are made consistent across time. The question of how we get to equilibrium is not possible: we are always already there. In the case of a static equilibrium, we can imagine starting in a disequilibrium state and moving towards equilibrium. If equilibrium spreads across time, there is no possibility of a pocket or era of disequilibrium. This comment is still valid in adjustment models: there is an equilibrium adjustment path to a long-run steady-state equilibrium.

5   CONCLUSION

In this chapter, some important equilibria have been looked at, and others have been ignored. What general lessons can be learned from the exercise? I will conclude with some personal thoughts.

First, although there is a loosely defined equilibrium method employed in economics, there are many different types of equilibrium which embody different views of the world. It makes little or no sense to talk of 'the equilibrium concept in economics'. At most there is a family resemblance present.

Second, the equilibrium method plays a crucial role in the process of explanation in economics. Out of equilibrium, actions of agents become inconsistent, or plans cannot be realised, or agents do worse than they could. Mistakes are made. With a formal notion of rationality, economists cannot explain mistakes. In equilibrium, in contrast, the interactions of agents are brought together and made consistent, and in some sense their actions are the right ones to take. We can thus explain things by saying: 'if everyone does as well as they can, then this happens'. This puts a great constraint on economics: because economists seek to explain, they seek to expand the equilibrium method to embrace more and more phenomena, real or imagined. Thus, what is initially seen as a disequilibrium situation becomes a challenge to economists, who invent new equilibria to cover it (as in the case of 'disequilibrium' macroeconomics resting on fix-price equilibria). This paradox is particularly acute in game theory, where equilibrium is defined by hypothetical deviations from equilibrium which should not occur if agents are rational. The answer to the problem might seem obvious: replace a formal model of economic rationality with a substantive model of rationality. If we model the actual decision-making process, we can then explain why it might go wrong. Whilst this may well prove to be the way forward in future, at present it seems an unacceptable alternative to most: to economists there is no obvious model of substantive rationality that is consistent with economics as practised today (which is of course based on formal rationality). Alternatively, the spread of equilibrium may represent an expansion of our explanatory power, an advance of knowledge.

Third, different types of equilibria embody different visions of the world, and with the passing of time economists' perspectives change. Thus, what economists view as the paradigmatic equilibrium has varied over time (as it may also vary geographically). Thus, recent years have seen a shift in interest from the Arrow–Debreu world of price-taking agents to a game-theoretic world of large or small agents strategically interacting within and across markets non-cooperatively. It will be interesting to see what comes next.

Part II
Mainly Macro

3 Of Coconuts, Decomposition and a Jackass: The Genealogy of the Natural Rate

1 INTRODUCTION

The concept of the natural rate of unemployment was formulated in 1968, by Friedman and Phelps. In Friedman, it plays the central role in his theory of the relationship between the short-run and long-run Phillips curve. However, in this chapter I will focus not on its role within the theory of inflation *per se*, but rather on the fundamental notion of equilibrium, the natural rate itself. The natural rate stands in a tradition of ideas that may be loosely called *classical* or *monetarist*. We may well ask, therefore, two questions: first, how does the idea of the natural rate (NR) differ from its predecessors; secondly, how have more recent ideas developed or diverged from it? A full and proper answer to both of these questions would require a degree of scholarship and comprehensive grasp of the broad sweep of the history of economic thought which, alas, eludes me. However, I intend to approach both questions in terms of a series of snapshots and observations which will be drawn together towards the end of the chapter. Without spoiling the story, I conclude that the natural rate as an *equilibrium* concept was largely derivative of Patinkin's concept of full employment, as laid out in his *Money, Interest and Prices* (first published in 1956). However, Friedman nowhere ever lays down a specific theory of the natural rate itself, and as such the concept has proven sufficiently loose and vague to fit a variety of subsequent models of equilibrium.

2 THE CLASSICAL DICHOTOMY

The origin of the notion of the natural rate lies in the view that (at least in the long run or some 'stationary state') real variables in the economy are determined by 'real things' such as preferences, technology, population and so on. To use Pigou's phrase, money acts as a 'veil', behind which the real economy operates (Pigou, 1941). The notion of the classical dichotomy itself was not formalised much by the classical economists. Perhaps its first formal statement was by Patinkin (1965), whose ideas I will discuss later. However, in a very revealing

essay written by Paul Samuelson in 1968, he defined the notion as a one-time
believer. To quote at some length:

> Mine is the great advantage of having been a jackass. From 2 January 1932
> until some indeterminate date in 1937, I was a classical monetary theorist. I do
> not have to look for tracks of the jackass embalmed in old journals and mono-
> graphs. I merely have to lie down on the couch and recall in tranquility ... what
> it was that I believed between the ages of 17 and 22 ... We thought that *real*
> outputs and inputs and price ratios depended essentially in the longest run on
> real factors such as tastes, technology and endowments. An increase in the
> stock of money ... would cause a proportional increase in *all* prices and values.
> (1968, pp. 1–2)

As Samuelson stated, the idea or concept was not formalised. The essential idea
was one of *homogeneity* of equilibrium equations in money and prices:

A. Write down a system of real equations involving *real* outputs and inputs,
    and *ratios* of prices (values), and depending essentially on real tastes, tech-
    nologies, market structures and endowments. Its properties are invariant to
    changes in the stock of money.
B. Then append a fixed supply of money equation that pins down (or up) the
    absolute price level, determining the scale factor that was essentially inde-
    terminate in set A ... (1968, pp. 2–3)

In statement A we have the real equilibrium of the economy in which real factors
determine *relative* prices, and in B the monetary side of the economy acts as a
scaling factor to determine *absolute* prices. This is stated most simply in the
quantity equation: real output Q is fixed, and the money stock (M) merely acts to
determine price (P) (via the well-known equation $MV = PQ$), with a direct pro-
portionality between M and P if the velocity (V) is constant.

However, the earliest notion of the dichotomy to my knowledge is in David
Hulme (1750):

> Money is nothing but the representation of labour and commodities, and serves
> only as a method of rating or estimating them. Where coin is in greater plenty –
> as a greater quantity of it is required to represent the same quantity of goods – it
> can have no effect, either good or bad, taking a nation within itself; any more
> than it would make an alteration in a merchant's books, if instead of the Ara-
> bian method of notation, which requires few characters, he should make use of
> the Roman, which requires a great many.

Similar statements can be found in a variety of subsequent writers including Walras,
Fisher and Cassel, Davenport, James Mill, Hawtrey (see Patinkin, 1965, note I,
pp. 454–62 for a brief history of the idea of the dichotomy).

3   PATINKIN AND FULL EMPLOYMENT

Money, Interest and Prices is perhaps as great in its vision as Keynes' *General Theory*. Whilst the latter has a greater abundance of originality, the former has a greater clarity of insight and formal expression. Don Patinkin states his theory of the labour market and corresponding notion of the full employment equilibrium in just three pages of *Money, Interest and Prices* (in the 1965 edn. pp. 127–30). These pages deserve great attention: they state the labour market model that became the standard foundation for the aggregate supply curve in the aggregate demand/aggregate supply (AD/AS) model. Although Patinkin himself did not formulate the AD/AS representation, it is implicit in his *Money, Interest and Prices*.

   Patinkin presents his model of full employment diagrammatically (in his figure 10 on p. 129) as has become standard in macroeconomics textbooks. Labour demand (N^d) depends on the real wage (and capital which is fixed), as does labour supply (N^s). Amending Patinkin's notation to reflect subsequent usage we have the familiar Figure 3.1. Two points need to be made about this model. First, Patinkin equates the notion of full employment with the competitive equilibrium in the labour market. Second, he suppresses the wealth effect on the labour supply. It is worth quoting at some detail from Patinkin on the suppression

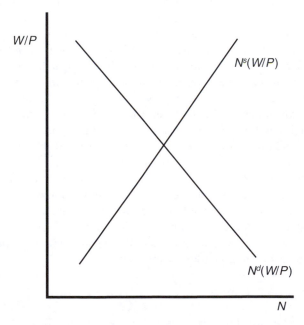

Figure 3.1   *Patinkin's model of full employment*

of the wealth effect:

> To the extent that an individual operates on the principle of utility maximisa-
> tion, the amount of labour supplied will depend on the real wage rate ... Thus
> we write $N^S = N^S(W/P)$ ... It will be immediately recognised that we have
> greatly oversimplified the analysis. Both the demand and supply equations
> should actually be dependent on the real value of bond and money holdings as
> well as the real wage rate ... Finally, full analysis of individual behaviour
> would show the supply of labour to depend on the rate of interest. If we have
> arbitrarily ignored these additional influences, it is because the labour market
> as such does not interest us in the following analysis; its sole function is to pro-
> vide the bench mark of full employment. (1965, pp. 128–9)

The suppression of the wealth effect from the labour supply is crucial, and has
proven to be most durable, giving rise as it does to the vertical aggregate supply
curve. It has the important feature that although the labour market functions in a
system of general equilibrium equations, it can be treated as a partial equilibrium
equation. Output, employment and the real wage are all determined in the labour
market without reference to the rest of the economy (usually the money and
goods markets).

Whereas the classical dichotomy rested on the *homogeneity* of equilibrium
equations, Patinkin's model of full employment went further. Patinkin made the
system of equilibrium equations *decomposable*, in that the labour market equation could be solved in isolation to the rest of the system of equilibrium equations. Since the level of output, employment and the real wage are determined by
the labour market equilibrium alone, changes on the 'demand side' of the economy (the goods and money markets in the IS/LM framework) can have no effect
on them. To see that this goes a lot further than the classical dichotomy, it implies
not only that money is neutral, but also that changes in *real* demand-side factors
will have no effect on output and employment. For example, an increase in real
government expenditure will have no effect on the level of output and employment (although it will of course reduce the other components of demand such as
consumption and investment – the 'crowding out effect'). If there is a non-zero
wealth effect on the labour supply, matters are rather different. Real balances (and
real bond holdings if Ricardian equivalence fails to hold) enter into wealth, and
these depend on the *nominal* price level. Hence the position of the labour supply
curve depends on the demand-side factors which determine the nominal price
level. The labour market equilibrium condition is now given by relation (3.1),
where for simplicity we assume that real balances are the only form of wealth,
and there is no taxation or non-labour income:

$$N^d(W/P) = N^s(W/P, M/P) \tag{3.1}$$

Note that (3.1) is still homogeneous to degree zero in (W, P, M), so that the
homogeneity underlying the classical dichotomy will not be affected.

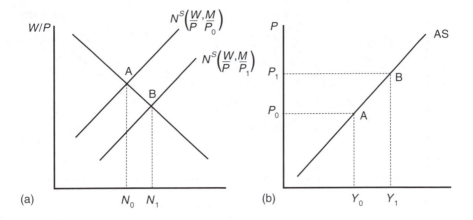

Figure 3.2 *Aggregate supply with a wealth effect*

However, the labour supply function will shift with P and M. Treating M as constant, if leisure is a normal good, a rise in P will reduce real balances, and hence increase the labour supply at any given real wage level, shifting the labour supply curve to the right, as in Figure 3.2a, thus tracing out the upward-sloping AS curve in Figure 3.2b.

With the wealth effect on labour supply unsuppressed, the equilibrium system of equations does not decompose, and in fact it is easy to show that an increase in real government expenditure will not have a zero multiplier: the expenditure multiplier will be strictly positive but less than unity. In Figures 3.3a and 3.3b we contrast the effect of an increase in the money supply and an increase in government expenditure. In Figure 3.3a we can see that the increase in real government expenditure Δg shifts the AD curve to the right, the distance of the shift being Δg if output markets clear. (For a formal derivation of the effects of fiscal and monetary policy with wealth effects, see classic graduate texts of the 1970s such as Ott, Ott and Yoo, 1975, ch. 12, and Barro and Grossman, 1976, ch. 1.) From equation (3.1) above, the increase in g has no direct effect on the AS curve. The equilibrium moves from A to B, with some crowding out of the initial stimulus provided by Δg as nominal prices (and wages) rise from P_A to P_B. Clearly the increase in government expenditure has a real effect on the level of aggregate output and employment. This stands in contrast to the effect of a proportional increase of the money stock: as depicted in Figure 3.3b, a proportionate increase in m to λM shifts both the AD and AS curves upwards equally, so that nominal prices rise proportionately to λP; the real side of the economy is unaffected.

Patinkin's notion of full employment added two things to the classical dichotomy. First, it identified the long-run equilibrium output with the now textbook competitive labour market, depicted in Figure 3.2. Second, it added the

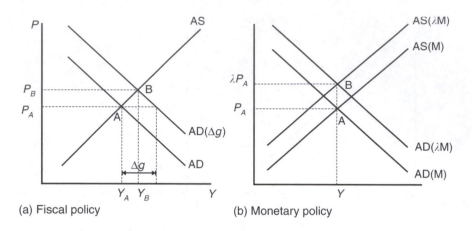

Figure 3.3   *Macroeconomic policy without decomposition*

property of decomposability, so that in addition to monetary neutrality total output, employment and the real wage were all independent of *any* change in the demand side of the economy, whether real or nominal. The vertical aggregate supply curve was born. The notion of decomposability has perhaps been the most crucial and pervasive. The notion that the labour market equilibrium might be non-competitive had always been recognised, but the first *formal* inclusion of imperfect competition in the output market in a Patinkinesque framework was done by Ball and Bodkin (1963). Following Joan Robinson's *Accumulation of Capital*, they introduced the 'degree of monopoly' into the labour demand equation:

> We add a profit maximizing condition: $(1-\mu)\cdot f'(N)=W/P$, where W is the money wage, P is the price level, and μ represents the degree of monopoly power existing in the economy. μ is equal to $1/\varepsilon$ where ε is the elasticity of demand, on an economy wide basis. (Ball and Bodkin, 1963, p. 61)

In this case, the familiar Figure 3.1 becomes as in Figure 3.4: imperfect competition in the output market shifts the 'labour demand curve' to the left (since with imperfectly elastic demand in the output market, the firm's marginal revenue product is less than marginal value product $P\cdot f'(N)$).

Output, employment and the real wage are less than under perfect competition. However, there is still a unique equilibrium level of employment. Furthermore, the equilibrium satisfies the classical homogeneity property, and also Patinkin's own property of decomposability if the wealth effect on the labour supply is suppressed. Thus Patinkin's notion of full employment was perfectly compatible with imperfect competition.

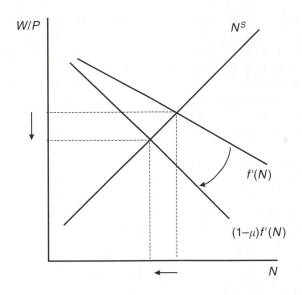

Figure 3.4 *Ball and Bodkin's (1963) model of full employment with price-setting firms*

4 FRIEDMAN AND THE NATURAL RATE HYPOTHESIS

Twelve years after Patinkin's *Money, Interest and Prices* had been published, and the same year that Samuelson had called his younger classical self a 'jackass', Friedman's Presidential Address to the American Economic Association (1968) was published. This paper is one of the great classics of economics: it turned out to be both prophetic and seminal. However, from the perspective of the study of the natural rate, it is elusive and frustrating. The other papers in which Friedman wrote explicitly about the natural rate are his IEA (Institute of Economic Affairs, a policy think-tank based in London) lecture *Inflation vs Unemployment* (1975), and his subsequent Nobel lecture of the same title (1977). Turning first to the 1968 definition of the natural rate, which has become ingrained in many generations of students, its meaning is more enigmatic than it seems:

At any moment of time, there is some level of unemployment which has the property that it is consistent with equilibrium in the structure of *real* wages ... The 'natural rate of unemployment' ... is the level that would be ground out by the Walrasian system of general equilibrium equations, provided there is imbedded in them the actual structural characteristics of the labour and commodity markets, including market imperfections, stochastic variability in demands and supplies, the costs of gathering information about job vacancies, and labor availabilities, the costs of mobility, and so on. (1968, p. 8)

This 'definition' is remarkable for its vagueness. It is not a definition at all, but rather a research programme! Certainly, Friedman himself never attempted to present a formal theory of the natural rate which included the various 'market imperfections' he lists. It is rather an assertion of the belief that the real side of the economy possesses a unique (long-run) equilibrium. The belief in the uniqueness of equilibrium is so deep that it is rarely stated as such by Friedman (although its implicit assumption permeates Friedman's work). In Friedman's IEA lecture (1975) we find only a few comments:

> The term 'the natural rate' has been much misunderstood ... It refers to that rate of employment which is consistent with the *existing real conditions* in the labour market – The purpose of the concept separates the monetary from the non-monetary aspects of the employment situation – precisely the same purpose that Wicksell had in using the word 'natural' in connection with the interest rate. (1975, p. 25)

The nearest we come to an explicit formulation of the microeconomic theory or the natural rate is also in Friedman's IEA lecture: turn to p. 16 figure 3, and what do we find? We find Patinkin's model of full employment, the competitive labour market with the labour supply depending only on real wages! Friedman's discussion of it is prefaced by the qualifier 'for example', but his discussion demonstrates the continuity with Patinkin in stressing both the homogeneity property of equilibrium and the decomposability of the labour market from the rest of the economy. The homogeneity comes across most clearly from Friedman's statement that what matters is the actual or anticipated real wage: 'the real wage can remain constant with W and P each rising at the rate of 10% a year, or falling at the rate of 10% a year, or doing anything else, provided both change at the *same* rate' (1975, p. 16). The notion of decomposability is implicit in his use of Patinkin's model, and the use of the phrase 'real conditions in the labour market' in the earlier quote from 1975.

Thus far, Friedman's natural rate seems to be nothing new: it is solidly in the classical tradition, and more specifically in the footsteps of his erstwhile Chicago colleague Don Patinkin. So what, if anything, was new about the concept of the natural rate as found in Friedman?

1   Friedman's main contribution was to restate the classical notion of a unique long-run equilibrium in terms of the then contemporary theories of the labour market: namely search models. Although he did not actually formulate any of these himself, he did describe the process of deviations from the natural rate in terms of 'reservation wages' and so on. In fact, although partial equilibrium models of search and imperfect information abounded, it was not until 1979 that Salop's model of the natural rate was published. The real question is whether the notion of a unique long-run equilibrium unaffected by macroeconomic policy can survive if put in these terms.

2   Furthermore, Friedman became explicit about the role of imperfect competi-
    tion in natural rate. This is clearest in his argument that whilst trade unions
    cannot cause inflation, they can influence the natural rate. The direct statement
    of this view is in an answer to a question after the IEA lecture:

> Trade unions play a very important part in determining the position of the
> natural level of unemployment. They play an important role in denying
> opportunities to some classes of the community that are open to others. They
> play a very important role in the structure of the labour force and the struc-
> ture of *relative* wages. But, despite appearances to the contrary, a *given*
> amount of trade union power does not play any role in exacerbating inflation.
> Industrial monopolies do not produce inflation; they produce high relative
> prices for the products they are monopolising, and low outputs for these
> products. (1975, pp. 30–1)

    Friedman argued that the only way to have a long-run influence on the level
    of unemployment was to reform the labour market (in the lecture text he talks
    of removing 'obstacles' and 'frictions').

3   Friedman *integrated* the classical theory with the Phillips curve to formulate
    the vertical 'long-run Phillips curve'. Essentially, this synthesis rested on
    restating classical notions of homogeneity in terms of inflationary expecta-
    tions. Whereas Patinkin had formulated it in terms of rates of *change*. Thus
    the natural rate becomes the level of employment which is consistent with
    fully anticipated inflation and constant real wages.

4   He also formulated a theory of *deviations* from the natural rate in terms of
    unanticipated inflation. Employment deviates from the natural rate because
    of forecast errors.

5   On the level of economic *policy* Friedman's formulation of the natural rate in
    terms of labour market equilibrium was very influential. In the UK it gave
    rise to the focus on labour market reform that characterised the Thatcher
    years (1979–91).

These are all important points, each one deserving as essay to itself. However, we
must hurry on to subsequent developments.

5   LUCAS–RAPPING AND THE LUCAS ARCHIPELAGO

Still staying at Chicago we turn to R.E. Lucas, who developed and formalised the
natural rate in terms of a competitive market-clearing framework. There are two
versions of this enterprise. The first was the Lucas–Rapping paper published in
1969 (written more or less contemporaneously to Friedman's address). This took
the basic demand–supply model of the labour market and added to it an *intertemporal*, dynamic model of household labour supply (even if it had only two periods). This introduced the notion of intertemporal substitution in the labour

supply: high wages today elicit a higher labour supply in part because it may mean that today's wages are high relative to future wages: the short-run responsiveness of wages is enhanced if the increase is seen as transitory as opposed to permanent.

The second paper was published a decade later (Lucas, 1979), and introduced the 'island' story of the natural rate in terms of a signal extraction problem. Each market is an island, and the aggregate economy is the archipelago. Agents in this economy have good information about their own 'island' market, but not the economy in general (the 'archipelago'). As rational agents, they have to distinguish between increases of nominal prices on their island that represent *real* increases in the price on their island relative to the general price level, and general inflation. Using optimal statistical forecasts based on the relative variances of aggregate economy-wide shocks and island-specific shocks, the agents apportion a certain proportion of any deviation of actual from expected prices to market-specific factors, and hence increase output, giving rise to a short-run Phillips curve.

Both of Lucas' models follow in the spirit of Friedman's definition of the natural rate, in that they put informational problems at the centre of the analysis; uncertainty about the future in the Lucas–Rapping model, and imperfect information about aggregates such as the price level and money stock in the 1979 one. In this sense, Lucas provided the micro foundations, the theory that was lacking in Friedman's notion of the natural rate. However, there was a different agenda as well. This agenda consisted in seeing all markets as competitive: unlike Friedman, Lucas gives little weight to the notion of non-competitive markets. The Lucas world view puts individual rational choice at the centre of a world of competitive markets. Institutional arrangements and customs are seen as irrelevant to the task of explanation: they are themselves endogenous, being designed 'precisely in order to aid in matching preferences and opportunities' (Lucas, 1981, p. 4). Fluctuations in economic activity are explained in terms of rational households varying labour supply in response to current and future wages and prices. For Lucas, this is the 'only account', there being 'no serious alternative' (1981, p. 4).

To others there were of course serious problems with Lucas's story. First, and perhaps most importantly, the two variables which the theory needed to be unkown to individuals on their islands were the aggregate price level and money supply. However, these are two of the variables for which regular (monthly) and reliable data are available in all developed economies. Second, with rational expectations the deviations form the natural rate are 'white noise': serially uncorrelated with mean zero. However, as we know, there is a *business cycle* with considerable serial correlation of output. This suggests that in order to understand the path of output we need to model the evolution of the equilibrium output itself rather than deviations from equilibrium. This brings us to real business cycle (RBC) theory.

6   REAL BUSINESS CYCLES

Lucas had formalised the notion of the natural rate in a way that rested, at least partly, on imperfect information of forecast errors. However, implicit in his conception of the importance of intertemporal substitution was the notion that even with full information and perfect foresight, fluctuations in economic activity would occur in response to changes in the underlying characteristics of the economy: changes in technology and tastes. The natural rate had been an essentially *static* concept. This is clear in the discussion of the real equilibrium in classical writers such as Pigou and even Patinkin where the adjectives 'stationary state' and 'comparative statics' are used. This carries over to Friedman's discussion of the natural rate which is in entirely static terms. In this framework, *dynamics* becomes the discussion of short-run deviations around the long-run static equilibrium.

In contrast, *real business cycle* theory took the notion of competitive equilibrium and extended it to a fully *dynamic* equilibrium (Prescott, 1986). In this view there is an intertemporal equilibrium that extends through time. Variations in output and employment represent the fluctuations in equilibrium as rational households and firms maximise over a relevant time horizon (usually infinite!). Real wages respond to productivity shocks: the labour supply responds to the profile of real wages over time, hence leading to the business cycle. Thus, if real wages in time t are relatively high, this may cause households to exploit this fact by supplying more labour in t. This development makes the concept of the natural rate irrelevant. In this dynamic setting there may exist no real distinction between the actual and the equilibrium level of employment: the equilibrium level of employment is itself fluctuating. In real business cycle theory, then, the concept of the natural rate itself has become largely redundant, although (as the adjective 'real' indicates) the spirit of the classical dichotomy is very much present.*

7   THE NAIRU: UNIONS AND IMPERFECT COMPETITION

Outside Chicago and Minnesota, matters were developing rather differently. At the London School of Economics (LSE) there emerged a framework for modelling the labour market which I shall call the CLE view (CLE being the Centre for Labour Economics, a research centre operating at the LSE in the 1980s). Friedman had put the labour market at the centre of his notion of the natural rate. Richard Layard and Steven Nickell developed an empirical model of the UK

---

*Editorial note. At the time of writing this chapter, there were many RBC researchers using real models without any monetary or financial sector. However, the notion that the economy can be built this way seems largely to have been rejected. Nearly everyone seems to have accepted the notion that nominal rigidities matter and nominal shocks can effect the economy at least in the short run. For a discussion of this see Chapter 5.

labour market which put imperfect competition at the centre of the natural rate, in distinct contrast to the Lucas developments. This empirical model became standard in much of European applied macroeconomics.

Two papers provided the basis for this approach (Layard and Nickell, 1985, 1986). One of the key features of the natural rate stressed by Friedman was that it is the only level of unemployment that is consistent with non-accelerating inflation. Layard and Nickell therefore renamed the natural rate the 'non-accelerating inflation rate of unemployment', or NAIRU. The approach reflected an increased interest in imperfectly competitive markets in the early 1980s. The notion of equilibrium in the CLE approach can be represented by a diagram which looks deceptively familiar (Figure 3.5).

The downward-sloping curve DD is a familiar 'labour demand curve', reflecting the fact that imperfectly competitive firms equate marginal revenue with marginal cost, which is the same thing as saying that the firm employs labour up to the point where the real wage equals the marginal product of labour scaled down by $(1 - \mu)$ as in Ball and Bodkin (1963). The upward-sloping curve WW is, however, rather more innovative. Layard and Nickell modelled the wage determination process as a bargain between the representative firm and union. The bargaining solution adopted was the Nash bargaining solution. The details of this need not concern us here; suffice it to say that the wage depends on the *outside options* (often called 'fallback positions') of the firm and union. The nature of the bargaining solution is that the better the outside option of an agent, the better that agent does. Layard and Nickell modelled the outside option of unions as the expected income of union

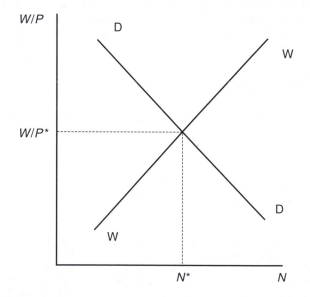

Figure 3.5   *The NAIRU*

members if they become unemployed. If unemployed, the worker obtains a job at the going wage W/P with probability $(1-u)$, where u is the unemployment rate, and stays unemployed with probability u. Hence the higher is employment in Figure 3.5, the better is the outside option facing the union's members, and the higher the wage which results from the bargain. Thus the upward sloping curve WW represents the fact that unions are able to obtain higher wages when employment is high (unemployment low), rather than labour supply conditions.

The great merit of the NAIRU approach is that it enables the natural rate to be modelled empirically. Nickell and Layard were able to classify factors into those which affected the WW curve (union power, labour mismatch, unemployment benefits, etc.), and those which affected the DD curve (world energy and commodity prices, capital stock, etc.), to track the changes in the NAIRU over time. This is an enterprise that Friedman himself never undertook, since he always emphasised the ineffable and unknowable quality of the natural rate (NR): 'One problem is that it [the monetary authority] cannot know what the natural rate is. Unfortunately, we have as yet no method to estimate accurately ... the natural rate of unemployment' (1968, p. 10).

8   AN EVALUATION OF THE NATURAL RATE HYPOTHESIS

I have given a brief sketch of some of the ideas giving rise to, and arising from, the natural rate. The history is by no means comprehensive, but I have given what I believe to be the main salient points (although I must apologise to search theorists for omitting them).

The concept of the natural rate is very solidly rooted in the classical tradition. In its simplest form it consists of two hypotheses:

(a) There exists a unique equilibrium for the economy determined by real factors in the economy (classical dichotomy).
(b) Equilibrium output, employment and the real wage are determined in the labour market (decomposability).

Hypothesis (b) is perhaps a little injudicious. Friedman himself only ever talked about *monetary* policy in the context of the natural rate: he clearly believed in the neutrality of money, and conceived of it in terms of the homogeneity of the system of equilibrium equations. However, in practice, both Friedman and others have followed Patinkin's approach in locating the real macroeconomic equilibrium primarily in the labour market: output, employment and the real wage are all tied down within the labour market. This notion of decomposability is common to all of the approaches we have explored from Patinkin's notion of full employment to new classical theories and the NAIRU.

The phrase 'natural rate' is itself a masterpiece of marketing, akin to the phrase 'rational expectations (RE)'. In terms of hypotheses (a) and (b) it is a blank space, an invitation for economists to insert their own ideas and fashions in order to define their own notion of the 'real equilibrium'. By not specifying any particular theory of the natural rate, Friedman avoided the problem of obsolescence. I commented that the definition of the natural rate given by Friedman was a research programme rather than a definition: after 25 years no one has yet managed to combine all of the elements identified by Friedman into one coherent model, and probably never will.

The only real difference between the concept of the natural rate and Patinkin's notion of full employment is that the latter is specific (a model of the competitive labour market), and furthermore the only concrete version of the natural rate offered by Friedman himself was the same as Patinkin. However, the phrase 'full employment' has lots of connotations, such as that there should not be much unemployment, and that workers are on their supply curve. One of the reasons that Friedman opted to stress search theory in his Presidential Address was that it focused on the *voluntary* decision of workers to accept or reject job offers. The terminology 'natural rate' served to divert attention from the word 'full', and hence to accept that in equilibrium there might be unemployment, and indeed that since this unemployment was 'natural' it was not necessarily a bad thing. In that sense the change of language Friedman introduced prepared the intellectual ground for the shift of political objectives away from full employment to reducing inflation, and the acceptance of ever-higher levels of unemployment in the ensuing 25 years. Another shift in policy emphasis resulting from this change of language was that unemployment was seen as a primarily *microeconomic* concern. The way to reduce unemployment was not through macroeconomic policy, but through policy towards the functioning of markets – the labour market in particular – in order to remove 'frictions' and 'imperfections'.

Thus far I have tried to clarify the concept of the natural rate, rather than criticise. However, I will now offer a series of critical observations on the natural rate from a theoretical and practical point of view. First and foremost, the notion that there is a unique equilibrium level of output and employment is an extremely strong assumption. Most macroeconomic models are highly stylised in their aggregative structure, using representative markets and agents, and these assumptions tend to bias models towards having a unique equilibrium. However, the possibility of multiple equilibria should not be dismissed as merely a curiosity. Friedman cast his 1968 discussion of the natural rate in terms of search theory. However, subsequent research has shown that the possibility of multiple equilibria in search models is endemic. The most notable model here is Peter Diamond's 'coconut' model (1982). Consider an island with coconut trees. Islanders eat coconuts, but there is a taboo against eating coconuts that you have picked yourself. In order to enjoy the succulence of a coconut and sample the delights of coconut milk you need to pick a coconut and then search for someone to swap coconuts with. The cost to you of getting a coconut (finding and climbing a tree) is a fixed production cost: however, the (expected) cost of finding a partner varies with the number of people searching for a partner. If there are many individuals wandering around the island with coconuts, the expected search cost of finding

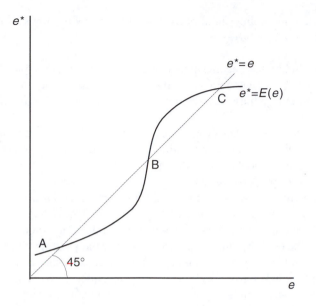

Figure 3.6 *Multiple equilibria in Diamond's (1982) coconut model*

one of them is low: if there are only a few of you, the search cost will be high. This is a basic *search externality*, in that the incentive to 'produce' a coconut depends positively on the proportion of the population similarly engaged. One obtains something like Figure 3.6, which follows Diamond more in spirit than detail.

Let us define the proportion of the islanders engaged in picking coconuts and searching for partners as e. As an individual, the marginal expected returns to picking a coconut are increasing in the proportion of people likewise engaged. Thus the more people are engaged in producing coconuts, the more individuals will find it in their interest to pick coconuts: this is captured by the function $e^* = E(e)$, where e^* is the proportion of people who want to pick coconuts given that a proportion e are doing so.

An equilibrium lies on the 45° line: the actual number of coconut pickers equals the number of would-be coconut pickers. Since E is upward-sloping, there may be multiple equilibria, as at points ABC in Figure 3.6. Furthermore, these equilibria may be welfare ranked: the more people eat coconuts the bigger is e. As Diamond stated:

> To see the importance of this finding, consider Friedman's (1968) definition of the natural rate of unemployment as the level occurring once frictions are introduced into the Walrasian economy. This paper argues that the result of actually modeling a competitive economy with trade frictions is to find multiple natural rates of employment. This implies that one of the goals of

macroeconomic policy should be to direct the economy towards the best natural rate. (1982, p. 881)

This sort of finding has become known as a *coordination failure* problem (Cooper
and John, 1988): the economy may have multiple equilibria which are Pareto-
ranked, and the free market may fail to ensure that the economy ends up at the
best one.

The second issue is that even if there is a natural rate, if it is not perfectly
competitive it will not be Pareto-optimal (indeed the coconut model shows that
even competitive models with externalities might not be so). In this case the
decomposability property of the natural rate model becomes rather suspect. It
rather artificially imposes a unique equilibrium on the labour market irrespective
of the demand side of the economy. Properly modelled, strong assumptions are
needed to rule out fiscal policy (or any other real demand 'shock') from having
an effect on the equilibrium. If we start from an initial position where there is too
little output and employment, then there is the possibility that if fiscal policy can
raise output, it will have a welfare improving effect. Indeed, if you drop the
decomposability assumption, you will not obtain a natural rate model, but rather
a *natural range* model: although there may be a unique equilibrium for a given
macroeconomic policy (mix of monetary and fiscal policy), there is a *range* of
equilibrium levels of output and employment available as policy is varied. If
these are welfare-ranked, then the government can choose from a range of equilibrium options (see, for example, Dixon, 1988, 1991). Both of the possibilities
discussed here: multiple (discrete) natural rates and a continuum (natural range)
are both more likely to be of interest in imperfectly competitive economies, since
non-competitive equilibria start off being Pareto-inefficient.

Third, one has to consider the empirical evidence for the natural rate hypothesis. This is discussed in some detail in Cross (1995), so I shall not dwell on it. It
is almost impossible to refute any hypothesis in economics on the basis of econometric evidence. However, the casual empiricist would be able to see huge fluctuations in employment over the past 25 years: these surely point strongly to the
presence of strong hysteresis effects, and possibly multiple equilibria (for empirical evidence on the latter, see Manning, 1992).

9   CONCLUSION

The natural rate has clearly been a powerful idea. It is a phase that captured and
continues to capture a point of view, a perspective: it views unemployment outcomes as 'natural' and unavoidable from the macroeconomic level. Indeed, the
phrase 'full employment' had much the same ideological force in the preceding
quarter of a century: it embodied the notion of abundance and stability as being
attainable through sound macroeconomic management. It is interesting to note
that the actual theory used to model both full employment and the natural rate

may be the same: we find the same demand and supply model of the labour market in Patinkin's 1956 model of full employment and Friedman's natural rate in his 1977 Nobel lecture. As economics moves on and develops, economists will no doubt continue to use the label 'natural rate' to apply to equilibrium states. The continuity in the label may belie a difference in substance. At some stage in the fullness of time someone will grasp the spirit of the age and think up a new name, a new attitude. I only hope that they do not simply relabel and recycle yet another version of Patinkin's diagram of the labour market.

4 The Role of Imperfect Competition in New Keynesian Economics

1 INTRODUCTION

The adjective 'new Keynesian' was introduced in the mid-1980s and refers to a body of work which was published over a period beginning in the mid-1970s. Whilst the term clearly applies to papers written since 1980, it has also been applied retrospectively to some work written before that. Much of this material is gathered together in a two-volume collection of reprinted papers edited by Mankiw and Romer (1991), although the coverage of this volume is somewhat parochial in that only American-based authors are included. There are other more recent surveys, most notably Silvestre (1993) and Dixon and Rankin (1994).[1] In order to understand the phenomenon of new Keynesian macroeconomics, it is essential to set it in an historical context.

2 WHAT'S NEW PUSSYCAT?

The epithet 'new' has been used many times in economics, particularly in recent times. Thus, for example, the 'new' industrial economics; the 'new' trade theory; the 'new' economic geography; are all labels that have come into use since 1980. In these cases the adjective 'new' designates some degree of a break with the 'old', but also some degree of continuity. For example, the 'new' in the new industrial economics literature represents the use of contemporary game theory in the analysis of oligopoly; see for example Vickers (1985), Dixon (1988) and of course the seminal graduate textbook by Tirole (1988). The 'new' in recent international trade literature represents the introduction of imperfect competition into the heart of trade theory.

Of course, new theories and ideas are always coming into being: economists come up with new ideas both from the incentive of theoretical invention, and the need to explain or attempt to understand contemporary economic phenomena. However, the adjective 'new' is introduced when there appears to be a shift in the approach by several economists at around the same time. In effect, a new school of thought or group of people with a common approach comes into being. However, if we look at the history of thought, the epithet 'new' has been used many times. In an academic environment where many people still had an education in Latin, the Latin 'neo' was preferred to the plain English 'new'. For example, the

74

phrase 'neo-classical' refers not only to an architectural style, or the musical idiom of Stravinsky, but also to the integration of perfectly competitive economics both with general equilibrium theory, and with macroeconomics.

In this chapter I shall argue that the fundamental 'new' idea behind new Keynesian models is that of *imperfect competition*. All of the major innovations of the new Keynesian school are made possible or worthwhile only because of imperfect competition. This is the key feature that differentiates the 'new' from the 'old' Keynesians: it differentiates the new from Keynes himself: it differentiates the 'new Keynesian' from the 'new classical' economists. Imperfect competition at its basic level means that agents (firms, households) are not price-takers: they have the power to set prices or wages. Even if all wages and prices are flexible, the presence of imperfect competition in itself means that the economy will be different in a fundamental way from a perfectly competitive economy. Before exploring the story of imperfect competition in the macro context, let us just remind ourselves how special the assumption of perfect competition is, and how it differs from imperfect competition. The fundamental idea can be illustrated within a simple microeconomic framework. The macroeconomic implications will commence after the interlude.

3   IMPERFECT COMPETITION FOR BEGINNERS: A MICROECONOMIC INTERLUDE

There are different ways of defining perfect competition:[2] however, for our purposes in this chapter, we can pick out two important features:

(a)   all agents are price-takers;
(b)   prices adjust to equate desired supply and demand.

When we say that agents are price-takers, we mean that they treat the 'market price' as given, they believe that they have no ability to influence the market price. Thus, when perfectly competitive firms decide how much output to produce, they treat the price as given and choose the output that equates supply with demand. This decision defines their supply function, which tells us how much they wish to supply at different prices. Similarly with consumers in deciding demand. When we say that prices adjust to equate supply and demand, we mean that the market price is determined (somehow!) at the point where the supply and demand curves intersect at point E in Figure 4.1a, at price P^* and quantity X^*.

One of the most important points to note about the competitive equilibrium is that it is in some senses a socially optimal outcome (in the absence of externalities etc.). In particular, we can say that it *maximises the sum of consumer and producer surplus*,[3] or, more simply, maximises *total surplus*. To see this, note that if we consider the competitive equilibrium in Figure 4.1a, the *producer surplus*, which is best thought of as profits, is given by the area between the horizontal price line $P = P^*$ and the supply curve, represented by the triangle between

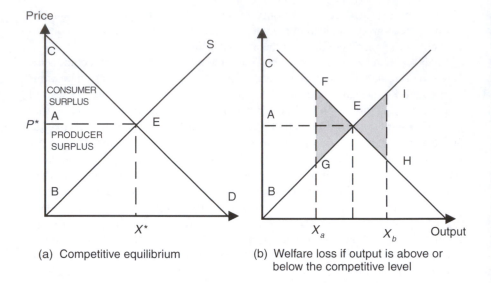

Figure 4.1   *The competitive equilibrium maximises total surplus*

points ABE. This is because the supply curve is simply the marginal cost curve of the firms supplying the market: thus the additional profit of producing one more unit is the difference between price and marginal cost at the current output. The *consumer surplus* is given by the triangle ACE, the area between the demand curve and the horizontal price line $P = P^*$. *Total surplus* is then the triangle BEC. Note that if the output was below X^*, for example at point X_a as in Figure 4.1b, then total surplus will be less: producer surplus is now given by the unshaded area below the price line, and consumer surplus by the shaded area above the price line. From the point of view of social welfare, the net gain to an additional unit of output is the vertical distance or 'gap' at that output between the demand curve (which represents the marginal value of output) and the marginal cost curve (which represents the marginal cost of output): at X_a this gap is GF. The total loss in surplus when we compare X_a to X^* is the triangle GEF. If output exceeds the competitive level as at point X_b, then this also reduces welfare, since now the marginal cost of output exceeds the marginal value: the loss is given by the triangle EIH.

The lesson of this illustration is that *the competitive equilibrium is in a Pareto-optimal outcome that maximises the sum of producer and consumer surplus (the total surplus). Any deviation from that output, whether it be an increase or a decrease, will tend to reduce the total surplus.*

Now let us consider an imperfectly competitive equilibrium, for example a monopoly. A monopolist will set its price as some mark-up over marginal cost. For example, in Figure 4.2, assume the profit maximising price of the monopolist is P^M, with resultant output X^M. As can be seen if we compare Figures 4.1a and 4.2,

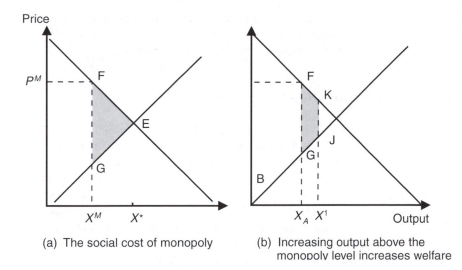

Figure 4.2 Welfare loss with imperfect competition

the monopoly outcome involves a loss in total surplus as compared to the competitive outcome: the net gain in producer surplus to the monopolist is more than offset by the loss of consumer surplus. The total loss is the triangle GEF in Figure 4.2a, which is often called the 'social cost of monopoly'. Thus if we compare the monopoly outcome to the competitive outcome, we observe that in comparison to the competitive outcome, (a) the level of economic activity is lower, and (b) the level of welfare is lower. However the difference does not end there: if for some reason the output is increased beyond X^M, then of course total surplus will increase. For example, if output increases to X^1 in Figure 4.2b, then the gain in total surplus will be the shaded area GFKJ. Thus if we start from an imperfectly competitive equilibrium, then an increase in output will increase welfare.

Hence we can see that there are two fundamental differences between the perfectly competitive equilibrium and the monopolistic equilibrium. First, *the monopolistic equilibrium involves a lower level of welfare than the perfectly competitive equilibrium*. Second, *starting from the monopolistic equilibrium, an increase in output increases welfare, a reduction reduces welfare*. This contrasts with the competitive equilibrium where any deviation of output reduces welfare. Although the above analysis was in terms of an output market, we could think in exactly the same way about a labour market, with *P* being the real wage, and *X* the level of employment.

Whilst the analysis of this section has been cast in terms of simple microeconomics, its lessons will carry over into macroeconomics. The extra dimension added in macroeconomics is that the approach is *general equilibrium*: we have to consider equilibrium of all of the markets in the economy, and how they interact.

Now, perhaps it is time to drop the general discussion of the word 'new', and to focus on what we mean by using the word 'Keynesian' after new. Let's take a look back in history to Britain, and more specifically Cambridge in the 1930s.

4   OF KEYNES AND THE KEYNESIANS

When Keynes first wrote *The General Theory* (Keynes, 1936) in the mid-1930s, he in effect gave birth to macroeconomics as a discipline. Before that, the study of large-scale aggregate phenomena such as employment and national income was based on a predominantly microeconomic and partial equilibrium perspective. Even the notion of national income and the measurement of macroeconomic phenomena was not at all developed in a coherent or useful way. Much of Keynes's contribution and that of the earliest macroeconomists was in providing a consistent and useful framework for national income statistics, and founding the accounting conventions that have now become standard.

However, whilst Keynes developed a new theory and new ideas, he was unable to develop a fully integrated framework which was clearly related to the existing approach of 'price theory', or standard supply and demand analysis in either its partial equilibrium version, or its general equilibrium version as developed by Walras. Keynes designated this corpus of theory as 'classical', and he was clear that his theory marked a definite departure from this classical approach. Thus, for example, he starts off *The General Theory* by stating two of the postulates of classical economics, which he defined as:

I   *The wage is equal to the marginal product of labour.*
II   *The utility of the wage when a given volume of labour is employed is equal to the marginal disutility of that amount of employment.*

(Keynes, 1936, p. 5)

Postulate I states that the labour market outcome is on the (competitive) labour demand curve; postulate II which Keynes rejected states that the labour market outcome is on the labour supply curve. Clearly, the rejection of postulate II introduces the possibility of *involuntary unemployment*, in that if the 'utility of the wage' exceeds the 'marginal disutility of work', then individuals will be willing to work more than they are able to at the prevailing wage. We will discuss this in more detail below.

However, this rejection of classical economics led to a tension within the postwar neoclassical synthesis. On the one hand, in much of microeconomics and subjects such as trade theory, the 'classical' approach largely dominated: agents were assumed to be price-takers; prices (and wages) adjusted so that markets cleared. Agents maximised something subject to some constraint. However, in macroeconomics, this approach was not taken; rather, a series of separate assumptions were made as necessary. For example, Keynes had been willing to assume that consumption was determined by a basic psychological law: he had either not seen it as necessary, or simply did not have the time to tinker with this aspect of his theory so as to show how it was related to the classical case.

The phrase *ad hoc* has often been used to describe this style of macroeconomics: wages were (for example) assumed to be downwardly but upwardly mobile. The most significant development in postwar Keynesian economics was probably the discovery of the Phillips curve (1958), and its integration into macroeconomic models with little or no theoretical underpinning; with the notable exception of Lipsey (1960). Of course, although the phrase *ad hoc* has usually been used perjoratively, there is nothing in principle wrong with *ad hocery* where it is better than the best non-*ad hoc* alternative. Thus Keynes himself was in my opinion quite right to freely develop a model of unemployment which was not fully worked out in the traditional sense when the next best alternative was a model for which unemployment was largely assumed away, at a time during the 1930s when mass unemployment was 'the' major policy issue.

Be that as it may, there was nevertheless a tension between macroeconomics as commonly practised and microeconomics. The success of Keynes's vision of macroeconomics brought to peoples' awareness the need to resolve this tension, and to somehow integrate it with the maximising behaviour which formed the basis of traditional microeconomics. At a more fundamental level, the notion of maximising subject to a constraint is fundamental to the enterprise of explanation by economists.[4]

There have been several different attempts to undertake this synthesis, and in order to understand the distinctive features of new Keynesian thought, it is essential to understand something of these previous attempts at integrating microeconomics and macroeconomics.

5 LITTLE AND LARGE: MICRO AND MACRO

Macroeconomics studies the behaviour of the macroeconomic system, of macroeconomic aggregates. Clearly, there is a relationship between the behaviour of the parts of the system (households, firms, the government) and the behaviour of the aggregates which macroeconomics studies. This relationship is not at all simple. For example, in physics and chemistry it is not always thought of as useful or possible to attempt to derive everything from quantum mechanics. However, in theoretical economics at least, it should be possible to trace through the relationship between the behaviour of the individual agents at the *micro* level in the economy and the behaviour of the economic system at the *macro* level, even if only in a stylised form. The attempt to do this was conceived as a search for the *microfoundations of macroeconomics*. However, this label indicates that the search is one-way: you do not need to consider macroeconomic aspects to get the micro level correct. This is of course not correct: there is a two-way street here, and the behaviour of the economic system at the macroeconomic level can of course influence what the microeconomics needs to be. There is in a sense a need for a *macrofoundation of microeconomics*. Thus when we think of an approach to macroeconomics such as the new Keynesian, we need to think of two levels of theory: the microeconomics of the firm/household/government, and the macroeconomics which corresponds to it. For the theory to be coherent, these two levels need to be consistent.

6   WALRASIAN MICROECONOMICS AND MACROECONOMICS

Léon Walras, a French economist, developed a vision of what we now call a 'general equilibrium system': that is the concept that all markets are linked through the price mechanism, and that in order to balance supply and demand in all markets, it is necessary to have all prices adjust at the same time. Demand for each good in principle depends on the prices of all goods, however indirectly. In his time, Walras was something of a visionary.

There are certainly assumptions which underlie the Walrasian model, which is the general equilibrium version of the standard supply and demand model. At the microeconomic level, it is assumed that agents (firms or households) are price-takers. This means that they believe that they can sell or buy as much as they want at the prevailing market price. This is usually justified by the notion that agents are 'small', too small to affect the market price (although recent work suggests that you can have competitive outcomes with only a few agents). This is a microeconomic assumption. However, in order for this microeconomic assumption to make sense, it is also necessary assume that all markets clear in the sense that prices are in place which equate planned demand with planned supply in all markets. When planned demand equals supply, and only then, can agents on both sides of every market trade as much as they want to at the going prices. This is in effect the *macroeconomic* assumption needed to underpin the microeconomic model.

To see why a global vision is needed, consider what would happen if for some reason the price deviates from that at which demand equals supply. This is depicted in Figure 4.3, where the price P is above the equilibrium price P^*. In this case the desired trades by agents do not match up: agents who are suppliers want to sell more than those demanding the good want to buy. In this framework, we can interpret this market as any market: for example, the 'price' of the 'good' could be the real wage, and the situation of excess supply corresponds to *involuntary* unemployment. In this case the labour that households wish to supply exceeds the quantity demanded by firms. Unemployment in this sense is seen as involuntary in that households are willing to supply more labour than is demanded. However we interpret this market, we can see that the offers by agents to trade (demands and supplies) are inconsistent: whatever happens, all agents cannot realise their planned transactions. Hence in this case to assume that agents behave as if they can buy and sell as much as they want to is hardly satisfactory. This contrasts with the case where the price is continuously at its competitive equilibrium value P^*: in that situation, agents are able to trade as much as they want to.

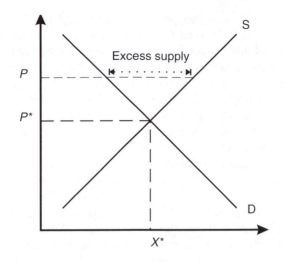

Figure 4.3 *Market clearing in competitive equilibrium*

Before we go on to look at other microeconomic set-ups, let us consider one of the fundamental conceptual problems associated with the Walrasian equilibrium. All agents are assumed to be price-takers, yet prices are assumed to instantaneously adjust to the level where supply equals demand. This is Arrow's paradox, named after Ken Arrow, the Nobel Laureate who pointed this out in his famous article published in 1959. Léon Walras was also aware of this problem, and he was familiar with the operations of the market-makers in the Paris Bourse (the stock exchange which still stands near Les Halles in Paris), who used to set the prices of the various stocks and shares. Léon Walras used the example of this market which he knew well and invented the 'auctioneer' for the whole general equilibrium system. This auctioneer was supposed to determine all prices in the economy (including the factors of production such as labour) so as to equate supply with demand. In a sense, this fictitious auctioneer is a central part of the macroeconomics of the Walrasian system.

7   NON-WALRASIAN MICROECONOMICS: NEO-KEYNESIAN MACROECONOMICS

What happens if prices do not instantaneously clear markets? What happens if people trade at prices other than the competitive or Walrasian prices? Whilst this is a subject that had been thought about by several economists previously, it was not until the 1970s that the subject was examined in full technical detail by the 'neo-Keynesian' economists, most notably Barro and Grossman (1971) and Bénassy (1973, 1975). Let us be clear why the term 'neo-Keynesian' was used in this context.

In the 1960s there was a 'reappraisal' of Keynes, primarily in the works of Clower (1965) and Leijonhufvud (1968). The full story of this reappraisal lies beyond the scope of this chapter, but without doing it full justice I will simply say that two tenets were central to it: first, it was claimed that underlying Keynes's theory was a *disequilibrium* story; secondly, underlying this theory was a coherent if imperfectly articulated microfoundation. The implication of this work was that traditional Keynesian analysis of the 'then' orthodoxy had in effect emasculated Keynes's original insights, and put them in a world of *ad hocery*.

Whatever the details of this phase, the result was the emergence of the neo-Keynesian school in the 1970s. The phrase 'neo-Keynesian' is not a universally accepted term, but it is one used by the main contributor during this phase: namely Jean-Pascal Bénassy. Bénassy studied at Berkeley in California under Gerard Debreu whose *Theory of Value* (1959) ranks as the main classic in the Walrasian tradition (along with John Hicks' *Value and Capital*, 1939). The result was Jean-Pascal Bénassy's thesis (1973), from which came three papers (1975, 1976, 1978) which defined the neo-Keynesian approach. The first contributions in this phase came from Barro and Grossman (1971, 1976), and there is much in common between the work of those authors and Bénassy. There is, however, also a big difference: whereas Bénassy adopted a primarily general equilibrium approach, the work of Barro and Grossman was primarily macroeconomic. This difference is one of perspective: both Barro and Grossman on the one hand, and Bénassy on the other, were trying to develop general equilibrium macromodels, that is microfounded macroeconomics. However, the emphasis was different: whereas Bénassy allowed for many commodities and looked at esoteric issues such as existence, Barro and Grossman adopted the standard aggregation of macroeconomic models and had just three goods (consumption, leisure and money). The neo-Keynesian approach was popularised by Edmond Malinvaud's (1977) book *The Theory of Unemployment Reconsidered*, which made these ideas known and accessible to a general audience; and Muellbauer and Portes (1978) also developed a simple textbook representation which was soon after included in William Branson's (1980) graduate macroeconomics textbook.

What was the essence of the neo-Keynesian school? In the Walrasian framework, all agents are price-takers, and an auctioneer is assumed to ensure that prices instantaneously clear markets, so that demand equals supply in every market. The microeconomics of this had been fully developed in a general equilibrium framework by Debreu and Hicks. The neo-Keynesian school kept the assumption that agents were price-takers, but dropped the assumption that prices adjusted to clear markets. What defines the approach of the neo-Keynesians is the *assumption that wages and prices are fixed*, or at least are *treated as exogenous*.

If the assumption that prices adjust to equate supply and demand is dropped, it then follows that the Walrasian model of firms and households needs to be modified, since it is based on the notion that agents can buy and sell as much as they want. In general this is only true in a competitive equilibrium. The neo-Keynesian school developed the theory of how households and firms would behave if they faced limits on how much they could buy or sell. These models were referred to as *quantity constrained* or *rationing* models (see Levačić and Rebmann, 1982 chapters 16 and 17). However, let us start from the beginning. Looking back at Figure 4.3, we need to consider what will happen in a situation where the price is fixed at a level where supply exceeds demand, as at price *P*. The first step is to establish what trades will take place. In this situation, it is argued that the 'min condition' holds: that is, where supply (S) and demand (D) are different, then the amount actually traded is the minimum (i.e. the smaller) of the two. In Figure 4.3, at price *P*, supply exceeds demand. Thus the min condition tells us that actual trading will be equal to demand D. This is depicted in Figure 4.4. For prices below the competitive price *P**, supply is less than demand (there is excess demand), so that actual trades equal the quantity supplied; for prices above the competitive price, demand is the smaller of the two, so that trades are demand determined. The notion underlying the min condition is simple enough: you cannot force people to trade more or less than they want to – trading is a voluntary activity. Thus, there is no way that the suppliers of a good can be forced to supply more than they want to if demand exceeds supply, and vice versa. In mathematical terms, the min condition can be written as the quantity traded *X* is:

$X = \min(S, D)$

Now, recall that in this approach, we treat the price as a exogenous variable, as something fixed. We then trace through the consequences of this. If the price is not equal to the competitive price, then the planned or desired trades of agents are not consistent: they cannot both be realised. Thus one side of the market must have their plans frustrated. This is in contrast to the Walrasian or perfectly

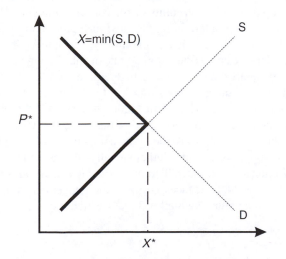

Figure 4.4   *The min condition*

competitive price at which supply equals demand. Here both sides of the market are able to realise their desired trades.

How will agents respond to finding that they are unable to trade as much as they would like to at the prevailing price level? If someone is unable to buy/sell as much as they want to, then we say that they are *rationed* or *quantity con-strained*. A new theory of the firm and household needed to be developed in which agents faced not only the standard budget constraint, but also possible quantity constraints (also called rationing constraints). Let us see very briefly how this theory developed, since it is crucial to understanding how the subsequent new Keynesian developments arose.

Traditional consumer theory assumes that the household maximises a utility function subject to a budget constraint. In a macroeconomic context, the utility function might have utility depending on consumption C and leisure L: the bud-get constraint might have total expenditure on consumption at price P being less than labour income and profits Π less tax etc. Ignoring taxes for now, and noting that work supplied, N, equals time endowment (set at 1) less leisure, then $N = 1 - L$, and we can write the household's maximisation problem as:

$$\max U(C, L) \tag{4.1}$$
$$\text{s.t. } P \cdot C = W \cdot (1 - L) + \Pi \tag{4.2}$$

The budget line (4.2) is written in such a way that there is no constraint on the amounts of C and L except the 'technological' ones (consumption C has to be non-negative; leisure L has to be less than or equal to the total time endowment 1, and cannot be negative). It is simply a straight line: when there is all play and no work ($L = 1$), consumption cannot exceed the non-labour (profit) income of the household; the slope of the budget line is the real wage, since for every unit of leisure it gives up it can buy W/P units of the consumption good.

The solution to this problem is represented in Figure 4.5a: it is the standard tangency condition at which utility is maximised at point $A(C^*, L^*)$, where the slope of the indifference curve (the marginal rate of substitution between consump-tion and leisure) equals the slope of the budget line ($-W/P$). Now suppose that the household faces a 'quantity constraint' in the labour market: it is unable to supply as much work as it wishes. In 'economist speak', this means that the household is forced to consume more leisure than it wants. This will occur if the 'price' in the labour market (W) is above the competitive price, and there is a sit-uation of excess supply of labour. Mathematically, we can add to the consumer's problem an additional constraint, called the *rationing constraint*, so that when the household maximises (4.1), it faces not only the budget constraint (4.2), but in addition there is a maximum amount of labour which it can sell, N^R so that:

$$(1 - L) \leqslant N^R \tag{4.3}$$

The situation of the household can is represented in Figure 4.5b, where the seg-ment of the budget line which involves the household selling more labour than N^R

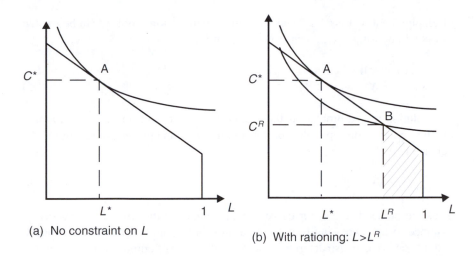

(a) No constraint on *L*   *(b)* With rationing: $L>L^R$

Figure 4.5 *Effective demand*

is now unshaded. The previous optimum (A) given this additional constraint, N^R, is now unfeasible. In effect, rather the consumption/leisure possibilities are represented not by the area between the origin and the budget line (called the 'budget set'), but rather the shaded area in the bottom right-hand corner of the budget set. The maximum utility that the household can attain is now represented by the point along the budget line which involves the household selling up to its constraint, at point B. This must mean a fall in utility from the unconstrained maximum U^* to U^R. This is of course a general result in mathematics: if you impose more constraints, it cannot make you better off!

If we compare the new quantity constrained optimum, we can see that the limit on the amount of labour supplied has not only reduced the labour supply (leisure has risen from L^* to L^R: it has also reduced consumption from C^* to C^R, although there was no direct constraint on consumption itself. This is of course common sense: if we are unable to work as much as we want to, it will mean that we are unable to afford to buy as much as we would like. This is often called a *spillover* effect from the labour market (where the household is constrained) to the output (consumption) market. This is in effect what can happen to the involuntary unemployed. The involuntary unemployed are people who would like to work more than they do at present for the same wage. If they were allowed to work more, then they would have more labour income, and thus be able to consume more. They would move along their budget line from point B towards point A.

We can make a similar analysis of the firm. In the Walrasian analysis, the firm is assumed to choose output and employment to maximise profits: no explicit constraint is put on the levels of output and employment that can be chosen. Suppose that the firm has a standard production function where output y is a function of employment N, $y=f(N)$. Then its profit maximisation problem can be written as one of choosing N (and hence y) to maximise profits:

$$\max P \cdot y - W \cdot N \qquad (4.4)$$
$$\text{s.t. } y = f(N) \qquad (4.5)$$

The solution to this problem is the standard one that the firm maximises profits by employing labour up to the point where the marginal product of labour (MPL) equals the real wage:

$$\frac{W}{P} = f'(N) \qquad (4.6)$$

Thus the demand for labour curve is represented by the MPL curve, which is assumed to be decreasing (due to the diminishing marginal product of labour). From (4.5), we can also determine the desired supply of output by the firm: to the level of employment N^* that solves (4.5) there corresponds the level of output $y^* = f(N^*)$. Clearly, the lower the real wage, the greater the amount of labour the firm will want to employ, and the greater the amount of output it wants to supply. Hence we can write both the demand for labour and the supply of output as functions of the real wage: both are decreasing in W/P:

$$y = y^s\left(\frac{W}{P}\right)$$
$$N = N^d\left(\frac{W}{P}\right) \qquad (4.7)$$

Now, suppose that the firm is rationed in the output market, and faces a quantity constraint on the amount of output it can sell. When the firm maximises its profits (4.4), it faces not just the technological constraint (4.5), but also the additional constraint:

$$y \leq y^R \qquad (4.8)$$

where y^R is the 'ration' on output that can be sold. The solution to maximising (4.4) subject to both (4.5) and (4.8) depends on whether the constraint (4.8) is 'binding': that is, whether the firm wants to sell more or less output than y^R. If the constraint is *non-binding*, then the amount that the firm wishes to sell is less than the quantity constraint y^R. In this case, output and employment by the firm are determined by the output supply function y^s and the labour demand function N^d given by (4.7). However, suppose instead that the firm wishes to sell more than y^R: in this case the firm will want to sell right up to the constraint, so that $y = y^R$. Since the amount the firm would like to sell is determined by the real wage, we can say that actual output y is determined by the following condition:

$$y = \min\left[y^s\left(\frac{W}{P}\right), y^R\right] \qquad (4.9)$$

What equation (4.9) tells us is that actual output y is the minimum (that is to say the smaller) of the amount that the firm would like to sell, given by the output supply function $y^s(w/p)$ and the demand constraint y^R. We can represent this in Figure 4.6a: on the vertical axis, we have the real wage, and output is on the horizontal axis; the function $y^s(w/p)$ is downward-sloping (a higher real wage means the firm wants to supply less output): the vertical line $y = y^R$ represents the *demand constraint*. The actual level of output depends on the real wage: if this is high, as at point a, the firm desires to supply less than y^R, so that output is given by the output supply curve y^s. However, at a point like b, where the real wage is low, the firm desires to sell more than the quantity constraint. In this case, we say that the firm is *demand constrained*.

In Figure 4.6b, we can see how the constraint in the *output market* affects the firm's demand in the labour market. The employment level N^R is the exact amount of labour needed to produce y^R: $y^R = f(N^R)$. At high wage levels, such as point a, there is no spillover from the quantity constraint in the output market to the labour market, and employment is determined by the usual labour demand curve.

There is thus an important potential spillover effect operating between rationing constraints in one market (in this example the labour market) and the behaviour of the household in another market (in this example the output or consumption good market). This link is crucial at the macroeconomic level, and forms the foundation for Keynes's theory of *effective demand* and the multiplier. Before we look at this a little more formally, let us consider the argument intuitively. From our example, the optimal consumption decision of households

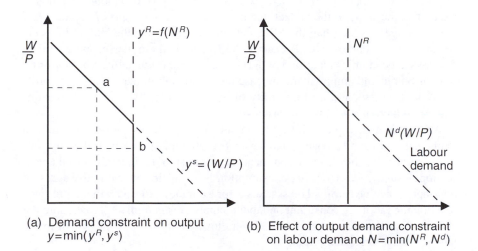

(a) Demand constraint on output
    $y = \min(y^R, y^s)$

(b) Effect of output demand constraint
    on labour demand $N = \min(N^R, N^d)$

Figure 4.6 *The spillover of demand constraints on output onto the firm's demand for labour*

depends not only on wages and prices (the factors which along with the profit income determine the position of the budget line represented by (4.5)), but also on the employment decision of firms, which determines the quantity constraint that the household faces. Hence we can get a feedback effect to operate, giving what is usually called the *multiplier*. If someone (e.g. the government) spends more on the output of firms, this will relax the quantity constraint that firms face: they will thus decide to hire more people in the labour market. If firms hire more people in the labour market, then the rationing constraint of the household is relaxed: it is able to supply more labour, which has the effect of increasing wage income and hence consumption. If consumer demand rises, then firms will increase employment; if firms increase employment then consumers will consume more, thereby increasing demand for firm's output…. This is a feedback process, by which the initial first round injection of demand into the economy is magnified. Now, of course, there are various details here that need to be satisfied: both the household and the firm need to be rationed, the firm in the output market, the household in the labour market. When this happens, the economy is said to be in the *Keynesian unemployment* regime (Malinvaud, 1977).

A necessary condition for the firm to be rationed in the output market is that price exceeds marginal cost (MC). To see why, note that the marginal profit from increasing output equals price less marginal cost: if the price is 6 and the MC of an extra unit is 4, the net profit from selling an extra unit at that price is 2 (since $2 = 6 - 4$). Similarly, if we look at the household, for the rationing constraint to be binding in the labour market, there must be *involuntary unemployment*, by which we mean that the household is willing to work more than it can at (or even slightly below) the current real wage. One way in which this is often described in the literature is that 'the real wage exceeds the disutility of labour'. By this is meant that the slope of the budget line in consumption/leisure (C, L) space – i.e. the real wage – is less than the MRS between C and L (i.e. the budget line cuts the indifference curve). This is exactly the situation where the second postulate of classical economics identified by Keynes is violated (see above). In this situation, as output and employment increase during the multiplier process, the profits of the firm increase, as does utility of the household. Everyone is better off, and hence there is a *Pareto improvement*.

We can formalise this a little further. For those readers who are allergic to mathematics, I would advise you to have a first attempt to read the following couple of paragraphs: however, if your head begins to spin, jump straight to the next section. Usually, we write that consumption is a function of the real wage, and non-labour income (profits Π less taxes T for example). However, in the presence of a binding rationing constraint on labour supply, this *quantity* N^R enters into the consumption function, representing the spillover from the unemployment in the labour market to consumption:

$$C = C(\frac{W}{P}, \frac{\Pi - T}{P}, N^R) \qquad (4.10)$$

All three derivatives are positive. Let us assume that the firm's technology takes a particular form: one unit of labour is used to produce one unit of output, so that output equals employment.[5] In this case we have $y=N$. We will now introduce the government into the picture: the government purchases g units of output, and pays for it by raising a lump-sum tax on the households T, or running down some asset. Given that, equilibrium in the economy can be written as:

$$N = C(W, \Pi - T, N) + g \qquad (4.11)$$

In order to write (4.11), we have assumed that the output price is the numeraire (i.e. we have set $P=1$).[6] We have also assumed that in the output market $y = y^R = C + g$, and in the labour market, $N = N^R$: using these we have substituted out the rationing constraints and expressed everything in terms of employment N. It is easiest to see what $C(W, \Pi - g, N)$ looks like if we take, for example, Cobb–Douglas preferences $U(C, L) = C^\alpha L^{(1-\alpha)}$. The 'unconstrained' consumption function[7] is then:

$$C = \alpha(W + \Pi - T) \qquad (4.12)$$

whereas the *constrained* demand when labour supply is limited to N^R is:

$$C = \alpha(W \cdot N + \Pi - T) \qquad (4.13)$$

An obvious interpretation of α is the 'marginal propensity to consume', since the household with Cobb–Douglas preferences consumes a proportion α of its income. Now, WN is total labour income, and Π is total profit income. The firm's budget constraint says that total revenue y must be divided between costs (labour is the only factor of production here, so costs equal wage costs $W \cdot N$) and profits Π: that is $y = W \cdot N + \Pi$. Hence, using the firm's budget constraint we can write (4.13) as:

$$C = \alpha(y - T) \qquad (4.14)$$

Now, what happens if g increases? Using (4.14) and noting that because of the firm's technology $y = N$, we have:

$$N = \alpha(N - T) + g \qquad (4.15)$$

Differentiating (4.15) with respect to g, yields (in two steps):

$$dN = \alpha(dN - dT) + dg$$

If $dT = 0$, and the expenditure is not tax financed, then

$$\frac{dN}{dg} = \frac{1}{1 - \alpha} = \frac{1}{1 - MPC} > 1 \qquad (4.16)$$

This is the classic Keynesian multiplier: the initial stimulus dg is magnified by the feedback process between employment decisions of firms and the consumption decision of households.

Has there been an increase in the welfare of everyone in this process? The simple answer is yes, there must have been. We can tell that from the fact that firms were willing to respond to the increase in the demand by increasing output, and also that the households were willing to supply more labour. Given that there is voluntary trade, any increase in output in this position must lead to an increase in welfare of the household and profits of the firm. In general, how can we tell when this will be the case. This turns out to be quite simple. In order to have a Keynesian multiplier like this, one need to start off from an initial position in which two conditions are satisfied:

 (i) There is an excess supply of output: $P > MC$
(ii) There is an excess supply of labour: $W/P >$ disutility of labour.

In order to understand (i), this simply says that the firm would like to sell more at the prevailing price P: a firm will always want to sell more so long as its marginal cost is less than price. Condition (i) simply says that the firm is quantity constrained or rationed in the amount of output it can sell, and hence its profits will increase if it can sell more. A similar observation applies to condition (ii) for households: as in Figure 4.5b, if the household can increase employment (reduce leisure), it can increase utility by moving from B towards A. Note that condition (i) corresponds to the relaxation of Keynes's Classical Postulate I, and (ii) to the relaxation of Classical Postulate II.

There is thus the question: under what assumptions will we be in an initial position where both (i) and (ii) are satisfied? *Here is the crucial link to new Keynesian economics.* In brief, the answer is that imperfectly competitive price/wage setting agents will ensure that (i) and (ii) are satisfied. Turning first to (i): if firms are price-setters, and face a non-perfectly elastic demand curve, then they will set their price as a mark-up over marginal cost: a monopolist, monopolistic firm or oligopolist will set the price above marginal cost as a consequence of profit maximisation. Turning to (ii) there are a variety of different stories. However, if we suppose that the labour market is unionised as in Blanchard and Kiyotaki (1987), then the union will aim to set the real wage above the competitive real wage, and hence to a position where the real wage exceeds the marginal disutility of forgone leisure. The argument is entirely analogous to the firm. Thus, *imperfect competition is crucial in creating the initial condition that households would like to sell more labour, and that firms would like to sell more output at the equilibrium prices.* That is, that *both households and firms are demand constrained.*

However, the mere fact that the initial condition is satisfied is not enough to obtain a Keynesian multiplier: rigid prices are also needed. This is the second key step taken by the new Keynesians: *nominal price rigidity is more likely when there is imperfect competition.* It is to this step that we now turn.

8   NOMINAL RIGIDITY

As we have seen in the previous section, if there is nominal rigidity (fixed wages or prices), then this can give rise to changes in *nominal* demand having *real* output and employment effects. One of the basic insights of new Keynesian economics was to link this idea to that of imperfect competition. This link was made by Michael Parkin (1986), George Akerlof and Janet Yellen (1985a,b), and Greg Mankiw (1985) in what has become known as the 'menu cost' theory.

However, before we go into the details of the menu cost theory, it is useful to briefly review another powerful idea: that of staggered contracts. The original new classical neutrality result of Sargent and Wallace (1976) showed that if prices adjusted instantaneously and agents held rational expectations, then only unanticipated changes in nominal demand could have an effect on real variables such as output and employment, and furthermore that these effects could only last one period. The reason for the transience of the effect was that agents with rational expectations will immediately update their beliefs and expectations in response to the information embodied in the shock. An early response to this was the Fischer (1977) and Taylor (1979) theory of overlapping or 'staggered' contracts: that is they took the basic Sargent and Wallace model, but added the real world assumption that firms/unions[8] do not all adjust prices/wages at once: rather the adjustment of nominal prices is usually spread over the year due to overlapping or staggered contracts. The key result of the staggered wage setting model is that the effects of shocks are no longer limited to the period in which they occur.

For example, suppose that 50 per cent of firms/unions adjust prices in a particular period (there are two groups who have two-period contracts, one group changes each period). Then when a shock occurs only those whose contracts are up for renewal are able to adjust their contracts: the other 50 per cent are still locked into their old contract. Thus the effect of an unanticipated change in nominal demand will last for at least two periods, and there will be what is technically referred to as 'serial correlation' in output: a positive shock will lead to high output for a couple of periods, and a negative shock to low output. However, the early work of Fischer and Taylor, while tracing out the real effects of nominal rigidities, did not provide any explanation of the structure of nominal wage and price setting. What was needed was a theory of why nominal rigidities persist through time.

9   ENVELOPES, MENU COSTS AND NOMINAL RIGIDITY

One of the key new Keynesian ideas was the notion that with price-setting firms, it was possible that nominal prices were more likely to be rigid. The argument is very simple. Suppose that we have a monopolist who sets the price for his good. If he maximises profits, we have the familiar first-order condition that marginal revenue equals marginal cost. Now, of course, at the optimal or profit maximising price, a small change in price will not lead to much change in profits. This is the meaning of the first order condition, that the derivative of profits with respect to price is equal to zero. To see why, let us consider Figure 4.7, which a visual representation of the relationship between price (on the horizontal axis) and profit

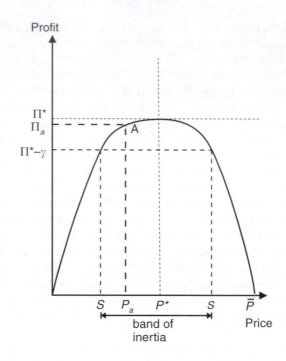

Figure 4.7   *Menu costs and the band of inertia*

(on the vertical). We can see that at a low price (zero, say), profits are zero, and that at a high price $\bar{P}$, the same is true. In between 0 and $\bar{P}$, however, profits are positive, and we have the 'profit hill'. As we set off from a zero price, profits at first increase: we are walking up the slope of the profit hill. However, as we get near to the top, the slope becomes flatter and flatter, until we reach the top. At the top, the hill must be flat: if it had an upward slope, we could not be at the top, since we could get higher by walking up the slope.[9] In mathematical terms, the derivative of profits with respect to price measures the slope: and the first order condition for a maximum states that at the highest level of profits (the summit), profits are flat as we change price (the derivative is zero). Now, this is of course just the intuitive explanation for the first order conditions for a maximum.

However, it has some powerful economic implications, and forms the basis for the 'menu cost'argument for nominal price rigidity. Different authors (Parkin, 1986; Akerlof and Yellen, 1985; and Mankiw, 1985) all saw that if there were some costs to changing prices, then even quite small costs could lead to significant price rigidity. The reason is very simple: suppose that we are near the top of the profit hill, say at point A in Figure 4.7. Furthermore, suppose that it costs a certain amount γ to change the price. In this case, we will only incur the cost of changing price if the benefit we derive in terms of extra profits is larger than γ.

Now as we can see, if we are at A, the benefit is less than γ: on the vertical axis the maximum profit is Π^*, and the profits at point A are Π_a, which is greater than $\Pi^* - \gamma$. Indeed, the fact that the hill is flat near to the top means that although we are not far from the top in terms of profits (the vertical height), the price might be quite far away from the optimal price P^* (the horizontal distance $P_a - P^*$). There is in fact a 'band of inertia' around the optimal price, representing all of those prices like P_a where the cost of changing price outweighs the benefits: this band is represented in Figure 4.7 by the range of prices on the horizontal axis between s and S; the reason for this notation will become clearer below, when we discuss (s, S) rules.

Whilst this all sounds as if it has more to do with geography than macroeconomics, that is not so. Suppose that there is a change in demand, for example the demand curve shifts. In terms of Figure 4.7, the mountain would move, or at least the profit hill would shift in some way: suppose that the whole thing might move to the right. Now rather than drawing the situation 'before' and 'after' the mountain moved, we can simply reinterpret Figure 4.7: P_a is the old optimal price before the mountain moved, and P^* is the new optimal price, and the profit hill drawn is the 'after' one. We can now see that if there is not a big move in the mountain (i.e. demand does not change too much), then the gain from adjusting our price (increasing profits from Π_a to Π^* will not be very much, since the old optimal price P_a is still near to the top of the hill, and the slope of the hill is flat. This mathematical result is known as the envelope theorem.[10]

What conclusion can we draw from this analysis? If a price-setting monopolist has some costs of adjusting price, then if there is a small change in demand (the mountain only moves a little bit), then he will not change price. Even quite small menu costs can lead to significant price rigidity. Indeed, it has long been observed that there is significant price rigidity in imperfectly competitive markets, and this is a possible explanation. However, whilst the menu costs might be quite small, as we have seen the welfare benefits of an increase in demand can be large. We know that a monopolist will mark up price over marginal cost: the more inelastic demand, the higher the gap between price and marginal cost. In terms of social welfare, the market price of the output exceeds the social costs of production (which will be equal to marginal cost if the factor markets are perfectly competitive). The increase in welfare is shown in Figure 4.8.

The demand curve Da is the initial demand curve corresponding to the optimal price P_a (you can link together Figure 4.7 and Figure 4.8): demand increases to Db, and the optimal price 'after' is P^*. However, suppose that the change in demand is small,[11] so that the potential gain in profits Π_a to Π^* from changing price from P_a to P^* is less than γ, so that the price remains fixed at P_a and output will have increased from X_a to X'_a. In this case there is a gain in total welfare: for each extra unit of output produced, the marginal value of this output to consumers (represented by the market price P_a) exceeds the social cost of production (represented by the marginal cost MC, here given). Note that the firm will of course earn more profits: the marginal profit on each extra unit sold is the

Mainly Macro

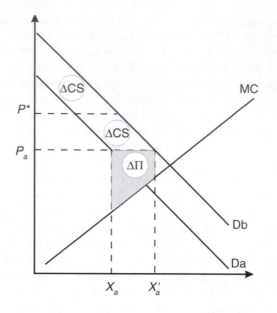

Figure 4.8 *Pareto improvement with a rigid nominal price*

difference between MC and price, the total increase in profits being represented by the shaded area $\Delta\Pi$. Furthermore, there is an increase in consumer surplus, the shaded area ΔCS (the whole area between the demand curves above the horizontal line P_a. Hence, if demand increases *and the price is rigid due to menu costs*, then there can be a Pareto improvement – consumers and the owners of firms are both made better off. Of course, the firm's shareholders would be even better off if there were no menu costs and the firm could raise its price to P^*: but the point remains that nominal rigidity of prices means that an increase in nominal demand can lead to a Pareto improvement whereby everyone is better off. This is obviously a very Keynesian result: if we interpret the increase in demand as being due to a tax cut or an increase in the nominal money supply, or a money financed increase in government expenditure, then when there are menu costs this sort of policy can lead to 'Keynesian' multiplier effects (since prices are rigid), and also 'Keynesian' welfare effects, since there is a Pareto improvement.

Now, all of this argument rests on the importance or size of the so called 'menu costs'. If menu costs are extremely small, then they will not cause much nominal rigidity. In terms of the band of inertia in Figure 4.7, the range (s, S) will be quite small. This means the ability of the government to take advantage of the rigidity is quite limited. There are three explanations of menu costs. Firstly, there is the literal cost of printing new price lists and informing customers of a price change. For a restaurant, this can be quite trivial. However, for some types of organisation this alone can be quite significant: for example, large banks and other institutions that provide variable interest home loans may have millions of customers. The cost of sending a letter to each one of these to inform them of a change in the loan interest rate (which they are required to do by law) is in itself very large (printing and postage costs). However, with a few specific exceptions, not many people think that these narrowly defined menu costs are what count. Rather there are two other types of argument which are really different ways of looking at the same thing.

First, there is the argument of bounded rationality (this was the original argument of Akerlof and Yellen, 1985): people do not really maximise, they adopt 'near rationality' in the sense of taking actions which tend to get them close to the optimum. Why should they behave in this way? This brings us to the second argument, which is that there are costs to decisions; we need to gather information, process it, decide what to do, and then implement our decision. These 'decision costs' mean that firms often adopt 'rules of thumb', guidelines for such activities as price-setting that seem to work. Indeed, one can put together the two arguments and say that bounded rationality is really full rationality but with decision costs taken into account.[12] Indeed, there has been a long tradition of literature which has argued that firms adopt simple 'rules of thumb' in their pricing decisions (see for example Hall and Hitch, 1939, and for a more recent and explicitly macroeconomic approach, see Naish, 1993). Certainly, there is strong empirical evidence that for variety of reasons some firms do not change their prices all that often (indeed, it is rare to find restaurants that vary prices frequently, despite the small menu costs).

However, even if we take the menu cost theory at the individual firm level, what are the macroeconomic implications? Caplin and Spulber (1987) came up with an interesting argument which showed that even if menu costs lead to price rigidity at the *firm* level, they might not lead to any significant rigidity at the *macroeconomic* level. In order to understand the argument, we need to look a bit more at the so-called (s, S) rule. The argument that we have advanced about menu costs was static: it looked at the effect of a one-off change in demand. In practice, of course, firms need to consider what is going to happen in the future when they set their prices now. If the general level of nominal prices in the economy is rising (there is background inflation), then setting a lower price now will lead to having to change prices sooner (and hence incur menu costs sooner) than if a higher price were set now. In practice there is a trade off between setting a price to optimise *current* profits, and the need to take into account future profits. This is a complex problem in dynamic optimisation which I will not explain here. However, some clever chaps have solved this sort of problem, and the solution is that firms adopt a (s, S) rule, which is really quite simple.

First, consider the optimal price in the absence of any menu costs at each instant t of time: $P^*(t)$. This is the price that equates current marginal revenue with MC. The optimal pricing rule[13] takes the following form. There is a lower barrier $P(t)^* - s$, and an upper barrier $P^*(t) + S$: these two barriers together define a band of inertia around the price $P^*(t)$ (and hence the two parameters (s, S)

define this sort of rule). If the price at any time is within the band of inertia, then the (s, S) indicates that it is optimal to leave the price where it is. However, if the price moves outside the boundary, then it should be adjusted, with the exact rule for setting the new price depending on the expected behaviour of future prices. We depict the sort of pricing behaviour by an individual firm when there is a constant background inflation, so that the 'optimal' price $P^*(t)$ follows a smooth upward trend equal to the rate of inflation, as in Figure 4.9.

The optimal pricing rule involves the following behaviour: the price is kept constant until the actual price hits the bottom barrier; at that point the firm will raise the price *above* the $P^*(t)$, and then hold it constant.[14] So, in Figure 4.9, we can see that the optimal behaviour involves the firm keeping the price constant most of the time, and having a periodic revision of the price to keep in line with inflation (depicted at time t_0 and t_1). This is realistic: we often observe firms which seem[15] to publish new price lists at regular intervals (every quarter or every year). Now Caplin and Spulber argued that this type of behaviour at the micro level is perfectly consistent with complete price flexibility at the aggregate macro level.

The argument is really quite simple. Imagine that we are in Ancient Rome,[16] and that there are ten months in the year. There are many firms, each with menu costs, following a (s, S) rule. The background inflation rate is 10 per cent per annum: each firm finds it optimal to change its price once per year. Thus, in terms of Figure 4.9, each individual firm keeps its price constant for 9 months of the year, and on the 10th it changes its price by 10 per cent. Now (and here is the

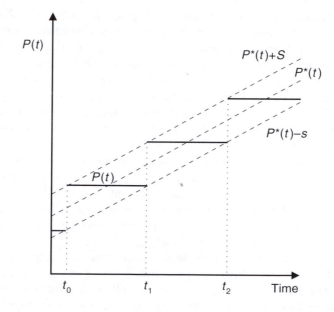

Figure 4.9   *Optimal pricing under an (s, S) rule*

interesting bit), if the critical month at which each firm changes its price are evenly spread over the year (1/10 each month), then the monthly inflation rate will be 1 per cent. To see why, in any one month 9/10 of prices are fixed, and 1/10 rise by 10 per cent: the average is therefore 1 per cent [(0 per cent $\times$ 0.9) + (10 per cent $\times$ 0.1) = 1]. Thus, each month we can see prices *on average* rising by 1 per cent: and over the 10 months there is a cumulative increase of 10 per cent.[17] Thus, although there is a nominal rigidity at the individual firm level, the aggregate price time series is perfectly smooth. Caplin and Spulber's argument rests on the notion that the incidence of price adjustment through time is even: each month sees an equal proportion of firms changing price. In fact they made a lot of very special assumptions to ensure that this was the case, and it is not a general result. Alan Sutherland (1995) analysed this in somewhat more detail, and found that 'clustering' was a more common phenomenon: firms would tend to arrange to change their prices together. In that case the aggregate price index would not be so smooth. In practice, we often observe such 'clustering': lots of prices change just after Christmas, and so on. Hence microeconomic price rigidity can lead to macroeconomic price rigidity.

One of the main empirical tests of the menu cost theory suggested by Ball, Mankiw and Romer (1988) was that there would be a relationship between inflation and the responsiveness of output to *nominal* demand shocks. In a high inflation country, the frequency with which firms adjust their prices will be higher. Hence any potential nominal rigidity will be less persistent, so that if there is a nominal demand shock (e.g. an unanticipated change in nominal national income), then the possibility of it translating into a *real* output change is less. The main prediction of the menu cost theory is therefore that the translation of nominal demand shocks into real output changes will be less in high inflation countries. They found some empirical evidence for this relationship looking at a large cross section of countries over a couple of decades.

10 IMPERFECT COMPETITION AND THE MULTIPLIER WITH FLEXIBLE PRICES

Imperfect competition plays a crucial role in the theory of new Keynesian macroeconomics. As we saw in the analysis of menu costs, it provides the basis of a theory of *nominal* price rigidity. However, it also provides the foundation of a theory of *real* rigidity: imperfect competition is an alternative equilibrium concept to the Walrasian one where supply equals demand. Imperfect competition provides an explanation of *how* prices are set by optimising agents rather than by fictitious auctioneers. However, the importance goes further than that, since the imperfectly competitive equilibrium may well be one where price exceeds marginal cost, and if the labour market is unionised, one where there might be involuntary unemployment. In short, the imperfectly competitive equilibrium might be 'Keynesian' in some sense. It is this possibility that I explore next. What does an imperfectly competitive economy without menu costs look like: is it possible to get something that is Keynesian even when prices and wages are perfectly flexible? I will look at this in two stages: first, I will examine an economy in which the labour market is competitive, and the only imperfection is that the product market is imperfectly competitive; secondly, I will look at an economy in which the labour market is not perfectly competitive.

10.1   Imperfect Competition in the Product Market

A few papers have looked at the effect of imperfect competition on the size of the fiscal multiplier (Dixon, 1987c; Mankiw, 1988; Startz, 1989; Marris, 1991; Dixon and Lawler, 1996). Three of the authors have made the claim that in some sense imperfect competition makes the economy Keynesian, and in particular that the traditional Keynesian multiplier $[1/(1-MPC)]$ can in some sense be said to arise in an imperfectly competitive economy. Let us look a bit more closely at this claim.

In order to keep things ultra simple, let us consider an economy in which labour is the only factor of production, and the marginal product of labour is equal to unity: output equals employment: $y = N$. There are two goods, leisure $L = 1 - N$, and consumption C. Households have the utility function

$$U(C, L) = C^{\alpha} L^{(1-\alpha)}$$

subject to the standard budget constraint we discussed earlier:

$$C = W \cdot (1 - L) + \Pi - T \tag{4.17}$$

Again, we are treating the output good as the numeraire. We can set up the Lagrangean for this problem as follows:

$$\Im = C^{\alpha} L^{(1-\alpha)} + \lambda [W \cdot (1 - L) + \Pi - T]$$

The first order conditions are then:

$$\frac{\partial \Im}{\partial C} = \alpha C^{\alpha - 1} L^{1-\alpha} - \lambda = 0$$

$$\frac{\partial \Im}{\partial L} = (1 - \alpha) C^{\alpha} L^{-\alpha} - \lambda W = 0$$

From the first equation we have[18] $\lambda = \alpha U/C$, and from the second equation we have $\lambda = (1 - \alpha) U/WL$. Combining these two, we have the equation:

$$\frac{C}{L} = \frac{\alpha}{1 - \alpha} \cdot W \tag{4.18}$$

We can represent this graphically in Figure 4.10. The household wants to consume consumption and leisure in fixed proportions, so that C/L is determined by its preferences (α) and the real wage (W) it faces. Thus, for any given value of W, the desired ratio C/L can be represented as a ray from the origin, with slope

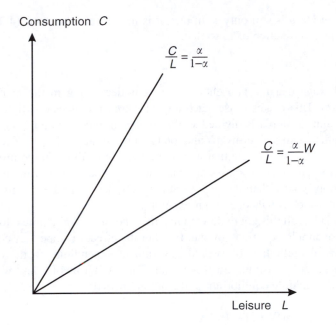

Figure 4.10   *Income expansion paths in consumption–leisure space with Cobb–Douglas preferences*

$(1-\alpha)/\alpha W$. In Figure 4.10, we have depicted two such rays,[19] one corresponding to a wage of 1 and the other a wage $W<1$. As the real wage falls, the household responds by consuming less and enjoying more leisure, since the rewards to work are less.

To find the actual level of consumption, you simply substitute equation (11) into the budget constraint (4.17), so that:

$$C=\alpha(W+\Pi-T) \tag{4.19}$$

Now comes the relevance of imperfect competition. Firms produce one unit of output with one unit of labour, so that marginal cost (MC) is W. Let us simply assume that there is some imperfect competition, so that the typical firm[20] is able to mark up the price over marginal cost: in particular, the so called 'price–cost margin':[21]

$$\mu=\frac{P-W}{P}=1-W \tag{4.20}$$

Since we are treating the output price as the numeraire, this has a very simple form. The meaning of (4.20) is really quite simple: the more monopoly power the firm has, the more it is able to mark up price over marginal cost, and hence the larger is $P-W$ relative to P (i.e. the larger is $1-W$), and μ is large. In the case of perfect competition, the firm sets a price equal to marginal cost, so that $W=1$, and $\mu=0$: there is no monopoly power. Note that μ lies in the range 0 to 1: even if wages are 0, μ is still only 1. In fact, it is more useful to invert (4.20), and to express W as a function of μ, so that:

$$W = 1 - \mu \tag{4.21}$$

The real wage that the household receives is decreasing in the market power of the firm. This makes sense: each unit of labour produces one unit of output, and this unit of output is divided so that μ goes in profits[22] and $1 - \mu$ in wages. Total profits are in real terms μN and total real wages are $N(1 - \mu)$. If we consider equation (4.21), we can see that with imperfect competition in the product market the first postulate of classical economics is broken: unless there is perfect competition ($\mu = 0$), then the real wage is strictly less than the marginal product of labour (which equals one in our example).

So, what has all this got to do with macroeconomics? Well, quite a lot, because with these simple equations we can find out the effect of imperfect competition on the fiscal multiplier. If we add government expenditure to the consumers expenditure, and substitute for wages and profits in terms of μ and we have the income–expenditure equilibrium in the output market:

$$y = C + g = \alpha(W + \Pi - T) + g$$

Since $y = N$, $W = 1 - \mu$ and $\Pi = \mu N$, also assuming a balanced budget ($g = T$), this becomes:

$$N = \alpha[(1 - \mu) + \mu N - T] + g$$

so that:

$$N = \frac{\alpha(1 - \mu) + g(1 - \alpha)}{1 - \alpha\mu} \tag{4.22}$$

This is the exact solution for equilibrium output and employment. As we illustrate in Table 4.1 below, as μ increases (firms have more market power), the level of output and employment decrease.[23] This is a standard result, which in no way depends on the functional form we have chosen. In order to obtain the multiplier, we differentiate (4.22) with respect to g:

$$\frac{dN}{dg} = \frac{1 - \alpha}{1 - \alpha\mu} \leqslant 1 \tag{4.23}$$

Equation (4.23) is very interesting: it shows that there is a direct link between the market power of firms μ and the size of the expenditure multiplier. Note first that the multiplier must be less than 1: even if μ takes its largest possible value of 1, the multiplier is just equal to unity. However, for all practical values of μ, the multiplier will be less than 1. This means that there is some crowding out of consumption, which is not surprising given that the increase in expenditure is financed by tax. Second, note that in a Walrasian world with perfect competition,

Table 4.1   *The relationship between the multiplier, output and the degree of imperfect competition*

μ	0.1	0.2	0.3	0.4	0.5
N	0.837	0.821	0.803	0.780	0.750
$\dfrac{dN}{dg}$	0.217	0.238	0.263	0.294	0.333

Note: Obtained from equations (4.22) and (4.23) setting $\alpha = 0.8$ and $g = 0.25$.

$\mu = 0$, and the multiplier is:

$$\left.\frac{dN}{dg}\right|_{\mu=0} = 1 - \alpha \tag{4.24}$$

Now what happens as we increase μ? From (4.23), it is clear that *an increase in μ increases the multiplier*: an increase in imperfect competition leads to an increase in the value of the multiplier. Let us take an example: suppose that $\alpha = 0.8$ (a very plausible value if we interpret α as the marginal propensity to consume). In Table 4.1 we give the value of the multiplier for different values of μ. For reference, we also compute the equilibrium output and employment level N, given $g = 0.25$. If we compare the Walrasian value (0.2) with the plausible empirical value for μ of 0.3, we can see that the multiplier is 19 per cent larger under imperfect competition. This means that the amount of expenditure necessary to yield a given increase in employment is smaller.

Whilst we can see the mathematics quite clearly, what is the intuitive reason behind this result? All three authors (Dixon, Mankiw and Startz) provide the same explanation, in terms of the *profit multiplier*, which is really quite simple to understand. Suppose that the government increases expenditure by an amount dg. Now, this will be received by the firms as income: they will pass some of the income to households in the form of profits. The initial increase in output associated with the increased expenditure is $dN = dg$: the extra profits resulting from this are then $\mu \cdot dg$, which will then appear in the household's budget constraint in the form of profits. The household will (from equation (4.19)), decide to spend a proportion α of this, thus causing an additional increase in output of $\alpha \mu dg$, and so on.[24] If there is perfect competition and no profits, then there can be no profit multiplier: but with more imperfect competition and a larger mark-up, this effect will be more powerful. Whilst we have looked at the impact of imperfect competition of the government expenditure, it will also apply to other real shocks, such as productivity and real exchange rate shocks.

We can show the effect of imperfect competition on the multiplier diagrammaticaly in Figure 4.11. The vertical and horizontal axes are consumption and leisure as before, and the income expansion paths correspond to those in Figure 4.10. The new feature is to include the production possibility frontier for the case

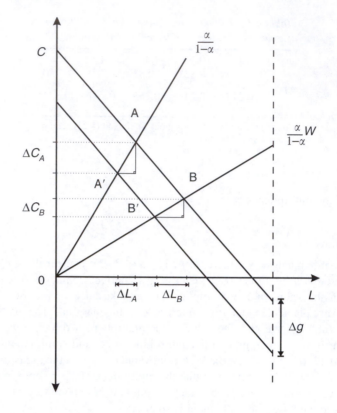

Figure 4.11   *Imperfect competition and the multiplier*

where there is government expenditure. There is one unit of time allocated to the household: it can spread this between work to produce output and leisure:

$$y + L = 1 \tag{4.25}$$

We can think of this as the production possibility frontier (PPF) for the economy. However, since output is divided between C and g, we can rewrite (4.25) as:

$$C = 1 - L - g \tag{4.26}$$

This is represented by the downward-sloping 45° line in Figure 4.11. Clearly, if $L = 0$ (the household works all of the time), then $C = 1 - g$; this is the intercept term for the PPF on the consumption axis. If $L = 1$ (the household does not work at all), then consumption should be equal to $-g$, a negative number: this is why we have allowed for negative consumption in Figure 4.11 (this makes for graphical clarity – the household would of course never choose $1 - L = N \leqslant g$).

   An increase in g means that the PPF in (C, L) space shifts downwards by the size of the increase in g, that is Δg. Now the initial equilibrium for the economy will occur where the relevant income expansion path intersects the production possibility frontier: in the Walrasian case at *A*, or for the case with imperfect competition at *B*. After the increase in *g*, the new equilibria will be *A'* and *B'* respectively. Clearly, in both of these cases, the level of consumption has been reduced in response to the increase in government expenditure (there is crowding out): however, the reduction is less than the increase in government expenditure (there is less than 100 per cent crowding out). In the Walrasian case, the reduction in consumption is ΔC_w, and in the imperfectly competitive case ΔC_μ. Clearly, since the slope of the imperfectly competitive IEP is less than the Walrasian IEP, it follows that the degree of crowding out is less, since:

$$\Delta C_w > \Delta C_\mu$$

Thus, the reason that the multiplier is greater in the imperfectly competitive case is that there is less crowding out.

As we can see from the above analysis, there is an important issue as to whether the multiplier is Keynesian or not: in Dixon (1987c), I called the multiplier 'Walrasian', since the mechanism by which output increases is that households are made worse off (since leisure is a normal good, if the labour supply increases, then the household must be worse off if the real wage is unchanged). Others (Mankiw, 1988; Startz, 1989) have interpreted such effects as Keynesian. However, whatever interpretation one has, the clear message is that imperfect competition matters here.

10.2   Imperfect Competition in the Labour Market

Whilst imperfect competition in the output market alone can give rise to some Keynesian effects, it cannot explain *involuntary unemployment*. If the labour market is perfectly competitive, then real wages will be such that households will be able to supply all of the labour they wish. Whilst there may be *underemployment* in the labour market (in the sense that the level of employment is lower than in the Walrasian equilibrium), any unemployment is voluntary.

Let us look a little bit more closely at the nature of underemployment, and consider again the model of the previous section. Equation (4.21) can be interpreted as the *demand curve* for labour: it states that the real wage *W* equals the marginal product of labour (which was assumed to equal 1) times $(1 - \mu)$. The usual demand for labour curve is of course assumed to be downward-sloping, because it is usual to assume a diminishing marginal product of labour. However, whether the marginal product of labour is constant or decreasing does not alter the argument. Suppose we depict a labour supply curve, and suppose that the labour supply depends only upon the real wage as depicted in Figure 4.12. In this case as μ increases, the labour demand curve shifts downwards: and hence the equilibrium level of employment decreases. The fact that employment is below its Walrasian level when $\mu > 0$ is defined as *underemployment*.

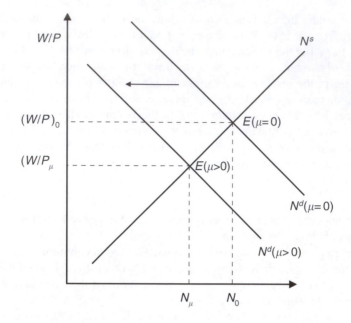

Figure 4.12   *Equilibrium employment and imperfect competition in the product market*

However, involuntary unemployment arises only if the household is off its labour supply curve. Imperfect competition is a way of explaining why this might be the case. The simplest idea is to imagine that the household/union acts as a 'monopolist' in its supply of labour, see for example Blanchard and Kiyotaki (1987), Dixon (1987c). It is able to restrict the supply of labour in order to increase the real wage (in effect it acts as union). For example, suppose that the union likes employment and real wages: that is, it has a union utility function defined over real wages and employment $V(W,N)$. Assuming that these have the usual properties of utility functions, we can represent them by downward-sloping indifference curves that are convex to the origin. Suppose that the technology of firms displays the usual diminishing marginal product of labour, so that we have the standard downward-sloping demand for labour. The utility-maximising union will choose the real wage and employment level so that the indifference curve is tangential to the labour demand curve, as at V^* in Figure 4.13. We have also drawn in the usual labour supply curve: the union will choose to restrict the level of unemployment to a position as represented in the figure at U, at which the marginal disutility of labour is less than the real wage: that is, there is involuntary (or 'union-voluntary') unemployment, represented by the horizontal distance from U to the labour supply curve. The equilibrium with perfect competition and no union is represented by N_0; the equilibrium level of employment and the real wage with imperfect competition only in the output market is represented by

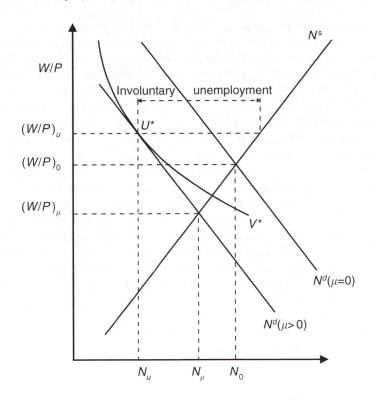

Figure 4.13 *Involuntary unemployment with a unionised labour market*

(W_μ, N_μ); the unionised equilibrium with the imperfectly competitive output market is (W_u, N_u). Clearly, $N_0 > N_\mu > N_u$; furthermore $W_0 > W_\mu$ and $W_u > W_\mu$; the relationship between W_0 and W_u is in general ambiguous, although we have depicted the case where the unionised wage with an imperfectly competitive output market exceeds the Walrasian wage.

11   THE CAMBRIDGE SOAP: WHAT MIGHT HAVE BEEN

In this chapter I have argued that imperfect competition is the key aspect of new Keynesian economics. It is interesting to look back and ask why did it not feature in Keynes's writing, or indeed in subsequent 'Keynesian' writing. On the former, Robin Marris (1991) has written definitively on the subject of Keynes and imperfect competition, and there is little doubt that Keynes rarely thought about imperfect competition. However, this is in a sense very surprising since at the same time as Keynes was developing his macroeconomic theory, the theory of imperfect competition was being developed at the same university by Joan Robinson and Richard Kahn. The explanation appears to have to do with social mores of

Cambridge in the 1930s, and personal tensions between the three. Unlike Keynes, Kahn and Robinson were very much heterosexual. Indeed they had an affair, with Keynes more than once entering Kahn's room to find them both on the floor. As Keynes observed: 'though I expect the conversation was only on the pure theory of monopoly' (Skidelsky, 1992, esp. pp. 448, 495, 536). The ensuing discussion no doubt included the topic of imperfect competition, and the resultant creation was Robinson's (1933) *The Economics of Imperfect Competition*.

Although Joan Robinson did indeed discuss the *General Theory* with Keynes, the link between imperfect competition and the ideas of the *General Theory* was never made.[25] It had been Richard Kahn (1931) who first thought of the multiplier and who helped Robinson (1933) develop her own theory of imperfect competition. Had Kahn and Keynes been able to work together, or Keynes and Robinson, the *General Theory* might have been very different. Another 'K' is of course Kalecki, a much more sensible person who ended up at Oxford. He certainly made the link between imperfect competition and Keynesian economics. However, the idea was buried in a review of Keynes written in Polish in 1936 which was not translated into English until 1982. Kalecki never developed the idea in English, nor in Polish so far as I know. Thus, although there are many 'might have beens', it is clear that in Keynes's writing, imperfect competition played no role, and it was really only with the new Keynesians that the idea was pushed to the forefront of macroeconomics.[26]

12   CONCLUSION

In this chapter, I have explored the key insights of new Keynesian economics as I see them. It is of course something of a presumption to batch together a range of individual people and denote them as 'new Keynesian'. Some individuals have certainly called themselves 'new Keynesian' (most obviously Greg Mankiw and David Romer): others have acquiesced in being so called.[27] However, there are certainly some common themes that seem to be shared in the ideas that we have explored in this chapter, and I will draw these together in this conclusion.

In a perfectly competitive or 'Walrasian' world, the price mechanism ensures that the economy is Pareto-optimal. Even if there are fluctuations in output (due, for example, to changes in technology and so on, as stressed by Real Business Cycle Theory), these fluctuations are optimal: just as a farmer 'makes hay whilst the sun shines', a prudent firm will try to produce more output in periods which are favourable to production. Deviations of output from the perfectly competitive equilibrium have no first order effects on welfare, and increases in output above the equilibrium will if anything tend to reduce the level of welfare.

However, an imperfectly competitive world is inherently non-Pareto-optimal: in such a world, fluctuations in output can have positive (negative) first-order effects on welfare. If there is equilibrium involuntary (union voluntary) unemployment, then an increase in output and employment can increase profits and the welfare of workers. There can be a Pareto improvement, with everyone better off. The microeconomics of the consumer and the firm with arbitrary fixed wages and prices was developed and perfected in the 1970s, and this was well-understood. The key contribution of new Keynesian economics has been to use imperfect competition as a foundation for an equilibrium in which firms and households both want to sell more, and also as a theory of nominal rigidity.

I started off this chapter by looking at the word 'new' in economics: how it applied to such areas as the new industrial economics and the new trade theory in the 1980s. I will conclude with the observation that in all of these fields, much of the 'newness' has arisen from the introduction of imperfectly competitive models into what were before either *ad hoc* or Walrasian approaches. In this sense, the new Keynesian macroeconomics is simply one aspect of the increasing recognition of economists of the importance of imperfect competition in explaining the economic world in which we live.

Notes

1   The latter is included in a collection entitled *The New Macroeconomics*, edited by Dixon and Rankin.
2   In macroeconomics, whilst we talk of perfect competition, the term 'Walrasian equilibrium' is often used instead of 'perfectly competitive equilibrium', in deference to the work of Léon Walras (of which more anon).
3   We do not wish to enter into the details of different measures of social welfare here: any good intermediate micro text will have a lot to say on alternative measures of welfare.
4   See Dixon (1990) for a detailed exploration of this theme.
5   This may seem a rather odd and special assumption. However, it is common to assume that there are constant returns to scale in production. Since labour is the only input here, that means that the marginal and average product of labour are both constant. The normalisation of this input/output coefficient to 1 can be achieved by choosing units.
6   Since there are two goods (C, L), there is really only one price, and we can choose either W or P as the numeraire, and set it to 1.
7   This is the solution to maximising $C^{\alpha} L^{(1-\alpha)}$ subject to $C = w \cdot (1 - L) + \Pi - T$.
8   Although the original papers were written with overlapping wage contracts, the analysis applies with price-setting firms as well.
9   The astute reader will note that I am assuming that the hill is *smooth*, i.e. that it does not have a corner at the top, as in the case (for example) of a pyramid.
10   I leave it to the reader's imagination to wonder what the envelopes have to do with mountains. However, you can also look it up. Sometimes the envelope theorem is also called the Theorem of the Maximum.
11   I have drawn it here as a big shift simply to make Figure 4.8 clearer, so it should not be taken as drawn 'to scale' with Figure 4.7.
12   I do not really agree with this interpretation: see Chapter 7.
13   Like many solutions in dynamic optimisation, this is not a general result in a mathematical sense, but economists (and engineers) usually assume that the world is sufficiently as it needs to be for this rule to be optimal.
14   This is called a 'one-sided' (S, s) rule, because only one barrier is ever hit: inflation means that the optimal price P^* is always rising, and the problem that the firm faces

is that once it has set its price, its real value is falling due to background inflation until it changes its price again.

15   I say 'seem', because there is a distinction between list prices (the advertised prices) and transactions prices (the prices at which the goods are actually sold). Obviously, discounts given to customers are hard to observe by an outside observer, but they clearly happen (in some markets a discount is expected – for example in the UK car market, no one expects to pay the list price).

16   The Roman setting is needed because an example with 12 months is slightly more complex.

17   The astute reader (or the aspirant bank clerk) will have noticed that I am ignoring the compounding of interest rates over the 10 months. The real annual inflation rate would be a little over 11 per cent if the monthly was 1 per cent. However, in the interested of keeping things simple, I return to the main text.

18   Note that this equates λ to marginal utility.

19   These rays are of course the Income Expansion paths for consumption and leisure.

20   The reader may need to be reminded at this point that although we talk about 'the' household, and 'the' firm, output and so on, this is just a simplifying device: the model is valid with many households, many markets and many goods.

21   This term is sometimes called the Lerner index of monopoly, after the economist Abba Lerner who invented it in 1933.

22   Profits are $\Pi = (P - W) \cdot N = (1 - W) \cdot N = \mu \cdot N$

23   We can find this by differentiating (4.22) with respect to μ, in which case we obtain:

$$\frac{dN}{d\mu} = \frac{-\alpha(1-\alpha)(1-g)}{(1-\alpha\mu)^2}$$

which is negative since for N to be positive, $g < 1$.

24   The multiplier is the sum of the infinite geometric series $dg(1-\alpha)[1+\alpha\mu+(\alpha\mu)^2+(\alpha\mu)^3+\dots]$.

25   On the details of the Cambridge soap, see Marris (1991, pp. 181–7).

26   Although, of course there were several people who recognised the importance of imperfect competition and macroeconomics; see Dixon and Rankin (1995, pp. 3–5).

27   In my own case, it is really the latter: my original (1987c) paper stressed the Walrasian rather than the Keynesian features of the multipliers.

5 New Keynesian Economics, Nominal Rigidities and Involuntary Unemployment*

1 INTRODUCTION

In this chapter, I seek to examine what the contribution of new Keynesian macroeconomics has been in the last 15 years and to consider the methodological lessons to be learned. I also want to outline what I believe to be the driving forces behind the innovations made. I would like to stress at the outset that this chapter is very much an expression of my own personal opinions and perspective rather than an attempt at scholarly objectivity. The new Keynesian umbrella has sheltered many different themes: financial market imperfections, coordination failures, endogenous growth, menu costs/staggered contracts, fiscal multipliers *inter alia*.[1] Here I wish to focus on two themes: nominal rigidities and involuntary unemployment. These have of course been part of the Keynesian approach since Keynes' *General Theory* and remain a major theme in *new* Keynesian economics.

I will argue that there is strong empirical evidence for the importance of nominal rigidities, making them an important ingredient in any serious macroeconomic theory. However, nominal rigidities can only be properly understood in a theoretical framework with price or wage-making agents. It is almost impossible to begin to understand nominal rigidities in the Walrasian framework where all agents are price-takers. It is precisely this shift that new Keynesian models made: they abandoned the notion of perfect competition and were then able to provide microfoundations for nominal rigidity. Much the same can be said for involuntary unemployment. There is now a growing body of evidence that reflects what has been obvious to the casual observer for some time: those who become unemployed are unhappy about the change in status. This is almost impossible to model in a Walrasian labour market. Indeed, in some Walrasian models the individuals who become unemployed suffer less than those who remain in employment. Again, the introduction of imperfect competition (e.g. efficiency wages, unions) is needed to make this explicable.

The outline of the chapter is as follows. In the following sections I briefly outline the new Keynesian 'idea'; look at the treatment of nominal rigidities in

*I would like to thank Roger Backhouse, Kevin Hoover, Andrea Salanti and Richard Lipsey for useful discussions. Shortcomings are solely my responsibility.

109

pre-new Keynesian models; explore nominal rigidities in the new Keynesian per-spective; consider the explanation of involuntary unemployment in Walrasian models and models with imperfect competition; look at the new consensus in macroeconomics; and finally conclude and draw out the methodological lessons explicitly.

2   THE NEW KEYNESIAN IDEA

I have written elsewhere in some detail about the origins and precursors of new Keynesian macroeconomics (Dixon and Rankin, 1995, and Chapter 4 of this vol-ume). However, for the purposes of this chapter, I will take as a starting point the discussion in the introduction to Mankiw and Romer's collection *New Keynesian Economics* (1991, pp. 2–3), Where the authors argue that New Keynesians *do* believe that:

- Nominal variables can affect real variables (the Classical Dichotomy is violated); and
- Market Imperfections are crucial for understanding the economy.

Indeed, putting together these two points Mankiw and Romer state that '… the interaction of nominal and real imperfections is a distinguishing feature of new Keynesian economics' (*op. cit.*).

What was the driving force that led economists to adopt this viewpoint? I shall argue as follows: first, the empirical evidence pointed to the importance of nom-inal rigidities; second, the theoretical motivation that the only way to explain nominal rigidities was to adopt a framework with price/wage-making agents. Indeed the theoretical motivation was even stronger, since the introduction of imperfect competition did not just solve the problem of explaining nominal rigidities, but also the explanation of involuntary unemployment[2] (see for exam-ple Blanchard and Kiyotaki, 1987; Dixon, 1988). Furthermore, it gives rise to very different welfare effects than the Walrasian model – for example, welfare increases in a boom and decreases in a recession. Thus the introduction of imper-fect competition simultaneously solved several problems at once: why wages and prices were at non-Walrasian levels; the possibility of involuntary unemploy-ment; welfare is increasing in output and employment, and so on. Again, the whole story is beyond this chapter, so I will instead focus on the two themes of nominal rigidities and involuntary unemployment.

3   NOMINAL RIGIDITIES BEFORE THE NEW KEYNESIANS

Let us pursue this core idea and see how it relates to previous economic para-digms.[3] Firstly, we have the *neoclassical synthesis* model, most notably associ-ated with the names John Hicks and Don Patinkin. From the perspective of the neo-classical synthesis the economy would in the long run be in Walrasian equi-librium. In the short-run, however, nominal (or real) rigidities could result in deviations from the equilibrium. The short-run equilibrium could thus be analysed by an IS/LM approach or the aggregate-supply/demand model for example. Alternatively, in an inflationary environment the Philips curve could be used to model price and wage adjustment. Nevertheless, the long run was a competitive equilibrium (the long run aggregate supply curve or Philips curve is vertical). Nominal rigidities are crucial here since they allow for the impact of nominal and real demand shocks to have real effects on the economy.

Here, however, is an incoherence at the heart of the neo-classical synthesis, summed up by *Arrow's paradox* (Arrow 1959).[4] For a perfectly competitive equilibrium, all agents need to act as price-takers. However, if everyone acts as a price-taker, how can prices change? This paradox is profound and not easy to resolve if you want to maintain perfect competition. If all agents are price-takers, the issue of nominal rigidity becomes almost impossible to investigate except in an *ad hoc* manner: if no one sets the price, it becomes difficult to ask why they do not adjust the price immediately![5] Of course, at the time (that is, in the 1950s and 1960s) this did not seem such a big issue: the model of price-adjustment used in general equilibrium was Walras's *tâtonnement* process: a fictional agent is invented, the auctioneer who adjusts prices in response to excess demands. However, you do not solve the issue of price-adjustment in a price-taking world by inventing a new category of supernatural economic agent.[6]

Friedman's account of the *natural rate* changed things.[7] He developed the surprise theory of the short-run Philips curve. In essence, deviations form the long-run equilibrium (the *natural rate*) were explained by *expectational* errors, not nominal rigidities. The central insight here was that supply decisions are based on expected (or perceived) prices or the current general price level. If demand caused the current level of prices to rise beyond what had been expected, this could stimulate supply. Workers might (mis)perceive concomitant nominal wage rises as real wage increases and supply more labour. This sort of idea was formalised by Lucas in his 'archipelago'[8] theory of the natural rate (Lucas, 1979). When allied to the notion of rational expectations, this idea gave rise to the notion of policy neutrality (Sargent and Wallis, 1976) and the notion that only unanticipated changes in the money supply have a real effect (Barro, 1977). This approach became central to much macroeconomic theorising in the decade starting around 1975. In particular, the 'Lucas surprise supply curve' embodied this view. Until Lucas's 'surprise supply function' became standard, people used to look at the Phillips curve as a relationship with inflation[9] on the left-hand side and output or employment on the right. The Lucas surprise supply curve inverted this relationship: inflation became the causative right-hand variable, whilst output and employment became the dependant variables. Governments made output and employment fluctuate by causing unanticipated inflation.

Whilst in the Friedman–Lucas story the notion of price-flexibility and market clearing is logically consistent with deviations from equilibrium, the consensus developed that perhaps this was not a very plausible story. The Lucas archipelago model rests on the notion that whilst individuals know a lot about their own market ('island'), they are not well-informed about the aggregate variables (the 'archipelago'). This means that they can misperceive a local nominal price/wage rise as a real increase, when in fact it may be a real decrease. However, the sort of aggregate variables that this story requires to be unknown are the aggregate price level and the money supply. But these are the two variables for which we have frequent, regular and accurate statistics regularly published and broadcast on the media.

Of course, much the same 'surprise supply' story can be told in terms of *contracts* made *ex ante*, before events unfold. Wages (and/or) prices are set *ex ante*, and nominal demand shocks can affect output via a standard aggregate supply curve based on fixed wages. But then the theory reduces to a model of nominal rigidities, with the same problems as the neoclassical synthesis.

There were two reactions in the 1980s to this problem of nominal rigidity in competitive models. One was the development of the new Keynesian school, which dropped the Walrasian assumption of price-taking behaviour and put imperfect competition at the centre of macroeconomic modelling. The other approach was to drop the nominal side altogether and model economic fluctuations as occurring due to real factors (technology shocks) in a dynamic general equilibrium model: the real business cycle (RBC) approach,[10] such as Prescott (1986).

4   NOMINAL RIGIDITIES IN NEW KEYNESIAN MODELS

Imperfect competition is central to the new Keynesian approach to nominal rigidity. The theory of menu costs as an explanation of nominal price rigidity in a macroeconomic context was developed more or less simultaneously by Parkin (1986), Akerloff and Yellen (1985a,b) and Mankiw (1985), although the idea had been around for sometime. I will not discuss the empirical evidence for the importance of menu costs here (these are examined in a companion paper, Dixon, 2000a): in this chapter I will provide a theoretical focus.

The approach states that there is some non-convex cost of price adjustment, a 'menu cost'. This can be thought of either as some explicit cost of price adjustment (as is implicit in the name), or rather as resulting from some sort of bounded rationality, which means that you do not change your current action unless it yields an improvement of more than ε (the technical term for this is ε-optimisation). Either way, it introduces some degree of nominal inertia at the individual level (price/wage-setter). The assumption of imperfect competition is important because it says that the nominal inertia will arise even when the menu costs are small.[11] Under imperfect competition the monopolistic price is optimal for the firm: hence any small deviations from it yield no first-order loss in profit. Thus only small menu costs can lead to price rigidity. The same sort of argument can be applied to the labour market: assuming the initial contract was in some sense optimal,[12] even small renegotiation costs can lead to nominal wage rigidity (in fact, people often accept that renegotiation costs might well be large, since they have to be agreed). Clearly, an efficiency wage model will have the same property even though the wage is set unilaterally by the firm.

Imperfect competition plays a dual role here: not only does it permit us to consider the price-making decision in labour and product markets explicitly, it also provides the argument for small menu-costs. In a Walrasian model neither of these roles is possible, since the act of price-setting is not modelled as the outcome of a maximising decision by an economic agent(s).

I would emphasise here that theories for labour markets based on contracts do not represent an *alternative* to menu-cost theory, but are properly seen as an inherent part of it. Whilst some authors (for example, Greg Mankiw) have tended to downplay the labour market and emphasise the product market, others such as George Akerlof and Janet Yellen have not. Indeed, most European new Keynesian[13] authors tend to focus more on unionised labour markets reflecting the relatively greater importance of unions in Europe. Furthermore, theories of overlapping contracts and related causes of nominal wage rigidity must be based implicitly on some renegotiation costs. The 'menu-cost' elements in the labour market are different in many ways to those in the output market, but the same general principles apply. I think it is not an exaggeration to say that so far as nominal wage and price rigidity goes, menu-costs are the only show in town.[14] The label 'menu-costs' was perhaps not judiciously chosen: it implies something trivial and restricted to restaurants. However, the fact that so many prices and wages are fixed in nominal terms over significant periods of time suggests that the menu-costs are large enough to cause significant nominal rigidities in practice (for a discussion of the evidence see Dixon, 2000a).

5   INVOLUNTARY UNEMPLOYMENT

The Walrasian equilibrium has some very special welfare features. The First Fundamental Theorem of Welfare Economics states that a Walrasian equilibrium is Pareto-optimal in the absence of certain well-defined market failures. In a representative agent economy this means that the equilibrium maximises the welfare of the representative agent. One big implication of this is that if we consider small deviations from equilibrium (caused for example by nominal rigidities or expectational errors), then not only is there is no first-order welfare effect, but the effect that is present is symmetric.[15] Booms are as bad as busts (recall Friedman's parable of workers being fooled into working too hard when there is unanticipated inflation).

Imperfectly competitive economies, however, are very different. Even if the behavioural features of an imperfectly competitive economy are similar to a Walrasian economy, the welfare properties will almost certainly be different. In particular, in an imperfectly competitive equilibrium there will tend to be too little output and employment. It is thus likely that welfare will be increasing in output and employment. This seems to mesh in with the common-sense view that 'unemployment matters'. Indeed, writing as a new Keynesian, Romer (1993) states that 'after all, accepting the belief that the labour market was continuously in Walrasian equilibrium would require denying that unemployment was an important phenomenon'.

Many economists, however, have doubted the importance of the concept of involuntary unemployment as a useful concept. For example, Lucas (1978) stated that:

> ... Involuntary unemployment is not a fact or a phenomenon to which it is the task of theorists to explain. It is, on the contrary, a theoretical construct which Keynes introduced [in order to explain] large scale fluctuations in measured, total unemployment.[16]

This viewpoint is (as I interpret it) that the concept of involuntary unemployment is of little use in explaining output and unemployment fluctuations and is immeasurable. However, even if this were the case, the *welfare* properties implied would be different. It is on this issue that I focus: what (if any) welfare effect is there when unemployment increases and how is it distributed across households?

There is no doubt that most people become unhappy when they become unemployed through redundancy; the empirical evidence for this is overwhelming (see Oswald, 1997a,b). This implies that we should have theories of employment determination which are consistent with this fact. One could of course argue with the facts: economists have largely ignored direct evidence on human happiness for the last half-century, on the basis that happiness could not be measured.

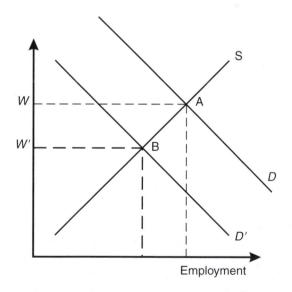

Figure 5.1   *A fall in the demand for labour*

However, the case for doing so is becoming less and less tenable (see for example Frank, 1997; Ng, 1997).

Walrasian theories of unemployment are not consistent with this fact. In order to understand the full extent of their inadequacy here, let us consider what happens in a labour market when there is an adverse technology shock, so that the demand curve[17] for labour shifts to the left in wage–employment space. For explanatory convenience we will adopt a purely partial equilibrium approach. In a competitive market, a fall in demand will lead to lower equilibrium (real) wages and employment: in Figure 5.1 we move from point A to point B. The key question on which I wish to focus is the following: *who is better off, the person who remains employed or the person who becomes unemployed?* In other words, how is the reduction in welfare shared out in a competitive market? Let us look at two different models of how the competitive market might work, both of which are commonly used in Walrasian macromodels.

5.1 The Representative Household

In this case, there is just one representative household in the economy. Implicitly, there are many identical households, all of whom supply the same labour, and all would have the same change in utility as a result of adverse productivity. One could think of this as being the case where all households work: the movement down the labour supply curve represents simply the reduction in working hours by the households. There is no room here for a distinction between unemployment and employment.

5.2 Heterogeneous Households, Indivisible Labour (HHIL)

In this model,[18] all households have a single unit of labour to supply and a reservation wage. If the market wage is at or above the reservation wage, they are willing to supply all of their labour: if it is below the reservation wage, they would rather supply no labour and consume the leisure. The market supply curve is simply the cumulative density function for the reservation wages of households. As we move down the market supply curve, two things are happening:

1   The real wage of those employed (for whom the real wage strictly exceeds their reservation wage) declines. This has a first-order effect on the utility of the employed, making them worse off.
2   However, those who become unemployed are almost indifferent. This is because, at the margin, the real wage and the reservation wage are (almost) equal. The gain in leisure (almost) exactly offsets the loss of wage income.

We thus have the conclusion that the reduction in welfare in the HHIL model is concentrated in the employed. The households who become unemployed have the smallest reduction (zero at the margin). This model clearly fails to pass the litmus test that the welfare loss should be concentrated on those becoming unemployed.

What sort of models do we need to fit the fact that those who become unemployed suffer the largest welfare reduction? I would argue that what we need is a model with equilibrium involuntary unemployment. There are different ways of modelling this, but let us consider a model with a fixed real wage as a good starting point.

5.3   Rigid Real Wages

In Figure 5.2, we see that the real wage is at W, which exceeds the competitive real wage Θ_A (the disutility of labour). The initial equilibrium is at A, with the level of involuntary unemployment being given by the distance A–C. After the adverse technology shock , the new equilibrium is at B, with the corresponding decline in employment from L_A to L_B. If we have a representative agent model this will result in a decline in hours for all households, with no individual being unemployed. The reduction in consumer surplus (taken to be the measure of household welfare[19]) is large and represented by the shaded area:

$$\Delta CS = (L_A - L_B)(W - \Theta_A) + \frac{1}{2}(L_A - L_B)(\Theta_A - \Theta_B)$$

The change in welfare ΔCS decomposes into two elements. First, there is the 'square' representing the loss in surplus due to the fact that the initial real wage is above the initial disutility of labour Θ_A; second, there is the 'triangle' representing the fact that the new employment level represents a deviation from the new competitive equilibrium. The triangle represents a second-order welfare loss; the square a first-order loss.[20]

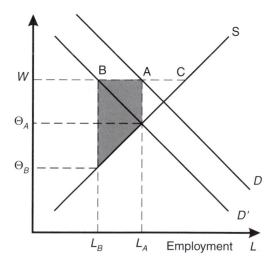

Figure 5.2   *Welfare loss with a rigid wage and involuntary unemployment*

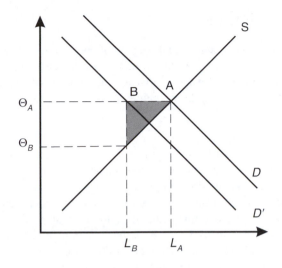

Figure 5.3   *Welfare loss in a Walrassian market with rigid wage*

If we started from a competitive equilibrium then $W = \Theta_A$, so that there is no (first-order) loss in welfare, only the second-order loss. This is represented in Figure 5.3, where the shaded area is:

$$\Delta CS = \frac{1}{2}(L_A - L_B)(\Theta_A - \Theta_B)$$

This follows because the initial employment level would be welfare-maximising given the wage: hence any reduction in employment from the initial position will not give rise to a first-order reduction in welfare (the envelope theorem again) but only the second-order 'triangle' loss. Hence, in this case it is not the real wage rigidity itself but the presence of involuntary unemployment in the initial equilibrium which is crucial in generating a first-order welfare effect of changes in employment in response to the adverse technology shock.

Now consider the same model, but with the employment change being one where people either work all they want, or not at all. In this case, as we go from A to B, those who remain employed suffer no reduction at all in their utility: *all of the reduction in welfare is concentrated on those who become unemployed.* In this model, the difference between an initial position with involuntary unemployment (IU) and market clearing is not so stark: even if the initial real wage were at the Walrasian level, there would be a concentration of the first-order welfare loss on those becoming unemployed. However, there is a problem here: how can a competitive market be reconciled with a situation where some households become involuntarily unemployed (as those who are made unemployed become, since they would be willing to work at a slightly lower real wage than the one prevailing). More on this later.

5.4   The Monopoly Union

The assumption of an exogenous real wage is of course not very satisfactory. Let us consider a standard monopoly union model. In this case, let us suppose that the union marks up the real wage so that it is a fixed markup over the marginal disutility of labour. For example, we can express the real wage as:

$$W = \frac{\varepsilon}{\varepsilon - 1} \theta$$

where ε is the elasticity of labour demand. Then, in effect, the 'supply curve' of the unionised labour market lies above the standard competitive labour supply, as depicted in Figure 5.4. The dotted upward-sloping line represents the marginal disutility of labour (which can be thought of as an increasing function of employment L). The solid upward-sloping line gives the markup on this. The reduction in demand leads to a shift from A to B: as in the competitive case the real wage and employment fall. The lost consumer surplus is given by the sum of three terms, representing the different parts of the shaded area in Figure 5.4.

$$\Delta CS = L_B(W_A - W_B) + (L_A - L_B)(W_A - \Theta_A) + \frac{1}{2}(\Theta_A - \Theta_B)(L_A - L_B)$$

In the case where people are either unemployed or employed, the loss in welfare to the employed is represented by the first term: the ones remaining in work are paid less. The second two terms represent the welfare loss to those becoming unemployed, who lose the entire surplus representing the gap between the marginal disutility of labour and the wage. Those becoming unemployed would suffer a far larger reduction in welfare than those who remain in employment.

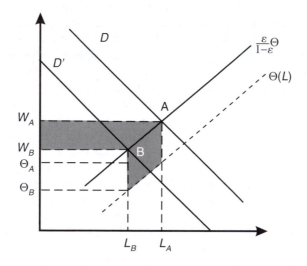

Figure 5.4   *Welfare loss in a unionised labour market*

5.5   Walrasian Models do not Fit the Facts

The assumption that labour markets clear all of the time is not consistent with the fact that when the total labour supply varies, the reduction in welfare is concentrated on those who lose their jobs. The oft-used model with reservation wages implies the exact opposite. It is almost impossible to reconcile in principle the idea of Walrasian market clearing with the notion that two otherwise identical households suffer different fates (one employed, the other unemployed). In the reservation wage model, the allocation of employment is efficient (it goes to those with the lowest disutility of work), which implies that those who become unemployed are those which get the least out of working. The marginal worker gets almost no surplus and so is indifferent between working and not working. Hence he loses little when he becomes unemployed.

One can of course introduce an *ad hoc* almost Walrasian model with long-run equilibrium, but which allows for short-term rigidities or other non-instantaneous market clearing. I have discussed this before: it is not in my opinion a coherent viewpoint (Arrow's paradox).

Lastly, if we return to Lucas' earlier statement, recall that the comparative statics of at least one of the non-Walrasian models we have considered (monopoly union) does look very much like the Walrasian (we simply use a different 'supply curve', the marked-up disutility of labour in Figure 5.4). However, the welfare effects are different in type and magnitude. The First Theorem of Welfare no longer holds sway.

6   NEW MACROECONOMICS, NEW CONSENSUS

As Neil Rankin and I argued in Dixon and Rankin (1995, p. 9), in the 1990s the distinctions between different 'schools' have tended to become reduced and a new consensus has arisen. In this section I want to talk a little about the nature of this consensus. Firstly, the notion that nominal rigidities seems to be emerging as a major part of the new consensus in macroeconomics; I will look at this in some detail. This in a sense marks a victory for new Keynesian economics, since this is the only sort of theory that can explain nominal rigidities.

Secondly, most economists have accepted the notion that we need to have dynamic models, and few macroeconomists write models that are completely static nowadays. Although the first models in dynamic macroeconomics tended to be Walrasian, the dynamic method in itself is not generic to the Walrasian equilibrium. For example, the RBC method can be applied to 'new Keynesian' models (see for example Hairault and Portier (1993), Danthine and Donaldson (1990, 1993), and Rotemberg and Woodford (1995, 1996)). The Ramsey model can be adopted to include unionised wage-setting (Aaronsen, Sjogren and Lofgren, 1998).

Perfectly competitive models are in general easy to solve – after all, they are just 'supply equals demand' dressed up in different ways. It is thus easier to develop new methods and ways of modelling when you have this simple equilibrium concept. For example, one of the special properties of 'supply equals demand' is that with a representative household the solution maximises welfare (this is implied by the First Fundamental Theorem of Welfare). Hence you do not even need to analyse the market process, but simply go first to a social planning problem to solve the model. Imperfect competition is generally more complicated to analyse; things are more intricate and require more thought. We should therefore expect people using perfectly competitive models to develop tools of analysis first.[21] We can then use these methods and address the real issues using models with imperfect competition.

Let us look at the first feature I highlighted in the new consensus – nominal rigidities. There is now a rapidly growing literature which puts an overlapping contract framework into a dynamic general equilibrium model – see for example Guido Ascari, 1997, 1998; Ascari and Rankin, 1997. In these models employment is determined by labour demand – there is involuntary unemployment – which enables the authors to explore the effects of policy in some detail. In particular, Ascari and Rankin (1998) shows the mechanics of how disinflation (both anticipated and unanticipated) causes a slump. There have also been writers who have been associated with the standard RBC approach who have been moving towards the integration of nominal variables into the dynamic general equilibrium model – for example Cooley and Hansen, 1995; Chari *et al.*, 2000. In fact, the literature integrating nominal rigidities into dynamic general equilibrium is growing so rapidly that it is not really appropriate to attempt to summarise it here.[22]

However, there is a more general move towards integrating nominal rigidities apparent in the monetary policy literature. For example, there has been a move towards modelling central banks as using the interest rate to try to control inflation. The usual way this is modelled is using a 'Phillips-curve' relationship which puts the rate of inflation as a (lagged) function of output (see for example Ball, 1997; Bean, 1998; Svensson, 1997). This marks an interesting change in perspective. The original policy credibility literature was based on the surprise supply function in which a surprise in inflation caused a change in output. The whole argument for central bank independence was that by delegating monetary policy to conservative central bankers the temptation to have a bout of inflation to reap the reward of some extra output and employment could be avoided. This model is perfectly compatible with the notion that prices and wages are perfectly flexible, with output variations caused by expectational errors (as in the Friedman/Lucas story). When authors are now modelling actual policy rules, they reverse the relationship and have changes in output (caused by interest rate policy directly or via the exchange rate) causing changes in inflation. This marks an interesting historical cycle.

7   CONCLUSION: THE LESSONS FOR METHODOLOGY

In this chapter I have given a personal view of the contribution of new Keynesian economics to macroeconomics in terms of providing a sound background for both nominal rigidities in prices and wages and for the theory of involuntary unemployment. A crucial feature of this contribution is the notion of imperfectly competitive markets with price-making agents. There were two main motivations for the theory. First, the empirical evidence pointing to the importance of nominal rigidities. Second, the fact that the introduction of imperfect competition enabled us to provide a sound theoretical framework for answering several issues at once.

Until new Keynesian macroeconomics, there was in macroeconomics one ruling theoretical framework, Walrasian equilibrium and, more generally, price-taking behaviour.[23] However, the Walrasian paradigm cannot in principle begin to explain two crucial macroeconomic features: nominal price or wage rigidity and involuntary unemployment. It should be noted that these facts had been known for a long time.

One response was to ignore these problems, introducing nominal rigidity as some *ad hoc* add on, not itself explained by the theoretical framework (that is, as the result of some maximising decision by economic agents). Involuntary equilibrium could then be generated as a transitory byproduct of non-market clearing prices. Another response was denial. This was essentially the route taken by RBC theory: nominal phenomena were completely ignored and involuntary unemployment seen as an irrelevant theoretical construct.

New Keynesian macroeconomics, however, managed to initiate a change in paradigm that is still going on. If we take nominal rigidities and involuntary unemployment seriously then we have to abandon the Walrasian framework. The key here is to set price-making agents at the heart of our macroeconomic framework: only once we have done this can we begin the task of explaining nominal rigidities and take unemployment seriously. The importance of this theoretical innovation is how it enables us to begin the process of understanding the mechanics of wage and price determination and the corresponding quantities in a manner consistent with standard economic theory.

Notes

1 For surveys of this literature see Dixon and Rankin (1994) and Silvestre (1993).
2 I have always used the concept of 'involuntary unemployment' in a purely technical sense that at the prevailing wage the household would like to supply more labour. When unions set wages, people sometimes prefer to use the term 'union-voluntary'. I do not think that it is worth arguing over terminology. However, with efficiency wages the firm sets wages so that there is clear and unambiguous 'involuntary' unemployment.
3 This is intended as a sketch which reflects my own interpretation of events. For a more scholarly and comprehensive treatment, see Hoover (1984, 1988). Although he deals primarily with monetarist and new Classical writings, he sets them in the context.
4 Arrow's comments were not directed at macroeconomic models. However, his reasoning applies as much to the neo-classical synthesis as it does to the Arrow–Debreu general equilibrium framework.
5 Arrow argues that in disequilibrium agents somehow gained market power that they lost when the equilibrium was reestablished. This idea has never been successfully formalised to my knowledge.

6   Of course, Walras himself based the notion of the auctioneer on the functioning of market-makers in the Paris Bourse. It is one thing to think of financial or commodity markets and another to apply this to the labour market.

7   I have discussed the Natural Rate concept in a historical and theoretical context at some length in Chapter 3.

8   An archipelago is a large collection of small islands. The 'island' is taken to be the individual market; the archipelago to represent the aggregate economy. The assumption is that the individual is well-informed about his own market/island, but not about the aggregate economy.

9   This comment applies to both the 'short-run' curve with given expectations, or the 'long-run' version. 'Inflation' should be meant to include 'deviations of actual inflation form expected'.

10   In fact the RBC movement was more than that. There was also a shift in focus towards a *quantitative* explanation of the business cycle, towards business cycle empirics (of a novel nature).

11   In Soviet Russia the price of bread was kept constant over decades, since Lenin had promised 'peace and bread'. The costs of price adjustment for bread producers were severe and terminal indeed!

12   For example, if the contract maximises some Nash-product of the employees and firm's payoffs.

13   For example, Andersen *et al.* (1996), Benassy (1995), Santoni (1996), Aloi and Santoni (1997) amongst many others.

14   Well, almost. The only alternative I can think of is a model with multiple equilibria. Even if something changes, the same nominal price might remain an equilibrium despite representing a real change. For examples of this, see for example Bhaskar (1990).

15   It was probably to avoid this problem that RBC practitioners sought to explain cycles by productivity shocks.

16   In a similar vein from about the same time, Fisher remarked 'I would maintain that involuntary unemployment as a phenomenon still lacks ... empirical support' (Fisher, 1976).

17   The labour 'demand curve' is not really a demand curve, but rather the equilibrium price–cost relationship. However, I bow to conventional usage.

18   This model has a long tradition. However, it has been used in RBC models (Hansen, 1985) since model 1 does not 'work' in the RBC context (individual elasticities of labour supply are too small).

19   I use the standard welfare measure of consumer surplus. Despite its failings, it is probably the best we have that can be measured in practice.

20   Since L is a function of W ($L=L(W)$), a linear approximation is

$$\frac{1}{2}(L_A - L_B)(\Theta_A - \Theta_B) = \frac{L'}{2}(\Theta_A - \Theta_B)^2$$

21   An obvious exception to this is Game Theory. Since this is inherently about strategic behaviour, it could only have been developed by people who rejected the competitive approach.

22   Some of the papers of particular interest are Ellison and Scott (1998), Erceg (1997), Kiley (1997), Jeanne (1997), all as yet unpublished.

23   The 'neo-Keynesian' economics of the 1970s based on fixed prices dropped the assumption of supply equals demand, but kept the price-taking behaviour of individual agents.

Part III
Mainly Micro

6   Oligopoly Theory Made Simple*

1   INTRODUCTION

Oligopoly theory lies at the heart of industrial organisation (IO) since its object
of study is the interdependence of firms. Much of traditional microeconomics
presumes that firms act as passive price-takers, and thus avoids the complex
issues involved in understanding firms' behaviour in an interdependent environment. As such, recent developments in oligopoly theory cover most or all areas
of theoretical IO, and particularly the 'new' IO. This survey is therefore very
selective in the material it surveys: the goal is to present some of the basic or
'core' results of oligopoly theory that thave a general relevance to IO.

The recent development of oligopoly theory is inextricably bound up with
developments in abstract game theory. New results in game theory have often
been applied first in the area of oligopoly (for example, the application of mixed
strategies in the 1950s – see Shubik, 1959, and more recently the use of subgame perfection to model credibility). The flow is often in the opposite direction: most recently, the development of sequential equilibria by Kreps, Milgrom,
Roberts, and Wilson arose out of modelling reputational effects in oligopoly
markets. Over recent years, with the new IO, the relationship with game theory
has become closer. This chapter therefore opens with a review of the basic equilibrium concepts employed in the IO – Nash equilibrium, perfect equilibrium,
and sequential equilibrium.

The basic methodology of the new IO is neo-classical: oligopolistic rivalry is
studied from an equilibrium perspective, with maximising firms, and uncertainty
is dealt with by expected profit of payoff maximisation. However, the subject
matter of the new IO differs significantly from the neo-classical microeconomics
of the standard textbook. Most importantly, much of the new IO focuses on the
process of competition over time, and on the effects of imperfect information
and uncertainty. As such, it has expanded its vision from static models to consider aspects of phenomena which Austrian economists have long been empha-
sising, albeit with a rather different methodology.

The outline of the chapter is as follows. After describing the basic equilibrium
concepts in an abstract manner in the first section, the subsequent two sections

---

*The material of this chapter is based on MSc lectures given at Birkbeck over the period
1985–86. I would like to thank students for their comments and reactions from which I
learnt a lot. I would also like to thank Ben Lockwood for invaluable comments as well as
Bruce Lyons, Steve Davies and the editors. Errors, alas, remain my own.

explore and contrast the two basic static equilibria employed by oligopoly theory to model product market competition – Bertrand (price) competition, and
Cournot (quantity) competition. These two approaches yield very different
results in terms of the degree of competition, the nature of the first-mover
advantage, and the relationship between market structure (concentration) and the
price–cost margin.

The fourth section moves on to consider the incentive of firms to precommit
themselves in sequential models; how firms can use irreversible decisions such
as investment or choice of managers to influence the market outcome in their
favour. This approach employs the notion of subgame perfect equilibria, and can
shed light on such issues as whether or not oligopolists will overinvest, and why
non-profit maximising managers might be more profitable for their firm than
profit maximisers. The fifth section explores competition over time, and focuses
on the results that have been obtained in game-theoretic literature on repeated
games with perfect and imperfect information. This analysis centres on the
extent to which collusive outcomes can be supported over time by credible
threats, and the influence of imperfect information on a firm's behaviour in such
a situation. Alas, many areas of equal interest have had to be omitted – notably
the literature on product differentiation, advertising, information transmission,
and price wars. References are given for these in the final section.

Lastly, a word on style. I have made the exposition of this chapter as simple
as possible. Throughout, I employ a simple linearised model as an example to
illustrate the mechanics of the ideas introduced. I hope that readers will find this
useful, and I believe that it is a vital complement to general conceptual understanding. For those readers who appreciate a more rigorous and general mathematical exposition, I apologise in advance for what may seem sloppy in places.
I believe, however, that many of the basic concepts of oligopoly theory are sufficiently clear to be understood without a general analysis, and that they deserve a
wider audience than a more formal exposition would receive.

2   NON-COOPERATIVE EQUILIBRIUM

The basic equilibrium concept employed most commonly in oligopoly theory is
that of the *Nash equilibrium*, which originated in Cournot's analysis of duopoly
(1838). The Nash equilibrium applies best in situations of a one-off game with perfect information. However, if firms compete repeatedly over time, or have imperfect information, then the basic equilibrium concept needs to be refined. Two
commonly used equilibrium concepts in repeated games are those of *subgame perfection* (Selten, 1965) and, if information is imperfect, *sequential equilibria* (Kreps
et al., 1982).

We shall first introduce the idea of a Nash equilibrium formally, using some
of the terminology of game theory. There are n firms, who each choose some
strategy a_i from a set of feasible actions A_i, where $i = 1, \ldots, n$. The firm's strategy

might be one variable (price/quantity/R&D) or a *vector* of variables. For simplicity, we will take the case where each firm chooses one variable only. We can summarise what each and every firm does by the n-vector $(a_1, a_2, \ldots, a_n)$. The 'payoff' function shows the firm's profits π_i as a function of the strategies of each firm:

$$\pi_i = \pi_i(a_1, a_2, \ldots, a_n) \tag{6.1}$$

The payoff function essentially describes the market environment in which the firms operate, and will embody all the relevant information about demand, costs and so on. What will happen in this market? A Nash equilibrium is one possibility, and is based on the idea that firms choose their strategies non-cooperatively; it occurs when each firm is choosing its strategy optimally, given the strategies of the other firms. Formally, the Nash equilibrium is an n-vector of strategies $(a_1^*, a_2^*, \ldots, a_n^*)$ such that for each firm i, a_i^* yields maximum profits given the strategies of the $n-1$ other firms a_{-i}^*.[1] That is, for each firm:

$$\pi_i(a_i^*, a_{-i}^*) \geqslant \pi_i(a_i^*, a_{-i}^*) \tag{6.2}$$

for all feasible strategies $a_i \in A_i$. The Nash equilibrium is often defined using the concept of a *reaction function*, which for firm i gives its best response given what the other forms are doing. In a Nash equilibrium, each firm will be on its reaction function.

Why is the Nash equilibrium so commonly employed in oligopoly theory? Firstly, because no firm acting on its own has any incentive to deviate from the equilibrium. Secondly, if all firms expect a Nash equilibrium to occur, they will choose their Nash equilibrium strategy, since this is their best response to what they expect the other firms to do. Only a Nash equilibrium can be consistent with this rational anticipation on the part of firms. Of course, a Nash equilibrium may not exist, and there may be multiple equilibria. There are many results in game theory relating to the existence of Nash equilibrium. For the purpose of industrial economics, however, perhaps the most relevant is that if the payoff functions are continuous and strictly concave in each firm's own strategy then at least one equilibrium exists.[2] Uniqueness is rather harder to ensure, although industrial economists usually make strong enough assumptions to ensure uniqueness.[3]

If market competition is seen as occurring over time, it may be inappropriate to employ a one-shot model as above. In a *repeated game* the one-shot *constituent* game is repeated over T periods (where T may be finite or infinite). Rather than simply choosing a one-off action, firms will choose an action a_{it} in each period $t = 1, \ldots, T$. For repeated games, the most commonly used equilibrium concept in recent oligopoly theory literature is that of subgame perfection which was first formalised by Selten (1965), although the idea had been used informally (e.g. Cyert and De Groot 1970). At each time t, the firm will decide on its action a_{it} given the past history of the market h_t, which will include the previous moves by all firms in the market.

A firm's 'strategy' in the repeated game[4] is simply a rule σ_i which the firm adopts to choose its action a_{it} at each period given the history of the market up to then, h_t:

$$a_{it} = \sigma_i(h_t)$$

If we employ the standard Nash equilibrium approach, an equilibrium in the repeated game is simply n strategies $(\sigma_1^*, \sigma_2^*, \dots \sigma_n^*)$ such that each firm's strategy σ_i^* is optimal given the other firms' strategies σ_{-i}^*. Thus no firm can improve its payoff by choosing a different strategy, given the strategies of the other firms.

However, a major criticism of using the standard Nash equilibrium in repeated games is that it allows firms to make 'threats' which are not *credible*, in the sense that it would not be in their interest to carry out the threat. For example, consider the example of entry deterrence, with two periods. In the first period, the entrant decides whether or not to enter. In the second period, the entrant and incumbent choose outputs. The incumbent could adopt the following strategy: if entry does not occur, produce the monopoly output. If entry does occur, produce a very large output which drives down the price below costs at whatever output is chosen by the entrant. In effect, the entrant is posed with a powerful threat by the incumbent: 'if you enter, I'll flood the market and we'll both lose money'. Clearly, with this powerful threat, the incumbent will be able to deter any entry. However, it is not a *credible* threat: if entry *were* to occur, then the incumbent would not wish to carry out this potent threat. Thus the incumbent's strategy is not credible, since he would be making unnecessary losses.

Subgame perfection was formulated to restrict firms to *credible* strategies. The basic idea of subgame perfection is quite simple. In a Nash equilibrium the firm chooses its strategy σ_i 'once and for all' at the beginning of the game, and is committed to it throughout the play (as in the above example). To rule out non-credible threats, however, in a subgame-perfect equilibrium, at each point in time firms choose their strategy for the rest of the game. The 'subgame' at any time t is simply the remainder of the game from t through to the last period T. Subgame perfection requires that the strategies chosen are Nash equilibria in each subgame. This rules out non-credible threats, since in effect it requires a firm to choose its strategy optimally at each stage in the game. In our example, the incumbent's threat to expand output is not 'credible': in the subgame consisting of the second period, it is not a Nash equilibrium. Indeed, if the market is Cournot and there is a unique Cournot equilibrium, then the unique subgame-perfect strategy for the incumbent involves producing the Cournot output if entry has occurred. One of the major attractions of subgame perfection is that it narrows down the number of equilibria: there are often multiple Nash equilibria in repeated games and imposing 'credibility' on strategies can reduce the number considerably, at least in finitely repeated games.

With imperfect information, a commonly used equilibrium concept is that of a 'sequential' equilibrium (Kreps *et al.*, 1982). This is formally a rather complex concept, but we shall provide a simple example in the section 'competition over time'. The basic idea of subgame perfection is employed, with the added ingredient of Bayesian updating of information.[5] Firms may be uncertain about each other's payoff functions (for example they do not know each other's costs or each other's objectives). At the start of the game, firms have certain prior beliefs, which they then update through the game. Firms may be able to learn something about each other from each other's actions. In such a situation, firms of a certain type may be able to build a 'reputation' by taking actions which distinguish themselves from firms of another type. For example, in Milgrom and Roberts' (1982b) paper on entry deterrence, low-cost incumbents are able to distinguish themselves from high-cost incumbents by following a 'limit pricing' strategy which it is unprofitable for high-cost firms to pursue. These reputational equilibria are very important since they can explain how firms might behave against their short-run interest in order to preserve their reputation intact, for example as a low-cost firm or as an aggressive competitor.

3   COURNOT AND BERTRAND EQUILIBRIA WITH HOMOGENEOUS PRODUCTS

The previous section considered the concept of a Nash equilibrium in purely abstract terms. To make the concept concrete we need to specifiy the exact nature of the strategies chosen and define the payoff function. Corporate strategy is, of course, very broad embracing all the activities of the firm – price, output, investment, advertising, R&D and so on. In practice, oligopoly theory abstracts from the complexity of real-life corporate strategy and concentrates on just one or two strategic variables. There are two basic ways of modelling how firms compete in the market. The first takes the view that the firm's strategic variable is its output and originates in Cournot (1838). The second takes the view that the firm's basic strategic variable is price and, originates in the work of Bertrand (1883), Edgeworth (1925) and more recently in models of imperfect competition with product differentiation (e.g. Chamberlin, 1933; Dixit and Stiglitz, 1977).

As we shall see, whether price or output is the strategy makes a difference to the equilibrium outcome. For example, one of the basic issues of interest to industrial economists is the relationship between concentration and the price–cost margin. The standard notion that higher concentration leads to a higher price–cost margin is based on the Cournot view, and does not hold in the Bertrand framework where there can be a perfectly competitive outcome with two or more firms. The distinction between price and quantity setting in the context of oligopoly is not present in monopoly, where it makes no difference whether the monopolist chooses a price or quantity (the monopolist simply chooses a point on its demand curve). In order to capture the distinction between the Cournot and Bertrand framework in its starkest form, we will first consider the simplest case of homogeneous goods. We will then discuss what arguments there are for choosing between the two competing approaches to modelling product market competition. In the next section we will pursue this fundamental dichotomy further in the context of the more realistic case of differentiated commodities.

3.1 Cournot–Nash Equilibrium with Homogeneous Goods

The basic view of the market taken by Cournot was that firms choose their outputs and that the market then 'clears' given the total output of firms. There are n firms $i = 1, \ldots n$, which produce outputs x_i, industry output being $x = \sum_{i=1}^{n} x_i$. We will make the simplest possible assumption about demand and costs:

A1   *Industry demand* $$P = 1 - \sum_{i=1}^{n} x_i \qquad (6.3)$$

A2   *Firm's costs* $$c(x_i) = c x_i$$

Equation (6.3) is called the *inverse industry demand function*. Normally the industry demand curve is seen as arising from the utility-maximising behaviour of consumers – the market demand curve tells us how much households wish to buy at a given price. The mathematical operation of taking the inverse, as in (6.3), has important economic implications: it assumes that there can only be one 'market' price. Thus firms have no direct control over the price of their output, only an indirect control via the effect that changes in their own output have on the total industry output.

Given A1–A2, we can define the firm's payoff function which gives firm i's profits as a function of the outputs chosen:

$$\pi_i (x_1, x_2, \ldots x_n) = x_i (1 - \sum_{j=1}^{n} x_j) - c x_i \qquad (6.4)$$

$$= x_i - x_i^2 - x_i \sum_{j \neq i} x_j - c x_i$$

Each firm has a reaction function, which gives its profit-maximising output as a function of the outputs chosen by the other firms. Since firm i treats the output of the other firm $j \neq i$ as fixed, the first-order condition for maximising (6.4) with respect to x_i is:[6]

$$\frac{\partial \pi_i}{\partial x_i} = 1 - \sum_{j \neq i} x_j - 2x_i - c = 0$$

Solving this defines the reaction function for firm i:

$$x_i = \frac{1 - \sum_{j \neq i}^{n} x_j - c}{2} \qquad i = 1, \ldots n \qquad (6.5)$$

Each firm has a similar reaction function, and the Nash equilibrium occurs when each firm is on its reaction function (i.e. choosing its optimal output given the output of other firms). There will be a symmetric and unique Cournot–Nash equilibrium which is obtained by solving the n equations (6.5) for outputs (which are all equal by symmetry),

$$x_i^* = x^c = \frac{1-c}{n+1} \quad \textit{Cournot–Nash equilibrium output} \tag{6.6}$$

which results in equilibrium price:

$$p^c = \frac{1}{n+1} + \frac{n}{n+1}c \tag{6.7}$$

For example, if $n=1$ (monopoly) we get the standard monopoly solution. For $n=2$, $x_c = (1-c)/3$, $p^c = 1/3 + (2/3)c$. The price–cost margin for each firm is:

$$\mu^c = \frac{p^c - c}{p^c} = \frac{1-c}{1+nc} \tag{6.8}$$

There is a clear inverse relationship between the equilibrium price–cost margin and the number of firms. As the number of firms become infinite ($n \to \infty$), the price–cost margin tends to its competitive level of 0: as the number falls to one, it tends to its monopoly level $(1-c)/(1+c)$, as predicted in Figure 6.1.

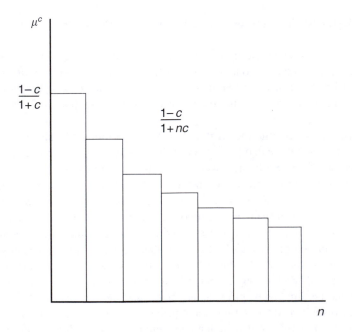

Figure 6.1 *The price–cost margin and the number of firms in the Cournot–Nash equilibrium*

What is the intuition behind this relationship between the number of firms and the price–cost margin? Very simply, with more firms, each firm's own demand becomes more elastic. With an infinite number of firms, the firm's elasticity becomes infinite and hence the firms behave as competitive price-takers. The representative firm's elasticity η_i can be related to the industry elasticity η:

$$\eta = \frac{p}{x}\frac{dx}{dp} \tag{6.9a}$$

$$\eta_i = \frac{p}{x_i}\frac{dx_i}{dp} = \frac{x}{x_i}\left(\frac{p}{x}\frac{dx_i}{dp}\right) \tag{6.9b}$$

Under the Nash assumption, firms treat the other firms' outputs as given and the change in industry output x equals the change in firm i's output. Hence $dx_i/dp = dx/dp$. Of course x_i/x is the ith firm's market share which, for our example, is in equilibrium $1/n$. Hence (6.9b) becomes:

$$\eta_i = n \cdot \eta \tag{6.10}$$

In equilibrium each firm's elasticity is equal to n times the industry elasticity of demand. As n gets large, so does η_i leading to approximately 'price-taking' behaviour.

3.2   Bertrand Competition with Homogeneous Products

In his famous review, Bertrand criticised Cournot's model on several counts. One of these was the reasonable one that firms set prices not quantities: the output sold by the firm is determined by the demand it faces at the price it sets. What is the equilibrium in the market when firms set prices, the Bertrand–Nash equilibrium?

If firms set prices the model is rather more complicated than in the Cournot framework since there can be as many prices in the market as there are firms. In the Cournot framework the inverse industry demand curve implies a single 'market' price. In the Bertrand framework each firm directly controls the price at which it sells its output and, in general, the demand for its output will depend on the price set by each firm and the amount that they wish to sell at that price (see Dixon, 1987b). However, in the case of a homogeneous product where firms have constant returns to scale, the demand facing each firm is very simple to calculate. Taking the case of duopoly, if both firms set *different* prices then all households will wish to buy from the lower-priced firm which will want to meet all demand (so long as its price covers cost), and the higher-priced firm will sell nothing. If the two firms set the *same* price, then the households are indifferent between buying from either seller and demand will be divided between them (equally, for example). If firms have constant marginal cost there exists a unique Bertrand–Nash equilibrium with tow or more firms where each firm sets its price p_i equal to marginal cost – the competitive equilibrium. This can be shown in three steps:

Step 1   If both firms set different prices then that cannot be an equilibrium. The higher-priced firm will face no demand and hence can increase profits by undercutting the lower-priced firm so long as the lower-priced firm charges in excess of *c*. If the *lower*-priced firm charged *c*, it could increase profits from 0 by raising its price slightly while undercutting the higher-priced firm. Hence any Bertrand–Nash equilibrium must be a single-price equilibrium (SPE).

Step 2   The only SPE is where all firms set the competitive price. If both firms set a price *above* *c*, then either firm can gain by undercutting the other by a small amount. By undercutting, it can capture the whole market and hence by choosing a small enough price reduction it can increase its profits.

Step 3   The competitive price is a Nash equilibrium. If both firms set the competitive price then neither can gain by raising its price. If one firm raises its price while the other continues to set $p_i = c$, the lower-priced firm will face the industry demand leaving the firm which has raised its price with no demand.

The Bertrand–Nash framework yields a very different relationship between structure and conduct from the Cournot–Nash equilibrium: with one firm the monopoly outcome occurs; with two or more firms the competitive outcome occurs. Large numbers are not necessary to obtain the competitive outcome and, in general, price-setting firms will set the competitive 'price-taking' price.

Clearly it makes a difference whether firms choose prices or quantities. What grounds do we have for choosing between them? First, and perhaps most importantly, there is the question of the *type* of market. In some markets (for primary products, stocks and shares) the people who set prices (brokers) are different to the producers. There exists what is essentially an *auction* market: producers/suppliers release a certain quantity into the market and then brokers will sell this for the highest price possible (the market clearing price). The Cournot framework would thus seem natural where there are *auction* markets. While there are auction markets, there are also many industrial markets without 'brokers' where the producers directly set the price at which they sell their produce. Clearly, the 'typical' sort of market which concerns industrial economists is not an auction market but a market with price-setting firms. How can the use of the Cournot framework be justified in markets with price-setting firms?

It is often argued that the choice of Bertrand or Cournot competition rests on the *relative* flexibility of prices and output. In the Bertrand framework firms set prices and then produce to order. Thus, once set, prices are fixed while output is perfectly flexible. In the Cournot framework, however, once chosen, outputs are fixed while the price is flexible in the sense that it clears the market. Thus the choice between the two frameworks rests on the relative flexibility of price and output. This is of course an empirical question but many would argue that prices are more flexible than quantities (e.g. Hart, 1982) and hence the Cournot equilibrium is more appropriate.

A very influential paper which explores this view is Kreps and Scheinkman (1983). They consider the subgame-perfect equilibrium in a two-stage model. In the first stage, firms choose capacities; in the second stage firms compete with price as in the Bertrand model and can produce up to the capacity installed. The resultant subgame-perfect equilibrium of the two-stage model turns out to be equivalent to the standard Cournot outcome. This result, however, is not general and rests crucially on an assumption about contingent demand (the demand for a higher-priced firm given that the lower-priced firm does not completely satisfy its demand) – see Dixon (1987a). An alternative approach is to allow for the flexibility of production to be endogenous (Dixon, 1985; Vives, 1986). The Bertrand and Cournot equilibria then come out as limiting cases corresponding to when production is perfectly flexible (a horizontal marginal cost curve yields the Bertrand outcome) or totally inflexible (a vertical marginal cost curve at capacity yields Cournot).

Another reason that the Cournot framework is preferred to the Bertrand is purely technical: there is a fundamental problem of the non-existence of equilibrium in the Bertrand model (see Edgeworth, 1925; Dixon, 1987a). In our simple example firms have constant average/marginal costs. If this assumption is generalised – for example to allow for rising marginal cost – non-existence of equilibrium is a problem.[7]

A common argument for the Cournot framework is its 'plausibility' relative to the Bertrand framework. Many economists believe that 'numbers matter': it makes a difference whether there are two firms or two thousand. Thus the prediction of the Bertrand model – a zero price-cost margin with two or more firms – is implausible (see, for example, Hart, 1979; Allen and Hellwigg, 1986). The Cournot equilibrium captures the 'intuition' that competition decreases with fewer firms. There are two points to be raised here: one empirical, one theoretical. Firstly, on the empirical level there exists little or no evidence that there is a smooth monotonic relationship between the level of concentration and the price–cost margin. Secondly, on the theoretical level, the stark contrast in the Bertrand and Cournot formulations has been exhibited here only in the case of a simple one-shot game. In a repeated game numbers may well matter. For example, Brock and Scheinkman (1985) consider a price-setting super-game and show that there is a relationship between numbers and prices that can be sustained in the industry (although the relationship is not a simple monotonic one). A related point is that the Nash equilibrium is a non-cooperative equilibrium. Numbers may well matter when it comes to maintaining and enforcing collusion and one of Bertrand's criticisms of Cournot was that collusion was a likely outcome with only two firms.

4   COURNOT AND BERTRAND EQUILIBRIA WITH DIFFERENTIATED COMMODITIES

In this section we will explore and contrast the Bertrand and Cournot approaches within a common framework of differentiated products with symmetric linear demands. As we shall see, there are again significant contrasts between markets where firms compete with prices and quantities. Firstly, we will compare the equilibrium prices and show that the Cournot equilibrium yields a higher price than the Bertrand equilibrium. Thus, as in the case of homogeneous products, Cournot competition is less competitive than Bertrand competition although the contrast is less.

Secondly, we contrast the 'Stackelberg' equilibrium (where one firm moves before the other) and the corresponding 'first-mover' advantage. In the Cournot framework, the leader increases his own output and profits at the expense of the follower and total output increases, reflecting a more competitive outcome than the standard Nash equilibrium. In the Bertrand framework, the Stackelberg leader will raise his price and increase his profits. The follower will also raise his prices and indeed his profits will increase by more than the leaders. Unlike the Cournot case there is then a 'second-mover advantage' in the Bertrand case. Overall, with price competition the Stackelberg equilibrium leads to higher prices and profits and a contraction in total output. These differences between the behaviour of markets with price and quantity competition have important policy implications which will be discussed at the end of this section in the context of the recent literature on strategic trade policy.

We continue to assume that firms have constant average/marginal cost, A2. However, we will drop A1 and assume that there is a symmetric linear demand system; in the case of two firms with differentiated products we have:

A3　　For $0 < \alpha < 1$

$$x_1 = 1 - p_1 + \alpha p_2 \tag{6.11a}$$
$$x_2 = 1 - p_2 + \alpha p_1 \tag{6.11b}$$

where $\alpha > 0$ implies the two outputs are *substitutes* (e.g. margarine and butter): if a were negative then they would be complements (e.g. personal computers and software). In the exposition we will assume throughout that the firms produce *substitutes* and for technical reasons that $\alpha < 1$ (i.e. quite plausibly the firm's own price has a greater absolute effect on its demand than the other firm's price).

The above equations express outputs (or more precisely, demands) as a function of prices.[8] If we want to explore the Cournot framework with differentiated products, we need to invert (6.11) to give the prices that will 'clear' the markets for chosen outputs.

Inverting (6.11) we have:

$$p_1 = a_0 - a_1 x_1 - a_2 x_2 \tag{6.12}$$
$$p_2 = a_0 - a_1 x_2 - a_2 x_1$$

where

$$a_0 = \frac{1 + \alpha}{1 - \alpha^2}; \quad a_1 = \frac{1}{1 - \alpha^2}; \quad a_2 = \frac{\alpha}{1 - \alpha^2}$$

Since $\alpha > 0$ both prices are decreasing in both outputs. Thus an increase in x_1 by one unit will decrease p_1 by a_1, and p_2 by a_2 (of course $a_1 > a_2$ for $\alpha < 1$).

4.1 Cournot–Nash Equilibrium

There are two firms which choose outputs, the resultant prices given by the inverse demand system (6.12). Firm 1's 'payoff' function is:

$$\pi_1 = x_1[(a_0 - a_1x_1 - a_2x_2) - c]$$

To obtain firm 1's reaction function x_1 is chosen optimally given x_2:

$$\frac{\partial \pi_1}{\partial x_1} = a_0 - 2a_1x_1 - a_2x_2 - c = 0$$

Solving for x_1 this yields:

$$x_1 = r_1(x_2) = \frac{a_0 - c - a_2x_2}{2a_1} \tag{6.13}$$

The slope of the reaction function is given by:

$$\left. \frac{dx_1}{dx_2} \right|_{r_1} = \frac{-a_2}{2a_1} = -\frac{\alpha}{2} < 0$$

With substitutes, each firm's reaction function is downward-sloping in output space as in Figure 6.2.

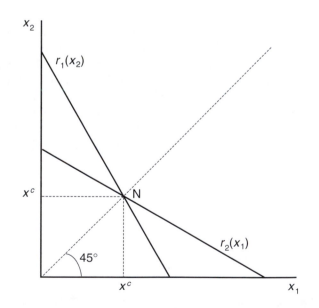

Figure 6.2 *Cournot reaction functions*

The firms are identical and there is a unique symmetric equilibrium at N with $x_1 = x_2 = x^c$:

$$x^c = \frac{a_0 - c}{2a_1 + a_2} = \frac{1 + \alpha - c(1 - \alpha^2)}{2 + \alpha} \tag{6.14}$$

with resultant price:

$$p^c = \frac{1 + c(1 - \alpha)}{(2 + \alpha)(1 - \alpha)} \tag{6.15}$$

4.2 Bertrand–Nash Equilibrium

Turning now to the Bertrand case, firms choose *prices* so that we use the direct demand system (6.11). Firm 1's profits are:

$$\pi_1 = p_1(1 - p_1 + \alpha p_2) - c(1 - p_1 + \alpha p_2) \tag{6.16}$$

$$\frac{\partial \pi_1}{\partial p_1} = 1 - 2p_1 + \alpha p + c = 0$$

Hence firm 1's reaction function in price space is:

$$p_1 = s_1(p_2) = \frac{1 + c + \alpha p_2}{2} \tag{6.17}$$

and the slope is:

$$\left. \frac{dp_1}{dp_2} \right|_{s_1} = \frac{\alpha}{2} > 0$$

Thus the two firms' reaction functions are upward-sloping in price space as depicted in Figure 6.3. There is a unique symmetric equilibrium price $p_1 = p_2 = p^b$ with corresponding output, price and price–cost margins:

$$p^b = \frac{1 + c}{2 - \alpha} \tag{6.18}$$

$$x^b = \frac{1 - c(1 - \alpha)}{2 - \alpha} \tag{6.19}$$

$$\mu^b = \frac{1 - c(1 - \alpha)}{1 + c} \tag{6.20}$$

How do the Cournot and Bertrand equilibria compare? Direct comparison of (6.18) with (6.15) shows that $p^b < p^c$: that is, the Bertrand equilibrium prices are *lower* than Cournot prices. We formulate this in the following observation.

Observation: If firms' demands are interdependent $\alpha \neq 0$ then:

$$p^c > p^b; \quad x^c < x^b; \quad \mu^c > \mu^b$$

If $\alpha = 0$ then each firm is, in effect, a monopolist since there are no cross-price

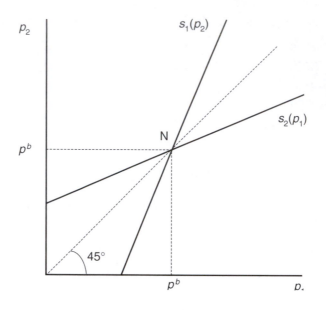

Figure 6.3   *Bertrand–Nash equilibrium*

effects and the two outcomes are, of course, the same. It should be noted that the above observation remains true when the goods are complements $(-1 < \alpha < 0)$.

With differentiated products, then, Bertrand competition will be more competitive than Cournot competition although the difference is less stark than in the case of homogeneous products. With product differentiation, firms have some monopoly power even with price competition and do not have the same incentives for undercutting their competition as in the homogeneous goods case.

What is the intuition behind the above observation that price competition is more competitive than quantity competition? Clearly, for a monopoly, it makes no difference whether price or quantity is chosen; it simply chooses the profit-maximising price–output point on its demand curve. There is a sense in which this is also true for the oligopolist: *given* what the other firm is doing, it faces a demand curve and chooses a point on that demand curve. However, the demand curve facing firm 1 will be different if firm 2 keeps x_2 constant (and hence allows p_2 to vary), from when firm 2 keeps p_2 constant (and hence allows x_2 to vary). From (6.11), if firm 2 has price as its strategy and holds p_2 constant, firm 1's demand is:

$$x_1 = (1 + \alpha p_2) - p_1 \tag{6.21}$$

with slope

$$\left.\frac{dx_1}{dp_1}\right|_{p_2} = -1 \tag{6.22a}$$

and elasticity

$$\left.\eta_1\right|_{p_2} = \frac{p_1}{x_1} \qquad (6.22b)$$

If, on the contrary, firm 2 has output as its strategy it allows its price p_2 to vary as p_1 varies (to keep x_1 constant):

$$p_2 = 1 - x_2 + \alpha p_1 \qquad (6.23)$$

Substituting (6.23) into (6.11a) we obtain firm 1's demand when x_2 is held constant:

$$x_1 = (1 + \alpha) - (1 - \alpha^2)p_1 - \alpha x_2 \qquad (6.24)$$

with slope and elasticity:

$$\left.\frac{dx_1}{dp_1}\right|_{x_2} = -(1 - \alpha^2); \qquad \left.\eta_1\right|_{x_2} = -\frac{p_1}{x_1}(1 - \alpha^2) \qquad (6.25)$$

Clearly, comparing elasticities (6.22) and (6.25):

$$\left.\eta_1\right|_{p_2} < \left.\eta_1\right|_{x_2} < 0$$

Thus the demand facing firm 1 is *more* elastic when firm 2 holds p_2 constant (and allows x_2 to vary) than when x_2 is held constant (and p_2 allowed to vary). For example, suppose that firm 1 considers moving up its demand curve to sell one less unit of x_1 with substitutes ($\alpha > 0$). If firm 2 holds x_2 constant, then as firm 1 reduces its output and raises its price the price for x_2 will rise (via (6.11b)). Clearly the demand for firm 1 will be more elastic in the case where firm 2 does not raise its price and expands output.

We have derived the above observation under very special assumptions A1, A3. How far can we generalise this comparison of Cournot and Bertrand prices? This has been the subject of much recent research – see for example Cheng (1985), Hathaway and Rickard (1979), Okuguchi (1987), Singh and Vives (1984), Vives (1985a,b). Vives (1985a) considers a more general differentiated demand system which need not be linear or symmetric (*ibid.*, p. 168) and derives fairly general conditions for which the Bertrand price is less than the Cournot price. Of course there need not be unique Cournot or Bertrand equilibria: with multiple equilibria the comparison becomes conceptually more complex. Vives (1985b) has established a result that for very general conditions there exists a Bertrand equilibrium which involves a lower price than any Cournot equilibrium.

Of course there are other contrasts to be drawn between Cournot and Bertrand–Nash equilibria. For example, there is the question of welfare analysis employing standard consumer surplus. A simple example employing the linear demand system (6.11), (6.12) is provided by Singh and Vives (1984; p. 76) which shows that the sum of consumer and producer surplus is larger in Bertrand than in Cournot–Nash equilibrium both when goods are substitutes and complements.

4.3   Stackelberg Leadership and the Advantages of Moving First

The difference between Cournot and Bertrand competition go deeper than the simple comparisons of the previous section. To illustrate this we will examine the advantages of moving first in the two frameworks. The standard Nash equilibrium assumes that firms move simultaneously. However, Heinrich von Stackelberg (1934) suggested an alternative in which one firm (the leader) moves first, the other (the follower) moves second. Thus when the follower chooses its strategy it treats the leader's choice as given. However, the leader will be able to infer the follower's choice and take this into account in its decision. The explicit algebraic analysis of the Stackelberg equilibrium is rather complicated and we will rather employ the familiar iso-profit loci.[9] In the following analysis it is important to note that under A1, A3 the model is perfectly symmetric; thus whether in price or quantity space the firms' reactions functions are 'symmetric' in the sense that firm 1's reaction is a reflection of firm 2's in the 45° line (see Figures 6.2 and 6.3). Similarly, firm 1's iso-profit loci are simply reflections of firm 2's in the 45° line and vice versa.

Firstly we analyse the Stackelberg equilibrium in the Cournot case. The follower (firm 2) will simply choose its output to maximise its profits given x_1 so that $x_2 = r_2(x_1)$. The leader, however, will choose x_1 to maximise its profits given that x_2 depends on x_1 via r_2. Thus by moving first the leader can pick the point on firm 2's reaction function that yields it the highest profits: this is represented in Figure 6.4 by the tangency of iso-profit loci π^L to r_2 at point A.

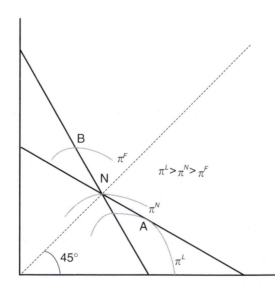

Figure 6.4   *First-mover advantage in Cournot duopoly*

If firm 2 were the leader and firm 1 the follower then, by symmetry, firm 2's Stackelberg point would be at point B – the reflection of A in the 45° line (at this point firm 2's iso-profit locus is tangential to firm 1's reaction function). Comparing points A, B and the Nash equilibrium at point N we can see that if firm 1 is the leader it earns π^L which is greater than in the Nash equilibrium π^N. If firm 1 is a follower it will end up at point B and earn only π^F which is *less* than π^N. Hence, in the Cournot framework we have:

$$\pi^L \quad > \quad \pi^N \quad > \quad \pi^F \quad \text{(Cournot)}$$

profits   Nash   profits
of   profits   of
leader   follower

There is thus a first-move advantage in two senses: the leader earns more than in the simultaneous-move case ($\pi^L > \pi^N$); the leader earns more than the follower ($\pi^L > \pi^F$). The leader increases his output and profits at the expense of the follower (in fact, the decline in the follower's profits from π^N to π^F is *larger* than the increase in the leader's from π^N to π^L: industry profits fall).

In the Bertrand case the story is rather different: there is a 'second-mover' advantage. The reaction functions and iso-profit loci of firm 1 depicted in price space are shown in Figure 6.5 and again are symmetric. The iso-profit loci for firm 1 are higher the further away they are positioned from the *x*-axis (firm 1 will earn higher profits the higher p_2 is). N is the Nash equilibrium, A occurs if firm 1 is the leader, B if 2 is the leader.

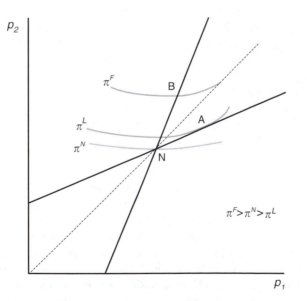

Figure 6.5 *Second-mover advantage in Bertrand duopoly*

If firm 1 is the leader it will choose to raise its price moving along firm 2's reaction function S_2 from N to A and profits will increase from π^N to π^L. However, if firm 1 is the follower it will end up at B with profits π^F. Note that the follower raises his price by less than the leader and that $\pi^F > \pi^L$. thus the leader will set a higher price than the follower, produce a lower output and earn *less* profits:

$$\pi^F > \pi^L > \pi^N \quad \text{(Bertrand)}$$

There is an advantage to moving 'second'. The second-mover advantage goes beyond Bertrand equilibria and extends to any game with upward-sloping reaction functions (Gal-Or, 1986). There is still a first-mover advantage in the sense that the leader earns more than in the simultaneous move case ($\pi^L > \pi^N$). In contrast to the Cournot case, in the Bertrand case Stackelberg leadership leads to higher prices, profits and lower outputs.

4.4   Prices vs Quantities

Price and quantity competition have very different implications for the nature of product-market competition between firms. Most importantly, from the firms' point of view, price competition leads to lower profits than does quantity competition in Nash equilibrium. As was discussed earlier, whether firms should be viewed as competing with price or quantity can be seen as depending on structural or institutional characteristics of the market – the flexibility of production, whether the market is an auction market, and so on.

An alternative approach is to treat the firm's decision to choose price or quantity as itself a strategic decision (Klemperer and Meyer, 1986; Singh and Vives, 1984). While it is perhaps not quite clear how firms might achieve this, it is at least a useful 'experiment' and will reveal the incentives which firms have to achieve one or the other type of competition.

Without uncertainty, this 'experiment' is not fruitful: firms are *indifferent* between choosing price or quantity. The reason is that from the individual firm's perspective it simply faces a demand curve and, like a monopolist, chooses a point on that demand curve. It can achieve any point on the demand curve by choosing either price or quantity. The firm's own price/quantity decision does not affect this demand curve which is rather determined by the *other* firm's choice. Firm 1's choice has a pure externality effect on the demand faced by firm 2: if firm 1 chooses price, firm 2's demand is more elastic than if firm 1 had chosen quantity. However, in the Nash framework, each firm will ignore this externality: given the other firm's choice, each firm will face a particular demand curve and will be indifferent between setting price or quantity itself. In the case of duopoly there will be four Nash equilibria in this strategic game: one where both set quantities (Cournot); one where both set prices (Bertrand); and two asymmetric equilibria where one sets price and the other quantity. With certainty, then, allowing firms to choose price or quantity tells us nothing about which may be more appropriate.

The presence of uncertainty (adding a stochastic term to A3, for example) can mean that firms have a strict preference between price and quantity setting. The results depend very much on the exact assumptions made (is demand uncertainty additive or multiplicative; is demand linear in prices?). For the simple linear demand system A3 with an additive stochastic term firms will prefer quantity setting if marginal costs are increasing; they will be indifferent if marginal costs are constant (as in A1); they prefer price setting if marginal costs are decreasing (Klemperer and Meyer, 1986; proposition 1). While this and related results are at present rather specific they do suggest that the presence and nature of uncertainty provide some insights into how firms view the alternatives of price and quantity setting.

5   PRECOMMITMENT: STRATEGIC INVESTMENT AND DELEGATION

In the previous section we explored the nature of the first-mover advantage in the Cournot and Bertrand framework. Clearly, if we start from the Nash equilibrium there is an incentive for the firm to precommit its output/price to obtain this first-mover advantage. By 'precommitment' it is meant that the firm takes some action prior to competing in the product market which commits it to a certain course of action. In the standard Cournot model it is not credible for one firm to produce the Stackelberg output in the simultaneous move game. For example, in terms of Figure 6.6, firm 1's Stackelberg point A is not on its reaction function – so that given firm 2's output, x_{2A}, firm 1 would like to produce x_1. The only credible equilibrium is the Nash equilibrium at N. In order to move towards its Stackelberg point the firm must be able to precommit its output in some way. In the previous section we simply assumed that the leader was able to move first. In some situations it is natural to assume a particular sequence of moves (e.g. entrant/incumbent, dominant firm). However, in the case of active incumbents which are competing on even terms, simultaneous moves seem more natural.

Given that there is an incentive for the firm to precommit how can this be achieved? This section will look at two methods of precommitment which have received much recent attention – precommitment through investment and precommitment through delegation. The basic idea is simple: the firm can take actions prior to competing in the market which will alter the Nash equilibrium in the market. Firms can take actions such as investment decisions[10] and choice of managers that are irreversible (in the sense of being 'fixed' over the market period) and which alter the firm's reaction function thus shifting the Nash equilibrium in the market. We will first consider how investment by firms can be used strategically to alter the market outcome.

For a wide range of industrial processes, economists since Marshall have taken the view that it is appropriate to treat the capital stock decision as being taken on a different time scale (the 'long run') to price/output decisions (the

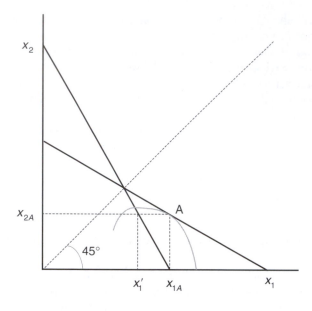

Figure 6.6 *Non-credibility of Stackelberg point for firm 1*

'short-run'). When firms compete in the product market it follows that they treat their capital stock as fixed. The capital stock chosen by the firm will influence its *costs* when it competes in the market. The fact that capital is committed 'before' output/price decisions means that it can use investment strategically to influence the market outcome. In essence, through its choice of capital stock, the firm will determine the short-run costs which it will have when it chooses output/price; the firm's marginal costs will determine its reaction function and hence the Nash equilibrium in the product market. Schematically:

Investment → short-run → reaction → market
marginal cost function equilibrium

For example, in the Cournot case the firm can increase its investment, reduce its marginal cost and hence shift its reaction function out so that the product market equilibrium moves towards the Stackelberg point. Of course, this precommitment is not costless: capital costs money and, as we shall see, such use of capital leads to productive inefficiency. Again there is an important dichotomy between the Cournot and Bertrand approaches: if the product market is Cournot then the firm will want to overinvest; if the product market is Bertrand then the firms will want to underinvest. We will briefly illustrate both situations.

The structure of strategic investment models is very simple: there are two stages to capture the distinction between the short and the long run. In the first 'strategic' stage, the firms choose their capital stock; in the second 'market' stage firms choose output/price. The choice of capital stock in the first stage will determine the cost function which the firm has. In the previous two sections we assumed constant average/marginal cost at c (A2). This can be conceived of as the long-run cost function. In order to keep the exposition consistent we will assume that firms have a production function of the form:

$$A4 \quad x_i = k_i^{1/2} L_i^{1/2}$$

$$c(x_i, k_i) = rk_i + \frac{x_i^2}{k_i} \tag{6.26}$$

where linear increasing marginal cost:

$$\frac{\partial c}{\partial x_i} = \frac{2}{k_i} x_i \tag{6.27}$$

Thus an increase in investment lowers the marginal cost of producing output. The production function A4 displays constant returns to scale and hence the long-run cost function has constant average/marginal cost in terms of A2,[11] minimum average cost

$$c = 2\sqrt{r}$$

We will first outline the strategic investment model with Cournot competition in the product market, a simple version of Brander and Spencer's (1983) article. If investment is used non-strategically, then the firm simply operates on its long-run cost function given by A2: capital and labour are chosen to minimise production costs. In the strategic investment framework, however, the firm's costs will be given by its short-run cost function (6.26). Turning to the market stage, the firm's profits are:

$$\pi_i = x_i(a_0 - a_1 x_i - a_2 x_j) - rk_i - \frac{x_i^2}{k_i} \tag{6.28}$$

The reaction function which the firm has in the market stage, conditional on k_i, is derived by setting $\partial \pi_i / \partial x_i = 0$:

$$x_i = r_i(x_j, k_i) = \frac{a_0 - a_2 x_j}{2a_1 + (2/k_i)} \tag{6.29}$$

By increasing its investment, firm i will reduce its marginal costs and from (6.29) it will shift its reaction function out as in Figure 6.7. Given the level of investment by the two firms (k_1, k_2) are obtained by solving (6.29) for x_1 and x_2, as depicted in Figure 6.8 (we leave this as an exercise for the reader). In general form:

$$x_i = x_i \left(\underset{+ \; -}{k_i, k_j} \right) \tag{6.30}$$

This notation signifies that firm i's equilibrium output in the market stage depends positively on its own investment and negatively on investment by the other firm. Suppose we start off at point A in Figure 6.9: an increase in k_1 to

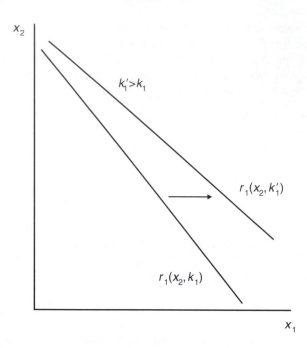

Figure 6.7   *Investment shifts firm 1's reaction function outwards*

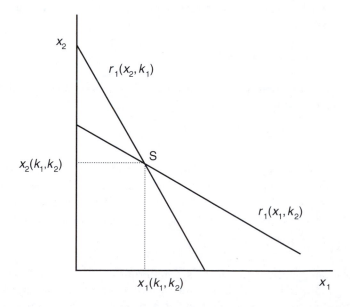

Figure 6.8   *Market stage equilibrium given investment k_1 and k_2*

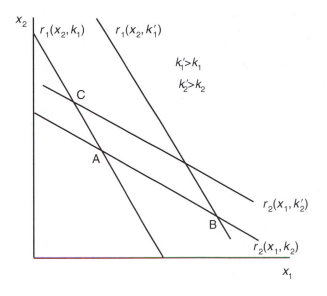

Figure 6.9 *Market stage equilibrium and changes in investment*

k_1' shifts out r_1 so that the market equilibrium goes from A to B, x_1 rising and x_2 falling. Conversely, an increase in k_2 shifts the equilibrium from A to C. Thus, by altering their investment, the firms can alter their reaction functions and hence the market-stage equilibrium.

How is the optimal level of investment in the first strategic stage determined? Firms choose investment levels k_i *given* that the second-stage outputs will be as in (6.30). We can see their profits as a function of capital stocks, so that for firm 1 we have profits:

$$\pi_1(k_1,k_2)=x_1(k_1,k_2)[a_0-a_1x_1(k_1,k_2)-a_2x_2(k_1,k_2)]-c(x_1(k_1,k_2),k_1)$$
(6.31)

The RHS term in square brackets is the price, which is multiplied by output to obtain revenue from which are subtracted costs.

The firm will choose k_1 to maximise its profits (6.31) hence:

$$\frac{\partial \pi_1}{\partial k_1}=\frac{\partial x_1}{\partial k_1}\left[a_0-2a_1x_1-a_2x_2-\frac{\partial c}{\partial x_1}\right]-a_2x_1\frac{\partial x_2}{\partial k_1}-\frac{\partial c}{\partial k_1}=0 \qquad (6.32)$$

Since firm 1 chooses x_1 to maximise profits given x_2 and k_1 in the second stage, the bracket on the right-hand side of (6.32) is zero (it is simply its reaction function (6.29)). Hence (6.32) becomes:

$$\frac{\partial c}{\partial k_1}=-a_2\frac{\partial x_2}{\partial k_1}x_1>0 \qquad (6.33)$$

What does (6.33) tell us? $\partial c / \partial k_1$ gives the effect of investment on the total costs of producing x_1. If $\partial c / \partial k_1 = 0$, as in the standard non-strategic case, then k_1 *minimises* the cost of producing x_1. If $\partial c / \partial k_1 > 0$, as in (6.33), then there is 'over-capitalisation': more investment than would minimise costs (a reduction in k_1 would reduce average costs). If $\partial c / \partial k_1 < 0$, then there is 'undercapitalisation': less investment than would minimise costs.

With a Cournot market stage, then, there is overcapitalisation of production in the market stage. The intuitive reason is quite simple. Given the other firm's reaction function, each firm can shift its own reaction function out towards its Stackelberg point. Of course there is a cost to: more investment leads to higher capital costs and inefficient production. The firms will shift out their reaction functions beyond their 'innocent' level and the final product market equilibrium will be at a point such as S in Figure 6.10. At the equilibrium level of investment the additional cost of investment equals the additional gains from moving out the reaction function further. In the strategic investment equilibrium S then, both firms produce a larger output than in the non-strategic equilibrium N.

In the Bertrand case an exactly analogous argument applies for strategic investment. However, there is the opposite result of *undercapitalisation*. The Stackelberg equilibrium results in higher prices and lower outputs than in the Bertrand case. Thus firms will *restrict* investment relative to the innocent Bertrand equilibrium in order to shift their reaction function *out* in price space, as in Figure 6.11. Starting from the 'innocent' Bertrand equilibrium at N, if firm 1 restricts its investment its marginal costs *rise* and its reaction function shifts

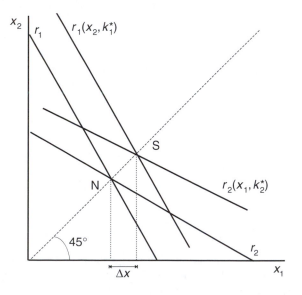

Figure 6.10 *Strategic investment equilibrium: the Cournot case. Overinvestment increases output and reduces the price*

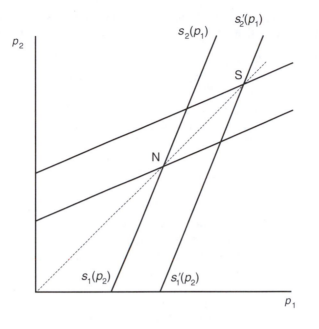

Figure 6.11   *Underinvestment raises prices: the Bertrand case*

outwards to s_1' (an outward shift because with higher marginal costs it will wish
to set a higher price and produce a smaller quantity given the price chosen by
the other firm). If both firms underinvest strategically the resultant equilibrium
will be at S with higher prices and lower output.

We will briefly sketch the algebra underlying this result. Under A1 and A4 the
firm's profits are:

$$\pi_i = p_i - p_i^2 - \alpha p_i p_j - \frac{1}{k_i}(1 - p_i - \alpha p_i p_j)^2 - r k_i \qquad (6.34)$$

Setting $\partial \pi_i / \partial p_i = 0$ firm i's reaction function $p_i = s_i(p_j)$ is:

$$p_i = \frac{1 + (2/k_i)}{2 + (2/k_i)} + \frac{\alpha(1 + (2/k_i))}{(2 + (2/k_i))} p_j \qquad (6.35)$$

Solving for p_i to p_j given k_i and k_j in general terms we have:

$$p_i = p_i\left(\underset{-}{k_i}, \underset{+}{k_j}\right) \qquad i,j = 1, 2, i \neq j \qquad (6.36)$$

The firms choose k_i to maximise (6.34) given that in the market subgame firms'
prices are given by (6.36) (i.e. a Bertrand–Nash equilibrium occurs):

$$\frac{d\pi}{dk_i} = \frac{\partial \pi_i}{\partial p_i} \cdot \frac{dp_i}{dk_i} + \frac{\partial \pi_i}{\partial p_j} \cdot \frac{dp_j}{dk_i} + \frac{\partial \pi_i}{\partial k_i} = 0 \qquad (6.37)$$

$$(0) \quad (-) \quad\quad (+) \quad (-) \quad\quad (+)$$

Note that $\partial \pi_i / \partial p_i = 0$, since firms are in their market stage reaction function (6.35) and, further, that $\partial \pi_i / \partial k_i = -\partial c_i / \partial k_i$. Hence (6.37) can be expressed as:

$$\frac{\partial c}{\partial k_i} = \frac{\partial \pi_i}{\partial p_j} \frac{dp_j}{dk_i} < 0 \qquad\qquad (6.38)$$

$$(+) \ (-)$$

That is, *undercapitalisation* of production results from the strategic use of investment with Bertrand product-market competition.

Clearly, the result of strategic investment models depends on the nature of product-market competition. Other papers have made different assumptions than the simple Cournot–Nash and Bertrand–Nash equilibria. Dixon (1985) considers the case of a *competitive* product market; Eaton and Grossman (1984) and Yarrow (1985) a *conjectural* Cournot equilibrium; Dixon (1986b) a *consistent conjectural* variation equilibrium in the product market.

Since production will generally be inefficient in a strategic investment equilibrium, firms have an incentive to try and precommit their labour input at the same time as their capital. By so doing, firms will be able to produce any output efficiently, while being free to precommit themselves to a wide range of outputs. In Dixon (1986a), precommitment is treated as a strategic choice by the firm: the firm can precommit either, neither, or both capital and labour in the strategic stage. Because of the strategic inefficiency in production that occurs when only capital is precommited, under almost any assumption about the nature of product market competition, firms would prefer to precommit both factors of production (Dixon, 1986a, p. 67). If firms precommit both factors of production in the strategic stage then, in effect, they have chosen their output for the market stage and the resultant equilibrium is equivalent to the standard Cournot equilibrium.

How might firms be able to precommit their output in this manner? One important method that may be available is choice of technology. More specifically, the firm may have a choice between a putty–putty technology that allows for smooth substitution of capital for labour in the market stage or an otherwise equivalent putty–clay technology that is Leontief in the market stage. If the firm chooses a putty–clay technology then its choice of investment and technique in the strategic stage effectively ties down its output and employment in the market stage. If possible, then, firms would prefer to have totally inflexible production in the market stage. This strong result ignores uncertainty of course. If demand or factor prices are uncertain there will be a countervailing incentive to retain flexibility.

In strategic investment models it is firms themselves which precommit. Governments, however, can undertake precommitments which firms themselves cannot make. In the context of trade policy there has been much recent research on how governments can improve the position of their own firms competing in international markets (see Venables, 1985, for an excellent survey). If domestic firms are competing in foreign markets the net benefit to the home country in terms of consumer surplus is the repatriated profits – total revenue less the production costs (with competitive factors markets production costs represent a real social cost to the exporting country). Government trade policy may therefore be motivated by what is called 'rent extraction': that is, helping their own firms to make larger profits which are then repatriated. Trade policy, usually in the form of an export subsidy or tax, is a form of precommitment by the government which enables domestic firms to improve their position in foreign markets. Brander and Spencer (1984) presented the first model based on the rent-extraction principle and argued for the use of export subsidies in the context of a Cournot–Nash product market. Subsidies have the effect of *reducing* the marginal costs faced by exporters and can thus be used to shift out their reaction functions to the Stackelberg point (the cost subsidies 'cost' nothing from the point of view of the exporting country since they merely redistribute money from the taxpayers to shareholders). As Eaton and Grossman (1986) argued, the exact form of the trade policy will be sensitive to the nature of product market competition. With a Bertrand product market, of course, rent extraction arguments lead to the imposition of an export *tax* since this will shift the Bertrand competitor's reaction function outwards in price space towards its Stackelberg point.

The incentive to precommit in oligopolistic markets also sheds light on one of the perennial issues of industrial economics – what are the objectives of firms? The divorce of ownership from control can be viewed as an act of delegation by shareholders, which can be employed as a form of precommitment by shareholders. What sort of managers do shareholders want to manage their firms? There is an obvious answer to this question which underlies the managerialist view of Marris (1964): shareholders want managers who maximise profits (share valuation) and work hard. This may be true in the context of monopoly: in an imperfectly competitive framework matters are rather different. Several recent papers (Fershtman, 1985; Lyons, 1986; Vickers, 1985a) have shown how higher profits for shareholders can be obtained when they have non-profit maximising shareholders. The reaction functions of firms in the standard Cournot and Bertrand models are based on the assumption of profit maximisation; by choosing managers with different objectives (e.g. a preference for sales, or an aversion to work) the firms' reaction functions will be shifted. We will illustrate this with a very simple example adapted from Lyons (1986). Managers maximise utility which depends on profits (remuneration) and sales R (power, prestige and so on). The utility is a convex combination of the two:

$$u = \gamma\pi + (1-\gamma)R \qquad 0 \leqslant \gamma \leqslant 1$$
$$= R - \gamma c$$

since $\pi = R - c$. The coefficient y represents the weight put on *profits*: $y = 1$ is profit maximisation, $y = 0$ yields sales maximisation.

Using the common framework A1, A2, assuming that managers choose outputs to maximise utility, we can derive the firm's reaction functions:

$$u_1 = x_1(a_0 - a_1 x_1 - a_2 x_2) - \gamma c x_1$$

$$\frac{\partial u_1}{\partial x_1} = a_0 - 2a_1 x_1 - a_2 x_2 - \gamma c = 0$$

which yields the reaction function:

$$x_1 = r_1(x_2, \gamma_1) = \frac{a_0 - \gamma c - a_2 x_2}{2a_1}$$
$$\qquad\quad (-)\ (-)$$

By choosing managers with a preference for sales (i.e. γ smaller than unity) shareholders can push out their firm's reaction function. In Figure 6.12 we depict the two extreme reaction functions: the one nearest the origin corresponding to profit maximisation $\gamma = 1$, the other to sales maximisation $\gamma = 0$. Given firm 2's reaction function, firm 1 can move to any point between N and T by choosing the appropriate value of γ. If, as depicted, the Stackelberg point A lies between N and T, then firms will be able to attain their Stackelberg point – note that since A will lie to the left of N, the choice of y will surely be less than unity, reflecting non-maximisation of profits due to some sales preference. In such a market, if one firm is a profit maximiser with $\gamma = 1$ and the other has management with $\gamma < 1$, the non-profit maximising firm will earn *more* than the profit-maximising firm! Of course, in a Bertrand market the shareholders would wish to choose managers who would restrict output and raise prices – perhaps lazy managers with an aversion to work (see Dixon and Manning, 1986, for an

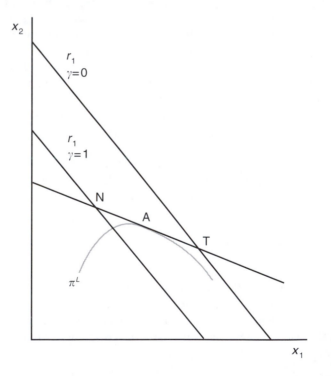

Figure 6.12 *Equilibrium outcome and managerial preferences*

example). While we have talked about different 'types' of managers, the precommitment made by shareholders can be seen as taking the form of different types of remuneration packages which elicit the desired behaviour from managers.

In an imperfectly competitive market, then, it can pay shareholders to have non-profit maximising managers. There need not be the conflict of interest between owners and managers that is central to managerialist theories of the firm. Also, 'natural selection' processes need not favour profit maximisers in oligopolistic markets since, for example, sales-orientated managers can earn larger profits than their more profit-orientated competitors. This is a comforting result given the apparent prevalence of motives other than profits in managerial decisions.

The presence of a first-mover advantage means that firms competing in an oligopolistic environment have an incentive to precommit themselves in some way. We have explored *two* methods of precommitment: through investment and through delegation. Strategic investment leads to productive inefficiency and, from the point of view of the firm, it may be cheaper to make its precommitment through its choice of managers rather than its choice of capital stock.

6   COMPETITION OVER TIME

In general, Nash equilibria are 'inefficient' in the sense that in equilibrium profits of all the firms can be increased. The fundamental reason is that firms' profits are interdependent (via the payoff function): each depending partly on what the other firms are doing. There is thus an 'externality' involved when each firm chooses its strategy. For example, in the Cournot framework if one firm raises its output, it reduces the prices obtained by the other firms, thus reducing their profits (a negative externality). In the Bertrand case, a rise in price by one firm is a positive externality since it raises the demand for other firms. Under the Nash assumption, each firm chooses its own strategy taking into account only the impact on its *own* profits, ignoring the externality.

The inefficiency of Nash equilibria can easily be demonstrated using the abstract notation of the section 'Non-cooperative equilibrium'. For simplicity we will take the case of duopoly. To obtain an *efficient* (Pareto-optimal) outcome between the two firms, simply maximise a weighted sum of firms' profits:

$$\max_{a_1, a_2} \lambda \pi_1(a_1, a_2) + (1 - \lambda)\pi_2(a_1, a_2) \tag{6.39}$$

where $0 \leqslant \lambda \leqslant 1$. The first-order conditions for (6.39) are:

$$\lambda \frac{\partial \pi_1}{\partial a_1} + (1 - \lambda)\frac{\partial \pi_2}{\partial a_1} = 0 \tag{6.40a}$$

$$\lambda \frac{\partial \pi_1}{\partial a_2} + (1 - \lambda)\frac{\partial \pi_2}{\partial a_2} = 0 \tag{6.40b}$$

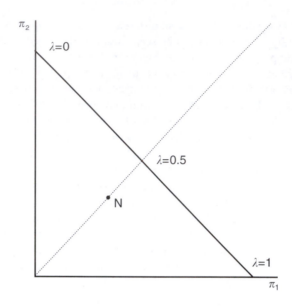

Figure 6.13 *The profit frontier*

The leading diagonal terms represent the effect of a_i on π_i, the firm's strategy on its own profits. The off-diagonal terms reflect the 'externality', the effect of a firm's strategy on the other firm's profits. Depending on the weight λ, a whole range of Pareto-optimal outcomes is possible (corresponding to the contract curve of the Edgeworth box). These outcomes can be represented as the profit frontier in payoff space, as in Figure 6.13. On the frontier, each firm's profits are maximised given the other firm's profits. As λ moves from 0 to 1, more weight is put on firm 1's profits and we move down the profit frontier.[12]

The Nash equilibrium profits are not Pareto-optimal and lay *inside* the profit frontier at point N, for example. To see why, note that for a Nash equilibrium to occur, both firms choose a_i to maximise their own profits (they are both on their reaction functions). Thus the first-order equations defining the Nash equilibrium are:

$$\frac{\partial \pi_1}{\partial a_1} = \frac{\partial \pi_2}{\partial \pi_2} = 0 \qquad\qquad (6.41)$$

If we compare (6.41) with (6.40) we can immediately see that if there is some interdependence captured by a non-zero cross-effect ($\partial \pi_i / \partial a_j \neq 0$), then (6.41) will not be efficient. If there is a *negative* cross-effect, then at the Nash equilibrium N:

$$\lambda \left.\frac{\partial \pi_1}{\partial a_1}\right|_N + (1-\lambda) \left.\frac{\partial \pi_2}{\partial a_1}\right|_N < 0 \qquad\qquad (6.42)$$

$$\quad (0) \qquad\qquad\qquad (-)$$

The marginal effect of a_i on the weighted sum of industry profits is *negative*: there is too much output chosen. Conversely, in the Bertrand case at the Nash equilibrium, the marginal effect of a price rise on the weighted sum of industry profits is *positive*.

This inefficiency of Nash equilibria means that there is an incentive for firms to collude – to choose their strategies (a_1, a_2) *jointly* and move from N towards the profit frontier. Of course, if the two firms could merge or write legally binding contracts, it would be possible for them to do this directly. However, antitrust law prevents them from doing so: firms have to behave non-cooperatively. However, since the efficient outcomes are not Nash equilibria, each firm will have an incentive to *deviate* from the efficient outcome: it will be able to increase its profits, for example from (6.40), at an efficient outcome where partial $\partial \pi_j / \partial a_j$ is positive (negative) then $\partial \pi_i / \partial a_i$ will be negative (positive) so that a slight reduction (increase) in a_i will increase i's profits.

Given that firms have an incentive to cooperate, how can they enforce cooperative behaviour if there is also an incentive for firms to deviate from it? One response is to argue that firms compete over time: firms can enforce cooperative behaviour by punishing deviation from a collusive outcome. Since firms are involved in a repeated game, if one firm deviates at time t, then it can be 'punished' at subsequent periods. In a repeated game, might not such 'threats' enable firms to enforce a collusive outcome over time? This question has provided the impetus for much research in recent years.

In a finitely repeated game with perfect information, it turns out that the unique subgame-perfect equilibrium will be to have the Nash equilibrium in each period (assuming that there is a unique Nash equilibrium in the constituent game). That is, if we restrict firms to *credible* punishment threats, then those credible threats will not enable the firms to do better than their Nash equilibrium profits in each period: the argument is a standard backwards induction argument. Consider the subgame consisting of the last period. There is a unique Nash equilibrium for this subgame which is that the firms play their Nash strategies. Any other strategy in the last period would not be 'credible', would not involve all firms adopting their best response to each other. Consider the subgame consisting of the last two periods. Firms know that whatever they do in the penultimate period, the standard Nash equilibrium will occur next period. Therefore, they will want to choose their action to maximise their profits in the penultimate period given what the other firms do. If all firms do this the standard Nash equilibrium will occur in the penultimate period. By similar arguments as we go backwards, for any period t, given that in subsequent periods the Nash equilibrium will occur, the Nash equilibrium will occur in period t as well. Hence finite repetition of the game yields the standard Nash outcome in each stage of the history of the market. This backwards induction argument goes back to Luce and Raiffa's (1957) analysis of the repeated prisoner's dilemma.

In finitely repeated games, then, there is no scope for threats/punishments to move firms' profits above their Nash level. The argument relied upon a known terminal period, 'the end of the world'. An alternative approach is to analyse *infinitely* repeated games, reflecting the view that market competition is interminable. This raises a different problem: there are generally many subgame perfect equilibria in infinitely repeated games. Clearly, the above backwards induction argument cannot be employed in infinitely repeated games because there is no last period to start from! It has proven mathematically quite complex to characterise the set of subgame perfect equilibria in infinitely repeated games. There are two types of results (commonly called 'Folk theorems') corresponding to two different views of how to evaluate the firm's payoffs over an infinitely repeated game. One approach is to view the firm maximising its discounted profits for the rest of the game at each period (Lockwood, 1984; Abreu, 1985; Radner, 1986). The other is to view that the firm does not discount but maximises its average per-period payoff.

Let us first look at the 'Folk theorem' for infinitely repeated games without discounting, which is based on work by Rubenstein (1979). The key reference point is the '*security level*' of firms: this represents the worst punishment that can be inflicted on them in the one-shot constituent game. This is the 'minimax' payoff of the firm, the worst payoff that can be imposed on the firm given that it responds optimally to the other firm(s). For example, take the simple Cournot model: the lowest level to which firm 1 can drive firm 2 is zero – this corresponds to where firm 2's reaction function cuts the x-axis and firm 2's output and profits are driven to zero. In the framework we have employed, each firms' security level corresponding to the worst possible punishment it can receive is equal to zero. An individually rational payoff in the constituent game is defined as a payoff which yields both firms their security level. The basic result is that *any* individually rational payoff in the constituent game can be 'sustained' as a perfect equilibrium in an infinitely repeated game without discounting. By 'sustained' it is meant that there corresponds equilibrium strategies that yield those payoffs for each firm. In our example this means that *any* combination of non-negative profits is possible! This will include the outcomes on the profit frontier of course but also outcomes that are far worse than the standard Cournot–Nash equilibrium! In terms of Figure 6.13, the whole of the area between the axes and the profit frontier (inclusive) represents possible payoffs of some subgame perfect equilibrium!

With discounting, the range of possible equilibria depends on the discount rate δ. At period t the future discounted profits for the rest of the game are:

$$\sum_{s=0}^{\infty} \delta^s \pi_{it+s}$$

where $0 \leqslant \delta < 1$ (if the interest rate is r then $\delta = 1/(1+r)$). The larger is δ, the more weight is put on the future: as δ tends to one, we reach the no-discounting case (since equal weight is put on profits in each period); with δ equal to zero, the future is very heavily discounted and the firm concentrates only on the current period. The analysis of infinitely repeated games with discounting is rather more complex than the no-discounting case, not least because it is more difficult to define the firm's security level which itself varies with δ (see Fudenberg and Maskin, 1986). The basic Folk theorem is that: (a) as $\delta \to 0$, then the set of perfect equilibrium payoffs shrink to the one-shot Nash payoffs; (b) as $\delta \to 1$, then any individually rational payoff is an equilibrium payoff. Again, the analysis is rather complicated here and the reader is referred to Lockwood (1987) for an excellent analysis of the issues. The basic message for games with discounting is that the set of perfect equilibria depends on the discount rate and may be very large.

From the point of view of industrial economics the game-theoretic results for repeated games are far from satisfactory. With finite repetition the equilibrium is the same as in the one-shot case: with infinite repetition there are far too many equilibria – almost anything goes! There seems to be little middle ground.

However, recent advances involving games of imperfect information may provide some answer to this dilemma (Kreps *et al.*, 1982). The basic idea is very simple. Suppose that the firms are uncertain about each other's objectives. In a repeated game, firms can learn about each other's 'character' from observing their actions through time. In this circumstance, firms are able to build up reputations. Let us take a very simple example: there are two firms A and B with two

$$
\begin{array}{cccc}
 & & \multicolumn{2}{c}{B} \\
 & & c & d \\
A & c & (1,1) & (-1,2) \\
 & d & (2,-1) & (0,0)
\end{array}
$$

strategies, cooperate (c) or defect (d). The resultant profits of the two firms are of the familiar prisoner's dilemma structure:

Defection is the 'dominant' strategy: whatever the other firm does, defection yields the highest profits hence the unique Nash equilibrium is for both firms to defect. This outcome is Pareto-dominated by the outcome where both firms cooperate. If there is perfect information and the game is repeated over time, then the unique subgame-perfect equilibrium is for both firms to defect throughout (by the standard backwards induction argument).

Now following Kreps *et al.* (1982), we introduce some uncertainty. We will take the case where firms are uncertain about each other's motivation. In general, firms are of two types: a proportion α are 'Rats' and play rationally; and a proportion $(1 - \delta)$ are 'Triggers' and play 'trigger' strategies – which means that the firm will play cooperatively until the other firm defects, after which it will punish the defector by playing non-cooperatively for the rest of the game.

In a multi-period game like this where there is imperfect information, each firm may be able to infer the other firm's type from its past actions. For example, if one firm defects when they have previously both been cooperative, then the other firm can infer that the other firm is a Rat (since a Trigger only defects in response to an earlier defection). By playing cooperatively, then, a Rat can leave the other firm guessing as to his true type; if a Rat defects he knows he will lose his reputation and 'reveal' his true nature.

To illustrate this as simply as possible, we will consider what happens when the above game is repeated for three periods and firms have discount rates δ. For certain values of α and δ it will be an equilibrium for both firms to cooperate for the first two periods and defect in the last period. Consider the following strategy from a Rat's point of view (a Trigger will of course follow a trigger strategy).

Period 1:   Cooperate
Period 2:   Cooperate if the other firm cooperated in period 1,
            defect otherwise
Period 3:   Defect

We will now show that this can be a perfect-equilibrium strategy for a Rat. Recall that the Rat does not know whether his opponent is a Trigger or a Rat following the same strategy.

In period 3 it is clearly subgame perfect to defect – whatever the type of the opponent, be he Rat or Trigger, defection is the dominant strategy and yields the highest payoff. In period 2 the decision is a little more complex. If the other firm (B, say) defected in period 1 then, of course, he has revealed himself to be a Rat and so defection is the best response for A for period 2. If firm B did not defect in period 1, then he may be a Trigger or a Rat (with probability $(1-\alpha)$ and α respectively). If firm A defects in period 2 then whatever the type of firm B, it will earn two units in period 2 and nothing in period 3 (since firm B will retaliate whether a Rat or a Trigger). Its expected discounted profits are 2. If, however, firm A cooperates in period 2 it will earn 1 unit of profit in that period: in period 3 its profit will depend on firm A's type—with probability a the other firm is a Rat and will defect anyway: with probability $(1-\alpha)$ the other firm is a Trigger and will cooperate in the last period. Thus if A cooperates in period 2 its expected period 3 profits are $\alpha 0 + (1-\alpha)2$. In period 2 firm A's expected discounted profits, if it cooperates, will be $1 + \delta(1-\alpha)2$. Clearly, firm A will cooperate in period 2 if the expected discounted profits doing so exceed those from defection, that is:

defect in $2 < 1 + \delta(1-\alpha)2$ cooperate in
period 2   period 2

This is satisfied for $\delta(1-\alpha) > \frac{1}{2}$. In period 1 the decision is similar. If it defects in period 1 it earns 2 then nothing thereafter. If it cooperates, then it expects to earn 1 in period 1, 1 in period 2 (from the foregoing argument) and $(1-\alpha)2$ in period 3. The expected discounted profits from cooperation in period 1 are thus $1 + \delta + \delta(1-\alpha)2$. If $\delta(1-\alpha) > \frac{1}{2}$ then, again, cooperation is period 1 yields higher expected profits than defection. Thus the above strategy is subgame perfect if the proportion of Triggers is high enough $(1-\alpha) > \frac{1}{2}\delta$.

With uncertainty, then, it can be an equilibrium to have both firms cooperating initially during the game and only to defect towards the end of the game (the last period in the above example). The intuition is simple enough: by playing cooperatively in the first two periods the Rat hides his true nature from his competitors. There is a 'pooling' equilibrium early on: both Rats and Triggers cooperate so that cooperation yields no additional information about the firm's type to alter the 'priors' based on population proportions α, $(1 - \alpha)$. One problem with this account – for neo-classical economists at least – is the need to assume the existence of non-rational players to sustain the collusive outcome. This is a problem in two senses. Firstly, there are an indefinite number of ways to be non-rational: alongside the Trigger, the bestiary of the non-rational includes the 'Tit-for-Tats' (Kreps *et al.*, 1982) and many other fantastical possibilities. Secondly, the methodology of most economics is based on an axiom that all agents are rational maximisers. It might be said that all that is required for such equilibria is the *belief* that there are some non-rational players. While this may be so, it would seem less than satisfactory if the belief were not justified by the existence of the required proportion a of Triggers.

This sort of equilibrium with imperfect information is called a *sequential equilibrium* and has the added ingredient that firms use the history of the game to learn about each other's type by Bayesian updating. The equilibrium strategies in the example need not be unique: for some values of δ and α it is also an equilibrium for Rats to defect throughout the game, as in the full-information case. However, there exists the possibility of sustaining cooperative behaviour for some part of the game even with a limited period of play. The use of sequential equilibria has been applied to several areas of interest and industrial economists – most notably entry deterrence (Milgrom and Roberts, 1982a,b).

7 CONCLUSIONS

This chapter has tried to present some of the basic results in the recent literature on oligopoly theory in relation to product market competition. Given the vastness of the oligopoly literature past and present, the coverage has been limited. For those interested in a more formal game-theoretic approach, Lockwood (1987) is excellent (particularly on repeated games and optimal punishment strategies). On the growing literature on product differentiation, Ireland (1986) is comprehensive. Vickers (1985b) provides an excellent survey of the new industrial economics with particular emphasis on its policy implications.

Notes

1 a^*_{-i} is the $n-1$ vector of all firms' strategies excepting i's.
2 See Debreu (1952), Glicksberg (1952) and Fan (1952). Strict concavity is a stronger condition than we need – it can be relaxed to quasiconcavity.
3 A sufficient condition for uniqueness is that each firm's reaction function is a 'contraction mapping' – see Friedman (1978) for a formal definition.
4 Note the change in the use of the word 'strategy'. In a one-shot game, the firm's strategy is simply the action it pursues. In a repeated game, 'action' and 'strategy' cease to be equivalent, 'strategy' being its 'game plan', the rule by which the firm chooses its action in each period.
5 Bayesian updating means that firms have subjective probabilities which they update according to Bayes' rule. Firms start the game with 'prior' beliefs, and revise these to take into account what happens. This is a common way to model learning in neoclassical models.

6   This simply states that x_i is chosen to equate marginal revenue with marginal cost.

7   The reason for this non-existence is quite simple – step 3 of our intuitive proof breaks down and the competitive price need not be an equilibrium. The competitive price is an equilibrium with constant returns because when one firm raises its price the other is willing and able to expand its output to meet all demand. However, if firms have rising marginal cost curves they are supplying as much as they want to at the competitive price (they are on their supply functions). If one firm raises its price there will be excess demand for the firm(s) still setting the competitive price. The firm raising its price will thus face this unsatisfied residual demand and, in general, will be able to raise its profits by so doing (see Dixon, 1987a: theorem 1). One response to this non-existence problem is to allow for *mixed* strategies (rather than firms setting a particular price with probability one, they can set a range of prices each with a particular probability). Mixed-strategy equilibria exist under very general assumptions indeed (Dasgupta and Maskin, 1986a,b) and certainly exist under a wide range of assumptions in the Bertrand framework (Dasgupta and Maskin, 1986a; Dixon, 1984; Dixon and Maskin, 1985; Maskin, 1986). However, the analysis of mixed-strategy equilibria is relatively complex and it has yet to be seen how useful it really is. It can be argued that it is difficult to see that mixed strategies reflect a genuine aspect of corporate policy.

8   The standard models of Bertrand competition assume that outputs are demand-determined (see (6.11)) : each firm's output is equal to the demand for it. This was the assumption made by Chamberlin (1933) in his analysis of monopolistic competition. This is appropriate with constant costs since firms will be willing to supply any quantity at the price they have set (for $p_i \geqslant c$, profits are increasing in output). More generally, however, it is very strong. Surely firms will only meet demand insofar as it raises the firm's profits. With rising marginal cost the output that the firm wishes to produce given the price it has set is given by its supply function (the output that the firm wishes to produce given the price it has set is given by its supply function). If demand exceeds this quantity and there is *voluntary trading* then the firm will turn customers away (otherwise marginal cost would exceed price). This approach is similar to Edgeworth's (1925) analysis of the homogeneous case – see Dixon (1987b) and Bénassy (1986). Bénassy (1989) has analysed the implications of including an Edgeworthian voluntary trading constraint on price-setting equilibria. While the Nash equilibrium prices will be the same there is, however, an existence problem: if demand is highly cross-elastic between firms then no equilibrium may exist.

9   The formula can be obtained by total differentiation of the implicit function $\pi_1(a_i, a_j) = \theta$.

10 'Investment' can be taken as any fixed factor – capital, R&D, firm-specific human capital and so on.

11 Long-run average cost is derived as follows. Minimise total costs $rK + L$ with respect to the production function constraint A4. Since the production function displays constant returns, long-run average and marginal cost are equal.

12 The profit frontier in Figure 6.13 is derived under the common framework A1–2. Linearity comes from constant returns with a homogeneous product. The actual solution is that *total* output on the frontier equals the monopoly output M, with total profits at their monopoly level μ. λ determines firms' share of output and profit:

$$x_1 = \mu M; \quad \pi_1 = \lambda\mu; \quad x_2 = (1-\lambda)M; \quad \pi_2 = (1-\lambda)\mu$$

With diminishing returns, i.e. a strictly convex function, the profit frontier will have a concave shape.

7 Some Thoughts on Economic Theory and Artificial Intelligence

1 INTRODUCTION

In this chapter I will offer some thoughts on the potential contribution of Artificial Intelligence (AI) to economic theory. I write as someone who is at present an orthodox economic theorist and who has only recently been introduced to the ideas and achievements of modern artificial intelligence. My overall impression is that artificial intelligence does have a potential to offer to economic theory, both in terms of providing a fruitful perspective from which to view currently problematic issues, and through raising new and interesting problems that have been hitherto marginalised or ignored.

In my view, the main potential contribution of artificial intelligence to economic theory lies in providing a practical methodology for modelling reasoning, and hence rationality. Economic decision-making is one of many human activities which can be said to display 'intelligence', since it involves potentially complex reasoning and problem-solving. Artificial intelligence is a branch of computing which aims to design machines which can perform such 'intelligent' activities; as such, it has much to say about how humans go about solving problems. There now exists a wide body of research on artificial intelligence in a variety of applications which may well prove useful to economic theorists.

However, the current orthodox approach of economic theory to rationality is well-established and simple. Advocates of artificial intelligence need to demonstrate clearly why there is a need to change perspective, and how it will pay off in terms of theoretical understanding. Therefore in the next section I explore both the current orthodox model of 'rationality without reasoning', and in particular I consider to what extent it can be extended to embrace 'bounded rationality'. As I will argue, I believe that by generalising strict optimisation to approximate optimisation we can maintain the simplicity of the current orthodoxy without needing explicitly to model problem-solving with artificial-intelligence techniques. Following on, I take the more positive approach of considering how artificial-intelligence techniques can make a useful contribution in modelling the behaviour of economic agents in complex decision situations. In particular, I describe the use of finite automata to model the complexity of strategies, and also the issues arising from the choice of strategies. To put matters very simply, insofar as agents tend to 'get things right' in the sense of choosing an action or solution close to the optimum, we (as economists) need not really worry about how the decision is arrived at. The role for artificial intelligence seems to me to have the greatest potential in situations where agents make mistakes. This potential is, of course, of great relevance to the study of disequilibrium, an area of economics that has proven notoriously difficult within the orthodox model of rationality. Lastly, in the fourth section I consider the implications of modelling reasoning in strategic environments. Insofar as the method of solving a problem might influence the action you choose, reasoning itself can be a method of pre-commitment. This is illustrated in the context of Cournot duopoly.

I would like to acknowledge my debt to the writings of Herbert Simon: whilst I have not referenced his works explicitly or in detail, his ideas were formative in my education and have clearly influenced the way I look at things.

2   ORTHODOX ECONOMIC RATIONALITY: RATIONALITY WITHOUT REASONING

At the heart of orthodox economics beats a model of rationality. The economic conception of rationality has become embodied by the mathematical theory of constrained optimisation. Put at its simplest, a rational agent is conceived of as choosing the best option open to him, given his constraints. The historical basis of this lies in utilitarianism, and in particular the Utilitarian psychology of individual action, which saw mankind placed 'under the governance of two sovereign masters, pain and pleasure' (Bentham, 1789, p. 33). Although more recently economics has eschewed utilitarian psychology due to problems of measurement of cardinal utilities, the notion of maximisation itself has become, if anything, more central. If we consider the salient features of economic rationality, three points are worth highlighting in the present context.

1   There is no modelling of reasoning. The process or procedure of reasoning is viewed as unimportant in itself, and the outcome inevitable. If a solution (maximum) exists, then the rational agent will arrive at that solution; agents costlessly choose their best option.
2   Technical assumptions are made to ensure that a well-defined maximum exists. This usually involves two sorts of assumptions: first, to ensure that a well-defined continuous objective function can be specified; second, to ensure that the agents' choice set is compact.[1] It is often easy to forget how many assumptions are made by economists just to ensure both of these criteria are satisfied, so as to ensure the existence of a maximum.
3   If it is not possible to impose plausible restrictions to ensure the existence of well-defined maximum, there exists no obvious, typical, or generally accepted solution to the problem.

Let us illustrate this with reference to standard consumer theory. A household is assumed to have preferences over possible outcomes, which are taken to be suitably defined bundles of commodities which it might consume. These preferences

are 'represented' by a utility function, which assigns to each bundle a real number, with the property that bundles which are preferred have higher numbers. If
we turn to the first issue, a well-defined utility function is ensured by four
assumptions: (i) the 'sanity clause' of reflexivity that each bundle is at least as
good as itself; (ii) that preferences are complete, so that any two bundles can be
compared to each other; (iii) that preferences are transitive, so that if A is preferred to B, and B to C, then A is preferred to C; (iv) continuity, so that if one
bundle is strictly preferred to another, there is a bundle in between that is also
strictly preferred. It should be noted that the assumptions of transitivity and
continuity in particular are required only for mathematical reasons, rather than
any fundamental notions of rationality. The second issue of compactness is rather
easier to ensure: the household is restricted to choosing its utility-maximising
bundle from its budget set, which is closed and bounded (at least if all prices are
strictly positive).

The main feature of the orthodox model of economic rationality is that there is
no modelling of the reasoning processes of agents, or of how decisions are reached.
The formal maximisation process is simply stated, and if a maximum exists it is
assumed that an action yielding the maximum is chosen. This can be seen as a
model of rationality without reasoning, a 'black box' or even 'empty box' approach
to behaviour. The great attraction of the approach is that it means that economic
theory can largely ignore the potentially complex and diverse processes of reasoning and decision-making underlying the behaviour of individual economic agents
and organisations. This yields a very simple model of rationality. Whilst it has been
criticised for its very simplicity, in that it ignores much real-world complexity, it
has certainly delivered results and proven itself in many contexts.

In order to convince economists of its value, advocates of artificial intelligence
need to demonstrate that there is both a clear need and payoff to model reasoning itself.

Whilst simplicity is perhaps the most cogent defence of orthodox economic
rationality, another important defence is that it can easily be extended to encom-
pass bounded rationality. Given that some economic environments are complex
and uncertain, so that strictly defined optimising may be inappropriate, it still
may be unnecessary to deviate from the orthodox model. Whatever line of reasoning, search procedure, or algorithm agents may use, rational agents may be
reasonably assumed to get 'near' to the strictly defined optimum. A very simple
way to model this is to assume that agents ε-optimise: they choose an action that
yields them within ε of their best payoff. Let us specify this a little more formally.
Suppose that an agent chooses an action, a, that is chosen from the closed interval $[0,A]$, and that its payoff function $U_i\colon [0,A]\to R$ is continuous. Then there
exists a maximum, U^*, which is yielded by some a^*:

$$a^* = \arg\max U(a)$$

This is depicted in Figure 7.1, where the optimal a^* is assumed unique. It might
be argued that in a particular context the agent will not be willing or able to

inevitably choose a^*. Rather, the agent might adopt some heuristic search procedure or rule of thumb that might get reasonably close to optimum in terms of payoff. The details of the precise line of reasoning taken need not (it can be argued) concern the economist. Rather, whatever the route taken, the agent can be said to be ε-maximising, or choosing actions which yield payoffs within ε of the maximum. Given the continuity of $U(\cdot)$, there will in general be a set of such acceptable solutions, defined for $\varepsilon > 0$ by:

$$A^\varepsilon = \{a \in [0, A]: U(a) \geqslant U(a^*) - \varepsilon\}$$

This set is depicted in Figure 7.1. Two points need making. Firstly, the concept of ε-maximisation is a generalisation of strict optimisation: a^* is always an acceptable solution, and when $\varepsilon = 0$ it is the only acceptable solution. Secondly, the choice of ε is more or less arbitrary, although it is usually taken to be more acceptable if it is 'small'.

A simple generalisation of the orthodox approach is thus sufficient to capture some elements of bounded rationality without the need explicitly to model reasoning. As in the case of strict optimisation, approximate optimisation goes straight from the statement of the problem to the set of approximate solutions. Corresponding to the notion of ε-maximisation is the notion of an ε-equilibrium. For example, a Nash ε-equilibrium is defined in much the same way as a 'strict' Nash equilibrium. Suppose now that there are two agents, $i = 1, 2$, choosing actions a_i from compact strategy sets A_i, and continuous payoff functions

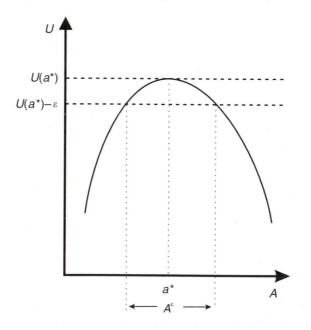

Figure 7.1   *ε-Optimisation*

$U_i(a_1, a_2)$. An ε-equilibrium occurs when both players choose actions (a_1^*, a_2^*) which yield them within ε of their best payoff given the action of the other player. Formally, for player 1 (and analogously for 2) (a_1^*, a_2^*) satisfies:

$$U_1(a_1^*, a_2^*) \geqslant U_1(a_1, a_2^*) - \varepsilon \qquad \text{for all } a_1 \in A_1$$

This can be represented by 'reaction correspondences', where a reaction *correspondence*[2] gives the player actions that yield within ε of his best response given the other player's action. For player 1, we have $r_1: A_2 \Rightarrow A_1$:

$$r_1(a_2) = \{a_1 \in A_1 : U_1(a_1, a_2) \geqslant \max_{a_1} U_1(a_1, a_2) - \varepsilon\}$$

These reaction correspondences are 'fat' because there is a set of ε-maximal responses to any action by the other agent. An ε-equilibrium occurs at any point in the intersection of the two reaction correspondences, as depicted in Figure 7.2. It should be noted *en passant* that in general there will be many (in the 'continuum' sense) ε-equilibria, and they may well be Pareto-ranked. To see this, merely consider what happens as ε gets large: for ε large enough, any conceivable outcome will be an ε-equilibrium! However, whilst multiplicity is endemic to ε-equilibria, it is not exclusive. There is no real reason why there should be unique strict optima and unique equilibria in strict Nash equilibria. They are usually ruled out for convenience sake, because models with unique and well-behaved equilibria are simpler to deal with.

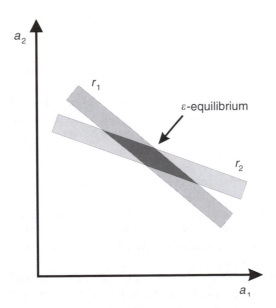

Figure 7.2 *Nash ε-equilibria*

The concept of bounded rationality as embodied in the notions of approximate optimisation and equilibria, whilst not in general usage, is certainly not uncommon. Well-known recent examples include Akerlof and Yellen's work on business cycles (Akerlof and Yellen, 1985), and Radner's work on cooperation in the finitely repeated prisoner's dilemma (Radner, 1980). The notion of ε-equilibrium has been often used when no strict equilibrium exists (see, *inter alia*, Hart, 1979; Dixon, 1987a).

The notion of ε-optimisation is a simple generalisation of strict-optimisation that maintains its parsimony. The details of reasoning need not be considered, and it is not mathematically difficult to deal with. However, there still seems to me to be further conceptually simple extensions of the more-or-less orthodox that can be used to try and capture aspects of bounded rationality without the need to model reasoning. One possibility that has not (I believe) been explored, is to treat the rational player's decision as a type of mixed strategy. The decision-making process might have general properties: it would be more likely to choose a better outcome; it might be able to avoid payoffs that are particularly bad, and so on. Again, this would be a generalisation of strict-optimisation (which puts a probability of one on the maximal, and zero elsewhere).

Whilst this approach has not been pursued, I believe it to be indicative of the fact that there are many possible extensions to the orthodox model that maintain its key advantages of simplicity and parsimony. The task for artificial intelligence is to show that it can yield something more than can be obtained by developing the orthodox approach.

3   COMPLEXITY AND ARTIFICIAL INTELLIGENCE

I have described orthodox economic rationality as 'rationality without reasoning'. If a problem is sufficiently simple and well-defined so that there exists a solution which is easily computable, the precise method of solution adopted may not matter. For example, a non-singular square matrix can be inverted by different techniques, all of which will yield the same solution if applied correctly. However, for complicated problems it may be the case that although we know a solution (optimum) exists, we do not know how to find it with certainty. Even worse, we may not know if a solution exists at all. In such a situation, the precise form of reasoning may be important, because it will determine the types of actions or decisions arrived at. In this context I am equating 'reasoning' with a particular method of searching for a solution (an algorithm). More importantly, different methods of searching for a solution may tend to yield different types of outcomes. In this context the choice of reasoning itself can become a strategic decision, as I will discuss in the next section.

There are two dimensions of complexity that deserve the particular consideration of economists, which I will outline in this section. Firstly, there is the complexity of *strategies*; secondly, there is the complexity of *choice of strategies*. I shall now briefly discuss these two issues.

Taking a cue from standard game theory, a strategy can be seen as a rule for choosing actions, in which the action chosen is a function of the information available to an agent. At any time, the 'information' available might be taken to consist of all of the past actions of various players, plus the realisations of various exogenous parameters. For example, an oligopolist at time t might know the history of play up to time t in the sense of knowing all the choices of outputs by itself and other firms, as well as (for example) the past realisations of demand. If we denote this 'history' at time t as h_t, a strategy is a rule (or in mathematical terms, a mapping) that tells the firm at any time t what action to take given h_t:

$$x_t = r(h_t, t)$$

In informal terms, the strategy can be seen as a 'game plan' for the firm, telling it what to do in every possible contingency. In standard game theory, there is no limit to the complexity of the strategies chosen by agents. Furthermore, some of the results of game theory require very complicated strategies to support equilibria (for example, the 'carrot and stick' punishment strategies supporting equilibria in Folk theorems).

Various authors (Rubenstein, 1986; Abreu and Rubenstein, 1988; Kalai and Stanford, 1988) have argued that some limits or constraints need to be put on the complexity of strategies chosen. A popular way of capturing 'complexity' in this context is to use the notion of a 'Moore machine' or 'finite automaton' as a way of representing a strategy. A finite automaton is a machine with a finite set of states, and a specified initial state. It then has two rules: one specifies what action it takes at time t as a function of its state at time t; the second is a transition rule which specifies what its state in time $t+1$ will be as a function of both its state in time t and the action of the other player at time t. The size of the automaton (its 'computing power') is captured by the number of states it has: '… the complexity of a strategy will be identical with the size (number of states) of the smallest automaton which is able to implement it' (Kalai and Stanford, 1988).

This can easily be illustrated by a couple of examples using 'transition diagrams' to represent the automaton (see Rubenstein, 1986, for a full and lucid exposition). Let us take the standard prisoner's dilemma game, where there are two agents, $i = 1, 2$, each with two strategies, C (cooperate) and D (defect), with payoffs as in Table 7.1. The automaton can be represented by $<Q_i, q^0, \lambda_i \mu_i>$ where Q_i is the set of states; $q^0 \in Q_i$ is the initial state; λ_i gives the action a_i as a function of state q_i, and μ_i is the transition rule giving the next period's state. The

Table 7.1   *The prisoner's dilemma (PD)*

		Player 2	
		C	D
	C	2, 2	0, 3
Player 1			
	D	3, 0	1, 1

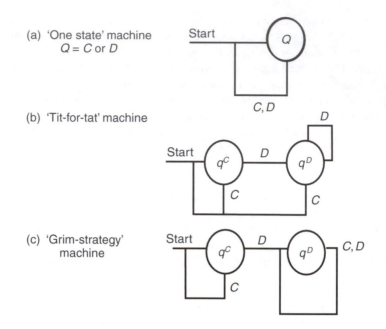

(a) 'One state' machine
    $Q = C$ or D

(b) 'Tit-for-tat' machine

(c) 'Grim-strategy'
    machine

Figure 7.3   *Strategies as finite automata*

simplest strategy is generated by a 'one-state' machine, where $Q_1 = q^0 = Q$, $\mu(Q) = Q$, and either $\lambda_i(Q) = C$ or $\lambda_i(Q) = D$. That is, a 'one-state' machine can only cooperate (or defect) all of the time: because it only has one state it can only ever choose one action, as depicted in Figure 7.3a. In order to respond, the automaton requires more states and more complicated transition rules. Let us consider a two-state machine, with one state, q^D, for defection, and one, q^C, for cooperation. The 'tit-for-tat' strategy is when the player cooperates until the other player defects, in which case he punishes the defection by playing D himself for one period before returning to C (see Axelrod, 1984). The automaton implementing this strategy is represented in Figure 7.3b, and is defined by a set of states $Q = \{q^C, q^D\}$, initial state $q^0 = q^C$, action rule $\lambda(q^a) = a(a = D, S)$, and transition rule $\mu(q, a) = q_a(a = D, S)$. The 'grim' punishment strategy punishes a defection forever, and is represented in Figure 7.3c. The 'grim punishment' automaton has an initial state, q^C. If the other automaton ever plays D, the machine switches to its defect state q^D, where it remains forever. The main point is that the automaton with more states can implement more complicated strategies.

Using the model of a finite automaton to represent a strategy, Rubenstein *et al.* have represented a game as involving agents choosing machines rather than strategies. The players 'optimise' over the choice of their machines (strategies), and then the machines play the game. As such, this approach ignores issues of computational complexity, and focuses merely on the issue of implementational complexity. Abreu and Rubenstein (1988) draw the analogy of sophisticated managers formulating simple operating rules for the firm.

The issue of computational complexity is central to artificial intelligence. Some problems are simple enough to have a deterministic method which will (nearly) always arrive at a solution. Consider the 'travelling salesman' problem:

> A salesman has a list of cities, each of which he must visit exactly once. There are direct roads between each pair of cities on the list. Find the route the salesman should follow so that he travels the shortest possible distance on a round trip, starting at any one of the cities and then returning there.

The solution to this problem can be found simply by exploring the 'tree' of all the possible paths, and picking the shortest one. This 'brute force' method will work, but it becomes very expensive in terms of computational requirements. With N cities, there are $(N-1)!$ different routes: each route has N stretches. The total time required to explore the entire tree is then of order $N!$ – with only 10 cities this method clearly becomes very lengthy (10! is 3 625 800). This is known as the phenomenon of *combinatorial explosion*. Since computations are not costless, rational agents need to trade-off the computational cost of a decision or search procedure with the benefits in terms of the eventual payoff. The notion of efficiency is important here: a search process is more efficient if it obtains a higher payoff (on average) for the same or fewer computations (on average). Evolving efficient search strategy involves using *heuristics*, which are guides, short-cuts or rules of thumb that we believe will get us near enough to the solution with reasonable computational requirements. For example, the travelling salesman problem can be solved using the useful general purpose heuristic of the *nearest neighbour algorithm*:

1   Select any city as your starting point.
2   To select the next city, consider the cities not yet visited. Go to the city closest to the one you are currently at.
3   Repeat 2 until all of the cities have been visited.

This algorithm requires far fewer computations than 'brute force': we need to visit N cities, and at each stage we need to consider the distances between where we are and the as yet unvisited cities, of which there will be on average $(N-1)/2$. Computational time is therefore proportional to $N(N-1)/2$, or more simply N^2, which is far superior to $N!$ The nearest neighbour algorithm need not yield the shortest route: Bentley and Saxe (1980) have found empirical evidence that when cities are distributed at random it performs on average about 20% below the optimum. Much of practical artificial intelligence involves the construction and evaluation of heuristic search procedures (see, for example, Polya's (1957) classic).

One response to the issue of computational cost and decision-making is to maintain the notion of maximising behaviour, but simply to add in a constraint reflecting costs of decision, computation or whatever. This may be reasonable in particular applications. For example, much of standard theory assumes that it is costless to change or adjust variables. It is simple enough in principle to introduce costs of decision or adjustment into our economic models (see, for example, Dixon, 1987, for a discussion of menu costs). However, this approach cannot answer the general problem. If one is unable to solve a simple optimisation problem X, it is unlikely that one can solve the more difficult problem, of optimising X subject to some computational constraint. This sort of *super-optimisation* is not the answer to an initial failure of a simpler optimisation problem. Rather, agents are forced to adopt reasonable decision procedures rather than the optimal.

The notion that many fundamental economic decisions are complex and uncertain has of course a long pedigree in economics, with its notions of rules of thumb (see Cyert and March, 1963; Hall and Hitch, 1939; Simon, 1947, *inter alia*). However, as I argued in the previous section, we can relax the assumption of strict-optimisation to ε-optimisation, which still largely maintains the 'empty box' methodology of rationality without reasoning. If agents use various heuristic techniques or rules of thumb, then presumably they will yield payoffs that are close to the optimal in some sense. In this case the precise nature of the heuristic need not bother us. The argument is really no different than in the case of 'perfect rationality', where we can predict the optimal choice irrespective of the method of solution. The only difference is that whereas the orthodox approach predicts that agents arrive at an optimal solution, we can relax this to a prediction that the agent will arrive close to the solution.

If economics is to abandon its model rationality without reasoning, it needs to be shown that there is a need to look at reasoning itself. In a complex decision problem, we may not be able to find a solution or optimum with certainty, and indeed may not even know if a solution exists. The method of reasoning, or searching for a solution may in these circumstances be important, because it will determine the actions and decisions of agents, and hence different methods may yield (or tend to yield) different types of outcomes. If we are not confident that the method of reasoning will tend to yield solutions close to the optimum, then the matter is different. I believe that the method of reasoning becomes most important when we need to understand and explain why agents make decisions that deviate considerably from the optimum. Almost paradoxically, reasoning is important only when it leads to mistakes. We only need to understand the mechanics of the rational agent's decision process when they fail.

Let me illustrate this with the example of the previous section, where an agent has to maximise a continuous function, $U(a)$, over the interval $[0, A]$. Suppose that the function is as depicted in Figure 7.4. We can see that analytically there exists a unique global optimum at a^*: this is the choice predicted by standard economic theory. Approximate optimisation would perhaps predict a point close to a^*. However, suppose that our agent is in the situation of having to optimise without knowing what U looks like. He can compute the particular value of U at particular point $a \in [0, A]$, and its gradient (or whatever) if defined, but only at a cost. The problem is rather like that of an econometrician trying to maximise a complicated non-linear likelihood function. There are different ways of going about this sort of problem, all of which are considered 'reasonable'. Several methods are variants of hill-climbing algorithms, as used from a point a_0 chosen at random (or by informed guess). You then compute both the value of the function and the gradient at that point: $U(a_0)$ and $U'(a_0)$. You then move a certain distance (perhaps specified by you) in the direction of steepest ascent. You stop when the function is sufficiently 'flat' and concave: usually this is defined by some predefined tolerance $d > 0$, so that 'flat' means $|U'| < d$. Depending on the costs of computing relative to likely gains, you may wish to start several ascents from different points. Two points are worth noting about such search procedures. Firstly, they will almost always fail to reach the solution A^*: $\{a^*\}$ is a singleton in the interval $[0, A]$, and is of measure zero, and hence in a loose but clear way, a^* will almost certainly never be chosen. However, as more and more points are computed, the sample maximum will tend towards the global maximum (this is ensured by the continuity of $U(a)$). For a survey of econometric applications see Quandt (1983, chapter 12).

The shortcomings of hill-climbing algorithms are well-known (and concern 'spikes', 'ridges' and 'plateaux'). It is clearly an 'intelligent' search process that is more efficient than random search. However, depending on what the functions to be maximised look like, hill-climbing may or may not be expected to get close to the optimum. Let us consider the example of Figure 7.4: there are three local optima $(0, a^*, a^{**})$. If the agent starts to hill-climb in the interval $[0, a']$ he will tend towards 0; in the interval $[a', a'']$, he will tend towards the global optimum

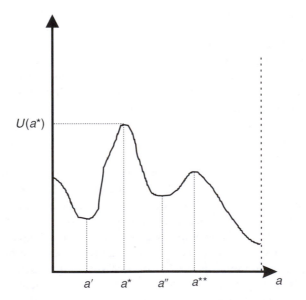

Figure 7.4   *Explaining a mistake*

a^*; if $[a'', A]$ he will tend towards a^{**} (assuming that at points (a', a'') the hill-climbing routine is equally likely to go in either direction). Our prediction of the agents eventual choice of action would depend upon the number of computations available. However, if $[a', a'']$ is small relative to $[0, A]$, we would certainly need to put a positive probability on all actions close to each local optimum. Furthermore, as drawn, it is clear that if only a few computations are made, then it is much more likely that the largest value computed will be close to $U(a^{**})$, since $[a'', A]$ is much larger than $[0, a']$ or $[a', a'']$.

Suppose that we observed an agent choosing action a^{**}, how might we explain it? Orthodox strict-optimisation would be powerless: the optimum is $U(a^*)$, and it has not been chosen. The mistake is inexplicable. In practice, no doubt, the route of super-optimisation would be pursued: the agent had a set of priors over $U(\cdot)$ and chose a^{**} to maximise the expected payoff. However, to repeat: *super-optimisation is not an adequate response to the failure of optimisation in the face of computational complexity. If you cannot solve a simple problem, it is unlikely that you can solve a more difficult one*! However, if we abandon the option of rationality without reasoning, matters are easier to explain: 'our agent adopted a hill-climbing algorithm. Given a limited number of computations this was quite likely to end near a^{**}. This can be explained even though a^{**} is nowhere near the optimal choice a^*, and $U(a^{**})$ is only half $U(a^*)$.

It is worth pausing here to state this argument so far, and put it in context. First, economists need not concern themselves with how economic agents solve problems if those agents successfully optimise or near optimise. We can explain and predict their behaviour as the solution of an optimisation or ε-optimisation problem. If, however, agents make 'mistakes' by choosing actions that are far from the optimal, and/or yield payoffs significantly below the maximum, matters are rather different. Then, in order to explain the specific choice, we will need to model the reasoning underlying the choice. I have given the example of a hill-climbing algorithm yielding a sub-optimal local maximum. Again, if we consider applying the nearest neighbour algorithm to the travelling salesman problem, from some starting points it will yield terrible solutions. The role for artificial intelligence in economics would then seem primarily to be in situations where economic agents make mistakes, and possibly bad mistakes. This is in some ways a paradoxical role for artificial intelligence.

However, it is a role with great potential, not least in modelling disequilibrium. I have discussed the concept of equilibrium elsewhere in *Equilibrium and Explanation* (1990, and Chapter 2 this volume). There are perhaps three properties that define equilibrium: firstly agents' actions are consistent (in some sense the actions of different agents 'add up'): secondly, agents are behaving optimally in equilibrium, and so have no incentive to deviate from their equilibrium actions; and thirdly, the equilibrium is the outcome of some adjustment process. If we focus on the second property, in a Nash equilibrium, each agent's actions I optimal give the action of other agents. In disequilibrium, however, agents' actions need neither be consistent, nor optimal. This causes agents to revise and adjust their behaviour, which may (or may not) drive the economic system under consideration towards equilibrium. It is the essence of disequilibrium that agents make mistakes. For this reason, the analysis of disequilibrium has been very problematic for economics. There seems to me to be a role for artificial intelligence in modelling disequilibrium systems, by specifying the decision rules used by economic agents. The firm, for example, can be viewed as an 'expert system' which will have some capacity for performing well in a variety of equilibrium and disequilibrium situations, but which may perform badly in others. Indeed, the standard 'myopic' adjustment rule used by Cournot in his analysis of stability can be thought of as just such a decision rule. The firm treats the output of the other as fixed and optimises against it. In disequilibrium this may not be a good decision rule, although in equilibrium it may be 'reasonable'.

4   REASONING AS PRECOMMITMENT: AN EXAMPLE

In the previous section I argued that artificial intelligence has a role in economics to explain how agents make mistakes in disequilibrium. In disequilibrium a perfectly reasonable decision rule may lead an agent to make sub-optimal decisions. As agents adjust their behaviour in response to such mistakes, there will (perhaps) be a movement towards equilibrium. In this section we will reverse the line of reasoning. In a strategic situation (e.g. oligopoly), there may be an incentive for firms to make 'mistakes'. In this case, agents may wish to adopt forms of reasoning that lead to actions which are in some strategic sense 'desirable', although they might in another sense not be optimal.

Perhaps the most important impact of artificial intelligence on economics will be that in modelling reasoning, it brings reasoning itself into the domain of choice, and hence opens it to strategic considerations. If an agent is perfectly rational, his behaviour is in a sense thereby restricted to a particular action (or set of actions), and hence becomes predictable. Given that a firm's objective is to maximise profits, it will choose its 'optimal' profit-maximising price/output. Even if it were in the strategic interests of the firm to do otherwise, the rational firm is 'unable' to do anything other than the optimal. This is essentially the insight that lies behind the concepts of subgame perfection and dynamic inconsistency. In each period, agents are restricted to behaving optimally; this fact can then be used to predict their behaviour and hence the future course and outcome of play.

However, suppose that we drop the assumption of rational intuition, that if a solution exists to a problem the rational agent intuits it directly. Suppose instead that an agent has to choose how to solve a problem. The choice of how he chooses to solve a problem, his decision rule, will determine (to some extent) his eventual choice of action. Economic agents can therefore use their choice of decision algorithm as a form of precommitment to certain actions. As is well-known, in a wide class of games there is an incentive for firms to precommit themselves.

This is perhaps best illustrated by an example, for which I will use Cournot duopoly. I have discussed this elsewhere, in terms of oligopoly (Chapter 6 this volume) as well as its general significance as an equilibrium concept (Chapter 2). There are two firms, $i = 1, 2$, who choose outputs $X_i \geqslant 0$. Given these quantities, the price P clears the market via the inverse demand curve $P(X_1 + X_2)$, giving each firm i's profits as a function of both outputs (assuming costless production):

$$U_i(X_1, X_2) = X_i P(X_1 + X_2)$$

A Nash equilibrium is defined as a pair of outputs (X_1^*, X_2^*) such that each firm is choosing its profit-maximising output given the other firm's output. Formally:

$$X_1^* = \arg\max U_1(X_1, X_2^*)$$

and similarly for firm 2. In this sense, then, neither firm has an incentive to deviate given the other firm's choice. This is often represented in terms of reaction functions. Firm 1's reaction function, r, gives its profit-maximising output as a function of firm 2's reaction function (and likewise for firm 2):

$$X_1 = r_1(X_2) = \arg\max U_1(X_1, X_2)$$

The Nash equilibrium (X_1^*, X_2^*) occurs where both firms are on their reaction-functions, i.e. $X_1^* = r_1(X_2^*)$ and $X_2^* = r_1(X_1^*)$. This is depicted in Figure 7.5 at point N. Without precommitment, both firms have to be on their reactions-functions, since it is assumed that firms are rational optimisers. However, if a firm can precommit itself to take any action, then it need not be on its best-response function. As is

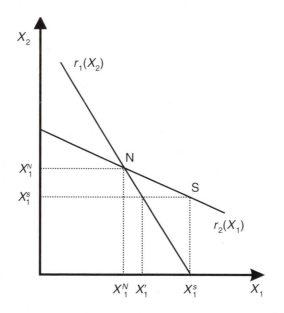

Figure 7.5 *Cournot duopoly*

well-known, if firm 1 can precommit itself to a larger output than X_1^*, it can increase its profits by moving down the other firm's reaction function. Under standard assumptions, the maximum profit for firm 1 to earn is at its Stackelburg point, S, to the right of N. At S, firm 1 is earning higher profits than it earned at N. There is thus an incentive to precommit. However, in the absence of precommitment, X_1^s is not a credible output for firm 1 to produce, since X_1^s is not the profit-maximising response to X_2^s (which is X_1'). In the absence of some form of precommitment, both firms are 'restricted' to being on their reaction functions, which result in the Nash equilibrium, N.

In standard economic models, with perfectly rational agents, precommitment has tended to be thought of in terms of some irreversible act or expenditure (e.g. investment in Brander and Spencer, 1983, or delegation in Vickers, 1985). However, in the case of bounded rationality, matters are rather different. *Firms can choose decision-making rules that tend to yield certain outcomes.* For example, in Cournot duopoly the firms have an incentive to precommit to an output larger than their profit-maximising Nash output, since this moves them towards their Stackelburg point. Thus firms might wish to adopt decision algorithms that tend to yield large outputs, that result in systematic overproduction relative to the 'optimum'. For example, if firms adopt some sort of hill-climbing algorithm, they can bias the solution to be above the optimum by tending to choose large outputs as initial positions. Such algorithms need to be told not only where to start, but when to stop. As mentioned in the previous section, the latter can be specified in terms of a threshold gradient: stop searching when the gradient falls below a certain level, $|U_i'| < d$. By starting from relatively large outputs and choosing a large d, the firm can precommit itself to choosing relatively large outputs.

5   CONCLUSION

In this chapter I have sought to achieve two objectives. Firstly, to state and defend the orthodox model of economic rationality. In particular, I wanted to explore the extent to which the orthodox approach has been and can be extended to embrace the notion of bounded rationality. Secondly, given this extended notion of orthodox rationality, I sought to explore what role artificial intelligence might have in economic theory. To conclude, I will simply summarise and restate the arguments in a schematic form.

Orthodox economic rationality is a model of rationality without reasoning. Insofar as economic agents tend to get things right – or almost right – we do not as theorists need to model how they solve their constrained-optimisation problems. In most economic models it is assumed that agents are 'strict' optimisers, who effortlessly optimise. Whilst this is an idealisation/simplification, it can easily be generalised to embrace bounded rationality by adopting the notion of ε-optimisation. In neither case is it necessary to consider in detail how agents actually decide what to do, their 'reasoning'. This is an advantage insofar as it means that economic theorists can avoid the complexities of the psychological and bureaucratic decision processes within individuals and organisations, and simply consider the objective problems (and solutions) themselves.

Given this extended notion of orthodox rationality, what role is there left for artificial intelligence? If orthodox rationality can handle decisions that yield optimal or near-optimal outcomes, it would appear that the main area for artificial intelligence to make a distinctive contribution is in situations where agents do not take decisions that yield optimal or near-optimal outcomes. I have highlighted two particular areas of possible research where this may be necessary: disequilibrium and strategic environments. In disequilibrium environments it is of the essence that agents make mistakes (otherwise we would be in equilibrium). For this very reason economic theorists have had great difficulty in modelling disequilibrium. In order to explain mistakes we need to understand not only the problem faced by agents, but the reasoning of agents, their method of solution. Artificial intelligence provides a practical framework for modelling the reasoning of economic agents in such situations. In strategic environments, agents can actually do better by behaving non-optimally. In such situations, it is thus in agents' strategic interests to make 'mistakes'. The actual method of reasoning used to solve the agents' problems can then be used as a form of precommitment, to influence the eventual outcomes.

This chapter has sought to define the limits and possibilities for artificial intelligence in economic theory, rather than make a positive and substantive contribution and application as found in other papers such as in Moss and Rae (1992). Whilst I do not see artificial intelligence as a new paradigm that will necessarily replace and supplant the orthodox economic model of rationality, it clearly has a great potential role, and one that will clearly become very important in future years.

Notes

1   'Compact' is a mathematical term meaning a set is closed and bounded.
2   A function $y = f(x)$ maps a value of x onto a single value of y; a *correspondence* maps a value of x onto one or more values of y.

8 Donut World and the Duopoly Archipelago: Social Learning and the Evolution of Competition

1 INTRODUCTION

The traditional approach to economics has been to assume that agents are rational and use all of the information they have in an optimal manner. However, as we have seen in the previous chapter, there are many arguments against this. At best, it is a modelling simplification, an 'as if' assumption made to make the process of understanding the economy and economic behaviour easier. There are *rationality fundamentalists* around, who believe optimising rationality is an essential part of human nature. I think that this is largely a credo with little or no justification, an act of faith by economists who want to have a single principle with which to understand economic phenomena. There are reasons why I reject the fundamentalists view. First, most economic decisions are made in the context of groups of people: the family/household, the firm, the union, the bank and so on. Even if individuals are 'rational', that does not imply that the decisions of groups will be 'as if' made by a single rational individual. Second, in practice individuals do not appear to act in ways consistent with rationality all the time:[1] they may learn to be rational, particularly in repeated situations where there is a lot to be gained or lost. But then again, some people end up making the same mistakes over and over again.

In recent years there has been a considerable revival of interest in the notions of learning in a *boundedly rational* context. This idea has of course been around for as long as economics itself. However, rather paradoxically, in the last decade the idea of boundedly rational processes has been revived in the field of game theory.[2] Game theory has traditionally been the area of economics where the belief in rationality has been the most intense. Indeed, many game theorists inhabit an artificial world where disembodied rational agents interact in a sea of common knowledge, able to perform all and any calculation the theorist might conceive. Without any constraints on the imagination, unencumbered by notions of firms or markets or any explicitly economic context, with a fascination for 2×2 games (the Prisoner's Dilemma an obsession) they create a *rationality wonderland*. In rationality wonderland, agents are perfectly rational, agents know the structure of the game and also know that all agents including themselves know that they know the game. This is called *common knowledge*. In order for a rational player to know what to do, she[3] needs do two things: first to guess what the other guy(s) are going to do; second to choose a best response to that action. Now, this problem involves an infinite regress: I need to predict the other player's behaviour to choose my best action; she needs to predict mine to choose her best action. So, I need to predict her prediction of my action; she needs to predict my prediction of her prediction of my prediction, and so on. This infinite regress is *solved* by game theorists uttering the incantation 'common knowledge' and then proposing that rational players would do what the game theorist wants them to. In my opinion the concept of common knowledge in incoherent, and arises because economists (in this case game theorists) try to extract too much from the basic idea of rationality.[4] However, dear reader, this is not the time nor place to explore this line of reasoning. Rationality wonderland is not our destination now: our destinations are *Donut World* and the *Duopoly Archipelago*. Before we set off, we will briefly consider *learning*.

Learning can be seen as taking place at two levels. *Individual* learning occurs when a single agent alters its beliefs and/or behaviour. Learning in this sense can take place if there is only one agent on its own without any interaction with another: for example, Robinson Crusoe was able to update his beliefs about farming and fishing techniques during his stay on the island. In the previous chapter on Artificial Intelligence and Economics I discussed some aspects of modelling the bounded rationality of individual agents. *Social* learning occurs within a population of agents and can only occur when there is more than one agent (indeed, usually a large number of agents is assumed). Whereas with individual learning it is the same individual who changes his behaviour, with social learning what matters is the evolution of the population behaviour: certain types of beliefs or behaviour might become more common within a population or society. Of course, some people would say that this is not 'learning' as such, since learning must involve some mental processes and the mental state of 'understanding'. However, this is an issue which lies beyond this chapter: I will simply follow the common usage and call all forms of adaptation and selection 'learning'.

An archetypal example of social learning is Darwinian natural selection. Suppose that we have a particular species: the giraffe. The giraffe develops a long neck so that it can eat leaves high up on trees.[5] Now, we can view this as a design problem: suppose that you were designing a giraffe. You can make the giraffe have a short neck or a long neck. There is a cost to a longer neck: it reduces mobility, uses up more energy and requires more food to keep it going and so on. It also has benefits: the giraffe has access to leaves that are beyond the reach of other land-based animals. The question is whether the costs outweigh the benefits. Individual giraffes never learn about this: they have the neck they are born with and that is it.[6] However, if the marginal benefit of a longer neck outweighs the marginal cost, the giraffes with longer necks will prosper and have more children who will tend to inherit the longer neck gene. This will go on until the point at which the marginal cost outweighs the benefits (or so the simple story goes). We can say that although no individual giraffe learns anything (they just hang out, eat leaves and try to avoid being eaten by lions), the giraffe species has 'learned' the solution to the problem of neck design. Now, this is perhaps a non-standard use of the term 'learn', but it is one which is standard in this literature, perhaps made more palatable in economics by the fact that we are not talking giraffes but humans. Darwinian natural selection is an extreme form of social learning: in economic models we might expect individuals to learn within the process of natural selection. There should be an interaction between individual and social learning.

The plan of this chapter is as follows. In the next section we will take a look at Antione Augustine Cournot's best response framework and the models of evolutionary biology (evolutionary stable strategies and the replicator dynamics). We will discover the close relationship between Cournot's concept of the Nash equilibrium and evolutionary equilibrium made clear by John Maynard Smith. As I shall argue, the assumption of random matching underlying the biological models are not appropriate for most economic phenomena. We shall then examine local interaction models which abandon the random matching assumption and replace it by agents interacting over time in a fixed network of relationships (Donut World), followed by an introduction to an explicitly economic context to the learning process. In the Duopoly Archipelago, there is a whole economy of markets, and within each market there are two firms playing some sort of market game. The new feature is that there is a capital market which imposes the discipline on all firms that they earn at least average profits in the long run: the capital market imposes a selection criterion, survival of those that manage to keep up with the population average – 'keeping up with the Joneses'. There we find the surprising result that each market in the economy is driven towards collusion.

2   SOCIAL LEARNING: FROM ANTOINE AUGUSTIN COURNOT TO JOHN MAYNARD SMITH

In this section I look at two types of learning model. The French economist Antoine Augustin Cournot (1801–77) is central to both, and in the 1980s John Maynard Smith extended the empire of economists from rational economic agents to the natural world of dumb beasts. First I will review Cournot's duopoly model as a learning model, and, second, I will review the biological model of evolution with random matching. What we shall see is that there is a very close relationship between evolutionary models and the economist's concept of a Nash equilibrium. Indeed, in his book *Evolution and the Theory of Games* the British evolutionary biologist John Maynard Smith showed that we can look at the outcome of evolutionary processes as a Nash equilibrium.

2.1   Cournot and Best-Response Dynamics

Let us start from the beginning, Cournot's familiar model of duopoly, as we have discussed in the previous Chapters 2 and 6. The process of adjustment to equilibrium involves an alternating move structure: we can think of time divided into discrete periods and firms alternately set their output for the next two periods. Cournot introduced the idea of the *myopic best-response* dynamic: the firm that sets its output in period t chooses the best response to the output currently produced by the other firm. Now, we can say two things about this simple 'society'. First, we can think of the firms as *learning* about each others' behaviour: each period they update their own beliefs about the other firm's output and adjusts their own behaviour appropriately. Also, the process will (under certain conditions) lead the firms to play the Nash[7] equilibrium in outputs. To see why, recall that any stationary point in this *learning* process occurs only when each firm is choosing a best response to the other firm, precisely as defined in the notion of a Nash equilibrium. We can see that there is a relationship between the learning process and the equilibrium here. The learning mechanism (myopic best response) defines a dynamic process (the time path of outputs); and the equilibrium can be thought of as a stationary point in this dynamic process that is stable. The Cournot adjustment process has been the subject of much criticism: why should firms be so myopic? However, in the context of bounded rationality, assuming agents are dumb is not such a bad thing! As we have discussed before, exactly how far to dumb down is a big issue.

2.2   Replication is the Name of the Game: Evolutionary Biology

Another type of social learning model comes from evolutionary biology. Although not easy to adapt to economic applications, lack of realism has not often deterred economists, so we proceed with the following model which can be seen as a metaphor or parable. Consider a population of economic agents who each live one period. They are randomly matched with each other in each generation. The economic agents have offspring: the payoff of the agent during its lifetime determines the number of its offspring. How will the population evolve over time? Well, we can define an agent by the action it takes (e.g. the level of output it chooses). We can then describe the population at time t by the proportions of each action which prevail at that time: for example, if there are three types of agent $\{A, B, C\}$, then we have the vector of the 3 population shares $[P_A, P_B, P_C]$ with $P_A + P_B + P_C = 1$. From an individual agent's point of view, what matters is the action played by its opponent when it is alive, since this determines its own payoff (it does not care about other agents' payoffs). However, from the point of view of the population, all that matters is how each particular type does: on the assumption of random matching, players of a particular type are evenly spread over the population. For example, if $P_A = 0.3$, $P_B = 0.2$ and $P_C = 0.5$, then if we take type A for example, 30% of type A agents will be playing type As, 20% type Bs and 50% type Cs. This can be represented by the array:

$$\begin{cases} P_{AA}=0.09 & P_{AB}=0.06 & P_{AC}=0.15 \\ P_{BA}=0.06 & P_{BB}=0.04 & P_{BC}=0.1 \\ P_{CA}=0.15 & P_{CB}=0.1 & P_{CC}=0.25 \end{cases}$$

The first row represents the distribution of type A: P_{AA} the proportion of type As matched with type As; P_{AB} the proportion of type As with matched with Bs and so on. The second row represents the distribution of type B agents over the population. With random matching, this distribution is easily calculated: $P_{Ai} = P_A \cdot P_i$ where $i = A, B, C$.

Now, let us suppose that there is a $n \times n$ payoff matrix Π with elements $\pi(i,j)$ which give the payoff to a strategy i when it plays a strategy j. With three strategies we have the 3×3 matrix:

$$\Pi = \begin{bmatrix} \pi(A,A) & \pi(A,B) & \pi(A,C) \\ \pi(B,A) & \pi(B,B) & \pi(B,C) \\ \pi(C,A) & \pi(C,B) & \pi(C,C) \end{bmatrix}$$

For example, the player 'type' or strategy might be outputs if the matched players play a Cournot duopoly game. This might not be very realistic: it is hard to imagine firms being randomly matched – one period you play a sock firm, the next a bicycle firm. However, continuing to ignore realism as an issue and for the purpose of exposition, let us suppose that the three types are actually output levels X_i:

Expository parable of the randomly matched Cournot duopolists

- When any two individual agents are matched, the industry demand they face is $P = 1 - X_i - X_j$.
- There are no costs.
- Type A produces output $X_A = 1/2$; type B produces $X_B = 1/3$; type C produces $X_C = 1/4$.

In this case we have the payoff matrix $\pi(i,j) = X_i(1 - X_i - X_j)$ – see Chapter 6 for more details – with payoffs both as exact fractions and decimals to 3 places.

$$\Pi = \begin{bmatrix} 1/8 & 5/48 & 1/16 \\ 5/36 & 1/9 & 1/15 \\ 1/8 & 1/10 & 0 \end{bmatrix} = \begin{bmatrix} 0.125 & 0.104 & 0.063 \\ 0.139 & 0.111 & 0.067 \\ 0.125 & 0.100 & 0.000 \end{bmatrix}$$

Clearly, there is a unique strict Nash Equilibrium here: both firms produce 1/3. This is the Cournot–Nash equilibrium. To see why, let us consider the best response of the row[8] player i. If firm j produced 1/4, then i's best response (look down the first column) is 1/3 (since $5/36 > 1/8$). If firm j plays 1/3, the best response is 1/3; if j plays 1/2 then 1/3 is also best. In fact, in this simple example, strategy B (1/3) is a *dominant strategy*: whatever the other player does, an output of 1/3 yields the best payoff – the second row has the largest element in each column. Of course, we could have constructed things so that there was no dominant strategy, but the types chosen are salient: 1/4 is the joint-profit maximising strategy; 1/2 is both the Stackelberg leaders output and half the Walrasian output. Having outlined the basic structure of the model, we now need to consider the population dynamics: we will take the example of the *replicator dynamics*.

2.3   The Replicator Dynamics: Even Educated Fleas Do It

The basic idea behind the *replicator dynamics* is simple: strategies that have a higher payoff have more offspring: their share of the population gets bigger. Success breeds success, failures fade away. Let us have a quick look at the mathematics (for those who do not like equations, move straight to the next section).

The average payoff of strategy i at time t ($\Pi_i(t)$) is defined as the weighted sum of its payoffs playing each strategy, where the weights are the population proportions. Hence for strategy A

$$\Pi_A(t) = P_A(t) \cdot \pi(A, A) + P_B(t) \cdot \pi(A, B) + P_C \pi(t)(A, C)$$

whilst the *average payoff* over all firms at time t is the weighted average of the payoffs off each strategy over the whole population

$$\Pi(t) = \sum P_i \Pi_i(t) = P_A(t) \Pi_A(t) + P_B(t) \Pi_B(t) + P_C(t) \Pi_C(t)$$

We can now model the process of evolution. The simplest form is to suppose that the population dynamics are given by the *replicator dynamics*:

$$g_i(t) = \frac{P_i(t+1)}{P_i(t)} = \left[\frac{\Pi_i(t)}{\Pi(t)} \right]$$

The growth of the proportion of type i is equal to the ratio of its payoff to the population average. The point here is that the proportion of a particular type increases (decreases) in proportion to the extent that its payoff is above (below) average. There is a simple story underlying this: the number of offspring is a linear function of the actual payoff.[9]

2.4   Alien Invasions and the Evolutionary Stable Strategy (ESS)[10]

John Maynard Smith, the British evolutionary biologist, introduced the concept of the evolutionary stable strategy. An ESS strategy is one which is stable if there is a small invasion by another strategy. Suppose the whole population is playing one strategy. Now let a small ε-invasion happen: an ε-invasion occurs when a proportion of size ε invades the population. The initial strategy is ESS if the ε-invasion will not succeed – it will die out. This can be expressed formally in the following way: suppose that we start from a situation where all of the population (earth people) is playing some strategy i: from our example, i can be one of $\{A, B, C\}$. The payoff of all firms will then be $\pi(i, i)$. Now, if a proportion of players of type j (other than i) invade the population, the average payoff of the alien invaders will be $(1 - \varepsilon)\pi(j, i) + \varepsilon \cdot \pi(j, j)$. The alien invaders are almost certain (with probability $(1 - \varepsilon)$) to meet someone playing strategy i; with a small probability ε they meet one of their own.[11] Likewise, the earth people playing i will have the payoff $(1 - \varepsilon)\pi(i, i) + \varepsilon \cdot \pi(i, j)$. The condition for strategy i to be an

ESS is as follows:

Definition 1:   Strategy i is ESS if for all j other than i,

$$(1-\varepsilon)\pi(i,i)+\varepsilon\cdot\pi(i,j)>(1-\varepsilon)\pi(j,i)+\varepsilon\cdot\pi(j,j)$$

In plain English, the alien invaders earn (strictly) less than the earth people. The left-hand side of the inequality is the payoff of the earth people; the right-hand that of the aliens. Hence, if population growth depends (positively) on payoff, the aliens will die out. Now, we come to an amazing result. First we have to understand the notion of a *strict* Nash equilibrium. A strict Nash equilibrium occurs when the equilibrium strategy yields *strictly* more than any other possible strategy: a *weak* Nash equilibrium occurs when the equilibrium strategy earns no less (i.e. *weakly* more) than any other possible strategy. In particular, a *sufficient* condition for strategy i to be ESS is that it is a strict Nash equilibrium strategy. In fact John Maynard Smith (1982) showed that the above definition of an ESS was equivalent to the following:

Definition 2: strategy i is ESS if,
    (a) $\pi(i,i)\geqslant\pi(j,i)$ for all j other than i
    (b) if $\pi(i,i)=\pi(j,i)$,   then $\pi(i,j)>\pi(j,j)$

As we can see, part (a) of the definition is simply the standard definition of a Nash equilibrium. If the Nash equilibrium is strict, then it is automatically an ESS. If we have a non-strict Nash equilibrium, we need to have the additional condition (b): the alien invaders do worse against themselves than the earth people. This result has the amazing implication that we can use game theory to model evolutionary biology! I recall in 1982 dining at Christchurch College, Oxford. Neither the fact that I was sat next to an elderly cleric called a 'cannon', nor the fact that the food was cold by the time it had reached the high-table from the kitchen were the most amazing thing that evening. No, I was most surprised by a zoologist who told me that he was applying game theory to animal behaviour. What seems a commonplace now seemed amazing then, since we all used to look at game theory in terms of rationality wonderland. Well, as the evening wore on (and after more glasses of wine and surreal conversations with the elderly cannon) it seemed pretty sensible.

However, the final relationship is between the replicator dynamics and the ESS concept. Again, there is a strong relationship between the two ideas: *every ESS is an asymptotically stable steady state of the replicator dynamics.*[12] A steady state is a state which is unchanging over time: in this case we can think of the state being the vector of population proportions. A steady state is *asymptotically stable* when the system returns to the steady state whenever there is a small deviation from equilibrium.[13]

What is the relationship between a Nash equilibrium and the replicator dynamics? Well, any steady state that is asymptotically stable under the replicator dynamics has to be a Nash equilibrium. This is both important and obvious.

A Nash equilibrium strategy has to be a best response to itself: this is also a necessary condition for the replicator dynamics to be stable around a steady state. To see why, suppose that a strategy was not the best response to itself: in terms of our example, let us suppose that we have a steady state where all firms are 'collusive' type A's. In this case, suppose that we move away from this a little and introduce some Cournot type B's. From the payoff matrix, the type B's will earn more than the type As, and so the proportion of type B's will increase, leading to a move further away from the initial steady state. This argument will hold for any non-Nash equilibrium strategy.

However, whilst all stable steady states are Nash equilibria, not all Nash equilibria are stable. For example, lets augment the strategy space to include a type D, which always produces 1 unit of output. This strategy yields a zero payoff for itself and any strategy it plays against.[14] In effect, the price is kept at zero whatever the opponent does: it seems appropriate to name it the 'Bertrand' or *party pooper* strategy. This strategy is a (weak) Nash equilibrium, the Bertrand equilibrium. However, it is certainly not stable: suppose that some collusive firms invade. These may earn zero most of the time when they play Bertrand firms: however, when they meet each other they earn a positive profit, so that they will thrive and increase in number whilst the Bertrand firms decline.

The relationship between the three concepts of Nash equilibrium, stability of the replicator dynamics and ESS for steady states is depicted in Figure 8.1. Here we have concentric circles, the largest of which is the set of all Nash equilibria;

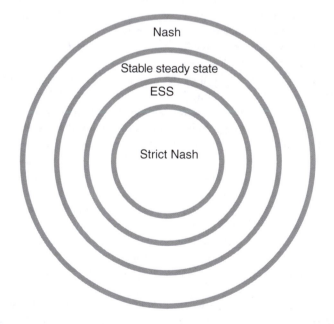

Figure 8.1 *Relationship between equilibrium concepts for steady states*

within that we have the set of stable steady states; within that is the set of ESS; within that is the set of strict Nash equilibria.[15]

We have come full circle. We started with Cournot and his equilibrium in which the equilibrium outcome results from a dynamic process of adjustment: the steady state arising out of it. The resultant Nash equilibrium has formed the basis for imperfectly competitive models, from Edgworth's price-setting duopoly model (1889) and the Robinson/Chamberlin model of monopolistic competition (1933), to the present day. We have also seen the same equilibrium concept playing a crucial role in evolutionary biology. In between, we have the more orthodox perspective of superrational agents with common knowledge playing games. It is amazing that the same equilibrium concept can be seen as arising from such different processes and perspectives.

2.5   Random Matching and Economics

The evolutionary models used in biology are perhaps not well-suited to economics. Most of them are based on the crucial assumption of random matching, whilst most economic interactions are repeated. We buy and sell with familiar traders over time. We work for the same firm, buy from the same shops, visit the same restaurants. This is the same whether we think of the household or the firm. If we are thinking of oligopoly or collective bargaining, then random matching is particularly inappropriate! In economics, the modelling of evolutionary forces by such biological models might be thought to be inappropriate except for special cases.

However, whilst I would myself council strongly against the unthinking and literal use of such biological models, we can think of the biological process not in terms of its microfoundations, which are inappropriate, but rather as a *metaphor*. The *evolutionary metaphor* merely says that forms of behaviour (strategies) that are more successful (earn higher payoffs) tend to become more common. That having been said, there can be no substitute for an appropriate framework for modelling economic and social interaction.

3   SOCIAL LEARNING IN HUMAN SOCIETIES: GABRIEL TARDE

> Whatever a great man does, the
> very same is also done by other men.
> Whatever the standard he sets,
> The world follows it.
> *Bhagavad Gita*, 3.21

There are powerful forces of learning in human societies that are not captured in the basic natural selection model. This was recognised by the French social theorist Gabriel Tarde (1843–1904), a lawyer and judge who for obvious reasons

Mainly Micro

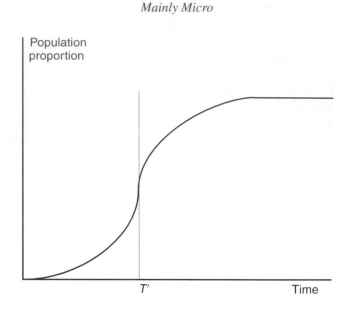

Figure 8.2   *The S-curve or logistic curve*

thought a lot about the causes of crime. He developed some general principles which he called the *laws of imitation*. He thought that people learn from one another through a process of imitation, and that activity or behaviour seen in others tends to reinforce or discourage previous habits. He also observed that the process of diffusion in human society often follows an 'S-curve', otherwise known as the *logistic curve*, as depicted in Figure 8.2.

What happens in the S-curve is roughly as follows. Someone has an idea: let us take the concrete example of a new method of breaking into a house. At first, only that person knows about it, plus possibly a few close friends whom he tells (possibly when he/she is in prison). But these friends can tell their friends, and so on, a process of growth which is exponential: each new person who catches on to the idea can pass it on to a few others. This explains the initial convex part of the curve: the absolute number of new people adopting the innovation in each period (the slope of the curve) is increasing up to time T'. This process cannot go on forever, however, since the population is finite! What happens eventually is that a saturation point is reached. Eventually when a new person learns of the idea, they will find that most people they tell the idea to will already know it. The process of growth will thus slow down and possibly there will remain some people (e.g. non-criminals) who will never adopt the new technique for house-breaking. After time T' the number of people adopting the innovation slows down and the curve becomes concave. Of course, ideas come and go and the world does not remain still. If lots of criminals adopt the new technique of housebreaking, then the police and security firms will develop countermeasures which house owners will start to adopt. After a period of time the new technique will become less useful and there may be a period of decline. In ancient Greece, one method of housebreaking was to tunnel through the walls of the house. This method relied on a mud-wall construction, and the technology died out when this construction technology became less common.

This theory of social diffusion has been widely developed and applied in a variety of contexts. In particular, it provides one of the basic models for marketing: firms are keen to look at ways of speeding up the process of adoption of a new product and extend the life of an existing one (see for example Kotler, 1986). It is also used by economists as a model for the diffusion of technical progress (the path-breaking paper here was Mansfield, 1961), and is applied in health (the theory of diffusion of medical practices and diseases, Coleman, 1966) amongst others.

Certain factors have been identified as important in the spread of an idea. For example, the adoption of the idea by opinion leaders can be crucial: if a widely known and respected individual is known to adopt an idea, it gives others the inspiration and confidence to try it out. A firm may not risk trying out a knew technology until it has seen that some of the large established players have taken it seriously. We can think of people having an agenda: these are the ideas or actions that people take seriously in the sense that they might actually think about adopting them. Because of the limitations of bounded rationality, people do not think about everything all of the time: they only think about a few things most of the time. We all know this from out own experience. We know that certain types of food and drink are bad for us: however, although we know and are aware of the healthier alternatives, we still end up eating the same old food most of the time. It takes some effort to change habits, to put new ideas (in this case a new diet) onto our agenda, so that we think about them seriously when we take decisions. Seeing someone whom we respect or identify with in some way adopting the idea is a way of putting it on our agenda, which makes it more likely that we will adopt it. This was exactly Krishna's argument to Arjuna quoted in the *Bhagavad Gita*.

3.1 Welcome to Donut World

One way of thinking about the process of interaction is to imagine society as a donut. A donut is a three-dimensional torus: a network without any edges. To make this clear, think about a network consisting of houses and paths. In each house there lives an economic agent, and the houses are connected by paths.[16] We can represent a society by a map of the houses and paths, as in Figure 8.3. Now, houses and paths can in theory be built anywhere: however, we can imagine that planning laws dictate a particular structure called a *lattice* or *grid* as in Figure 8.3. In a lattice, the houses are built in equally spaced rows and columns, whilst the house is connected to other houses by paths which are either east–west or north–south. Thus a house is only connected to its four immediate neighbours (going clockwise and starting at the top, north, east, south and west): it is not connected with its other four neighbours (who are northwest, northeast, southeast and southwest). We can think of the *neighbourhood* of the agent: these are the other agents with whom the agent interacts directly. The neighbourhood is defined by a number r, which is the number of paths the agent can travel to interact. If $r = 1$, then the neighbourhood of the agent consists of its four imme- diate neighbours. If $r = 2$, then the neighbourhood expands to include eight other houses (a total of 12). Lets keep life simple, and suppose that $r = 1$: the neigh- bourhood consists only of the folks next door.

In Figure 8.3, there is an edge to the lattice, where the houses stop. If we live in the middle of the page, we have the regular four neighbours. However, if we live on the edges, we will only have three neighbours: if we live at the corners, we will only have two neighbours. Now, lets talk donuts. First forget the origami: *do not attempt to tear out the page and fold it at home* (it won't work[17]). In your mind, consider what would happen if you joined up the top and the bottom row together and also the left and the right. Think about it for a while: the end result would be a donut, a surface without edges or corners. This is a very useful concept, since it means that every house is the same: all houses have the same number of neighbours. A one dimensional torus can be repre- sented in two dimensions as a circle:[18] the two-dimensional torus can be repre- sented in three dimensions as a donut. The important thing is that the dimension of the torus is one less than the dimension it occurs in (much the same as saying

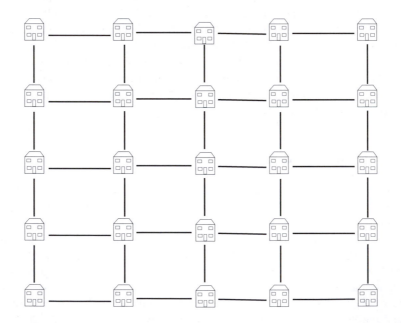

Figure 8.3 *Donut world*

the surface of the earth is two-dimensional,[19] but occurs in three-dimensional space). Rather than trying to draw a real donut, we can represent it by imagining that in fact there are paths going from all of the houses on the left side of Figure 8.3 to the houses on the right side, and those on the top to those on the bottom (corner houses would thus have two new paths). Maybe one day fast-food outlets will sell 'flat pack' donuts to be assembled before eating.

So, here we have our simple society. Let us suppose that each household is growing food (indeed some of the earliest studies of diffusion were in agriculture, Ryan and Gross, 1943); each agent can see the gardens of the houses in his neighbourhood and the methods of gardening. Now, suppose that one household innovates in period 1: it works out that if it rotates the crops in a certain way disease is reduced and output increases. We can take the idealised case first: suppose that neighbours see exactly what is going on and will always adopt a new technology with certainty if it is beneficial. In this case, in period 1 all neighbours will have seen what was done in period 1 and also that it yielded a greater harvest. So, in period 2 they will do the same thing: there are now five households rotating crops. In period 3 their neighbours will also do the same thing: an additional eight households bringing the total to 13. Now, suppose that this is an infinite lattice (it goes on forever): then the growth will result from each new house in period t generating $4(t-1)$ new houses in the next period. The sequence with one house starting is thus: 1, 5, 13, 21, 37 .... The total number of houses with the new technology at time t, denoted $H(t)$ is thus given by the recursive relationship $H(t) = H(t-1) + 4 \cdot (t-1)$, along with the assumed initial value $H(0) = 0$, $H(1) = 1$.

Now, let us assume that we are in Donut World, in a 5×5 3-D torus. In this case we have the constraint $H(t) \leqslant 25$. What will happen? Well, for the first three periods, everything is as in the infinite lattice case: $H(1) = 1$, $H(2) = 5$, $H(3) = 13$. Now, in period $t = 4$, only eight new houses adopt the innovation: the four houses at the 'edge' of the square in period $t = 3$ are next to houses that have already adopted the technology. Hence $H(4) = 21$. The four households at the 'corners' of the square are not reached until the next period: in $t = 5$ there are four new houses adopting the new technology, so that $H(5) = 25$, and $H(t) = 25$ for $t \geqslant 5$. In Figure 8.4 we can plot the diffusion of the technology: it indeed follows a roughly S-shaped curve: the increases in absolute terms are: 1, 4, 8, 8, 4.

This simple story is deterministic; now let us introduce some uncertainty or randomness into it. For example, suppose that households will not be looking at each others' gardens all the time and may (due to fog or rain) not observe them with great accuracy; the output of the farms has a random element; the households that see a high output might not bother to adopt the new technology (due to inertia or laziness). Let us suppose that we start from a situation where all gardeners are doing the same thing: they will obtain the same yield as each other, subject only to a random element (the luck of the draw) each harvest. This randomness means that the actual path of diffusion will be random, depending on what happens. For example, the diffusion might take some time to get started: the household with the new method might be unlucky for a few periods

Mainly Micro

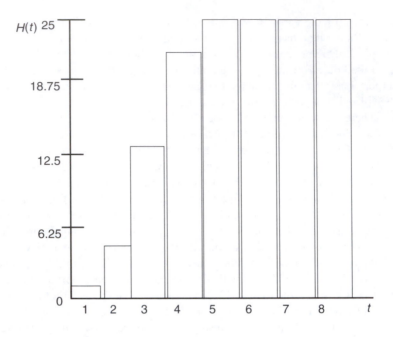

Figure 8.4 *Diffusion in donut world*

and its output might not be particularly high; even if it is high, the neighbours might not notice; even if they do notice they may not do anything about it straight away. However, *the important thing to note about randomness and uncertainty is that if there is enough time, then everything that can happen will happen.* From the perspective of eternity, everything is possible. The exact timing of events is random: but as the time available becomes longer and longer, even quite unlikely things can happen. It is like throwing dice: we are fairly unlikely to throw a double six in any one throw, but as we keep throwing the event becomes more and more likely. Throw the dice a thousand times and it is almost certain we will throw a double six at least once. This is why, in social learning models, researchers often concentrate on the asymptotic or long-run properties of the system (modelled mathematically as what happens when t tends to infinity). In terms of social learning, the effect of the randomness is merely to slow up the path of diffusion and make the exact path and timing uncertain. The end result will not necessarily be changed (see for example Bala and Goyal, 1998, for an analysis of learning from neighbours with local interaction with an explicit model of learning).

3.2 Diffusion in a Strategic Context

The case of an innovation is *non-strategic*: my method of cultivating vegetables does not affect yours.[20] Now let us think of a strategic interaction, where I actually undertake some sort of economic activity with my neighbours. For example, consider the Prisoner's Dilemma (PD). There are two strategies: cooperate C or defect D. The payoffs to the farmer of playing strategies i against j $\pi(i,j)$ are as follows: $\pi(C,C)=2$, $\pi(C,D)=0$, $\pi(D,D)=0$ and $\pi(D,C)=a$ which we represent as the payoff matrix

$$\Pi_{PD} = \begin{bmatrix} 2 & 0 \\ a & 1 \end{bmatrix}$$

Each farmer plays the PD with all of his four neighbours. However, he[21] cannot customise: at time t he can only play one strategy with each neighbour, either C or D: one size must fit all comers.

Now, clearly, since D is a dominant strategy, the issue might seem pretty trivial: choose D, since it is the best strategy whatever the competition does. However, if everyone had that attitude, all game theorists would be unemployed. So let us assume that things happen differently. Each farmer does what he does. However, he observes the payoffs of his neighbours. If a neighbour is doing better than him, he will imitate the neighbour: if more than one is doing better, he will imitate the one with the highest payoff. Let us call this process '*imitate your best neighbour*'.[22] Now, the payoff of a particular agent will be the sum of the payoffs he earns from his four neighbours. If we take the case of the PD, we then have a variety of possibilities: for a given strategy chosen by farmer Giles, there are four possible combinations of strategies he can face: {C,C,C,C}, {C,C,C,D}, {C,C,D,D}, {C,D,D,D}, {D,D,D,D}. Since there are two possible strategies farmer Giles can choose, we can represent the payoffs of the farmer in Table 8.1, with $a=2.5$. Now, consider what might happen here. Let us do a few thought experiment in Donut World. What will the learning rule 'imitate your best neighbour' generate at the social level?

Case 1: Suppose the torus is an even-numbered square (for concreteness a chess board, 8×8); 50% of farmers choose C, and 50% choose D. Furthermore, suppose that, like a chess board, the Cs and Ds alternate. Every farmer will have two Cs and two Ds in his neighbourhood. Looking down the table, the C farmers will be earning 4; the Ds 7. In this case, the C farmers will look enviously at their D counterparts, and imitate them. So, the next period all firms will choose D,

Table 8.1 Payoffs and the neighbourhood strategies with PD $(a=2.5)$

	C	D
CCCC	8	10
CCCD	6	8.5
CCDD	4	7
CDDD	2	5.5
DDDD	0	4

which is of course the Nash equilibrium of the PD. The equilibrium under the 'imitate your best neighbour' is a steady state where all farmers adopt D.

Case 2:   As in case 1, but the Cs and Ds are partitioned into two separate blocks. The top half of the donut is all D, the bottom is all C. There are four different payoffs here. The D surrounded by Ds earns 4; the C surrounded by Cs earns 8. The more interesting case are the two borders, where Cs meet Ds. Given that the torus is an even square (8×8) these are straight lines. In this case, each borderline C will have three fellow Cs and one D, hence earning 6; each borderline D will have three Ds and a C, earning a total of 5.5. Thus, in the next period, all of the borderline Ds will switch to Cs. Each period, cooperation will spread two more rows,[23] until the whole of Donut World is playing C after two periods. Again, we have a steady state equilibrium, but with all farmers adopting C , the opposite outcome to case 1.

Case 3:   As in case 2, except that the square torus is of odd size (e.g. 7×7) depicted in Figure 8.5. An exact 50/50 split is not possible here. In this case, the top three rows are all D; the bottom three rows all C; the middle row will be a mixture of Cs and Ds. Now, let us take the case where there are 25 Ds and 24 Cs: the middle row will have four Ds and three Cs alternating. In effect, the middle border between the Cs and Ds is a zig-zag. Every border C in row 4 will have three Ds and one C as neighbours, thus earning 2; two of the border Ds have three Cs and a D as neighbours and earn 8.5; the end two have two of each and earn 7. Clearly, all of the Cs in the mixed border row 4 will switch to D. There

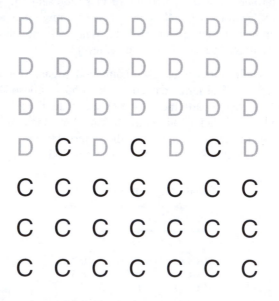

Figure 8.5   *Cooperation and defection in donut world*

are also four Cs in row 5 who have one D neighbour in the mixed row: they will be earning 6, and hence will also switch to D. Hence in period 2, row 4 has become all D and row 3 becomes mixed (the same as row 4 in the previous period). At the same time, there is a straight border between row 1 (all D) and row 7 (all C). As in case 2, the Ds in row 1 will all switch to C. Hence, the state of the Donut economy in period 2 is the same as in period 1, except that it has been 'rotated': the borders move 'up' one each period (like an Escher figure, going up from row 7 means going to row 1). Thus any particular farmer will spend three (or four) periods D and four (or three) C depending in which column he finds himself. This is the attractor of the imitation dynamics: it is not a steady state, but a cycle: it is rather like the human wave of hands that passes around the football stadium as people raise their arms if the person next to them does.

What these three thought experiments show us is that in the world of local inter-action, there is no inevitability about the Nash equilibrium coming about, even in the stark case of the PD where there is a dominant strategy. We can get cycles (case 3), or convergence to uniform populations of either all C (case 2) or all D (case 1). The history depends very much on the initial conditions and the exact structure of the payoff matrix. For example, the larger $\pi(D,C)$ (i.e. a), the less likely is C to survive; also, the Cs need to live together and apart form the Ds to survive.

In this section we have seen how social learning can be modelled in both a strategic and a non-strategic setting. Essentially, we can represent social interaction as a network (in the case of Donut World, a lattice torus): agents repeatedly interact within a neighbourhood. Clearly, Donut World looks a bit more like a real economy than the world of random matching. However, lets go a step fur-ther and try to construct something that looks even more like an economy: time to move on to the *Duopoly Archipelago*, a place where all aspirations are met in the long run and everything is possible for he who decides to experiment.

4   ECONOMIC NATURAL SELECTION: KEEPING UP WITH THE JONESES

The best monopoly profit is a quiet life.

John Hicks (1935)

This is the criterion by which the economic system selects survivors: those who realize positive profits are the survivors; those who suffer losses disappear.

Armen Alchian (1950, p. 213)

The idea of natural selection in economics is not new: it has long been argued that firms must earn at least normal-profits to survive in the long-run.[24] Failure to achieve this will activate some market mechanism which will lead to the ownership or the control of the firm changing. These mechanisms include:

- Bankruptcy: the firm becomes insolvent and is forced to stop trading. Its assets are then sold off.
- The shareholders replace the existing managers.
- The shares of the firm are purchased by the managers of another firm who replace the existing managers.
- Debtors are able to reschedule outstanding debts and impose changes on the firm.

In general, we can think of the mechanisms as reflecting the operation of the capital market in its widest sense. The performance of a particular firm is measured against the performance of other firms. The ultimate bottom line for the capital market is the profitability of the firm and its ability to deliver dividends to shareholders and/or keep up scheduled loan repayments. An extreme form of failure is insolvency or bankruptcy which occurs when a firm is unable to cover its expenditure with current income: the cash coming in is less than the liabilities it is incurring. It is against the law to continue to trade when insolvent: when a company is insolvent an outside agent is called in to take over responsibility for the company (in Britain, this person is called the *receiver*). The decision may be taken to liquidate the company: that is, sell off its assets and meet as many of the outstanding liabilities as possible. Alternatively, the decision may be taken to find new managers to continue running the company as a going concern.

However, even if managers of the firm are making a profit and have no cash-flow problems, there are still constraints. There are a variety of benchmarks against which they are judged by the capital market. In the first instance, the benchmark is provided by similar firms in the same or related lines of business. If firm X and firm Y are in the same industry, their profitability (rate of return on capital) should be the same: if firm X consistently underperforms relative to Y, then this is a good indicator that the strategy of X is not the best. However, in the long run there is an *arbitrage condition*: the rate of return must be the same for all possible investments.[25] The argument here is the same as all arbitrage arguments: if capital is earning less in one place than another, then shift it to the place earning more. So, the capital market links together all of the firms in the Duopoly Archipelago. Be they selling pizzas, making air conditioners, or an airline, the capital market evaluates them and reduces them to the same thing: money-making machines. *The capital market requires them to be equally efficient money-making machines.*

The capital market reflects the aggregate performance of the economy as represented by average profitability. In this chapter the level of normal profits is taken to be the average level of profits in the economy and explores the implications of this hypothesis in the context of an economy consisting of many oligopolistic markets. Under fairly general assumptions there are powerful long-run forces pushing the firms in each market towards collusion. What differentiates the approach here is that the evolution of the economy is inherently social, in that it is the level of average profits in the whole economy over time which drives the behaviour of firms.

In this section I model the behaviour of firms using an aspiration-based model of bounded rationality. *The key feature of this model is to link together the aspirations of firms with the level of normal profit by requiring that in the long run the aspiration level of all firms is to have at least normal profits.*

4.1 Welcome to the Duopoly Archipelago

Imagine an archipelago of islands: each island represents a market. On each island there are two firms, and the markets and firms on each island are the same in terms of size, costs and so on. We can picture the economy in terms of each island having two houses (firms) linked by a single path. The neighbourhoods of each firm consist only of its competitor on that island (the economy is not directly interconnected as in Donut World).

Firms have a finite strategy set with K pure strategies $i, j = 1 \ldots K$. For concreteness, we can think of the strategies as output levels X_i as previously, with no cost and linear demand. We need assume very little about the structure of the payoff matrix Π of the constituent duopoly game, except that the joint payoff can be maximised by a payoff-symmetric outcome. An outcome can be thought of as a pair of strategies (i,j): it is payoff-symmetric if the payoffs are the same for both firms: $\pi(i,j) = \pi(j,i)$. Clearly, the leading diagonal of the matrix Π is payoff-symmetric: however, it is possible in general that off-diagonal terms might also be payoff-symmetric. In the case of outputs as strategies, the payoff-symmetric outcomes will consist exclusively of the leading diagonal. We will therefore assume for simplicity that equal profits for the duopolists on a particular island means that they are producing the same output ($\pi(i,j) = \pi(j,i)$ implies $i = j$).

We will make the following assumption about the payoff matrix. The state of a market is fully described by the pair of strategies chosen by the firms in that market: which firm chooses which does not matter (except, of course, for the firms concerned!). Suppose we are free to choose any pair of outputs $\{i,j\}$: the joint profit maximising pair(s) S is (are) the pair(s) that maximise the joint profits of the firms, with the maximum joint profits denoted *JPM*:

$$JPM = \max_{\{i,j\}} \frac{\pi(i,j) + \pi(j,i)}{2}$$

In the case of the simple Cournot oligopoly, S consists of the unique pair of outputs $(\frac{1}{4}, \frac{1}{4})$, each firm producing half of the monopoly output: the *JPM* profits are then $\frac{1}{4}$ (each firm earns 1/8). Now, let us assume that we maximise joint profits, restricting ourselves to cases where both firms produce the same output:

$$SJPM = \max_{i=1 \ldots K} \frac{\pi(i,i)}{2}$$

Now, the assumption we need to make is that the joint profits are at their maximum when payoffs are symmetric. One way of saying this is:

Assumption 1:   JPM=SJPM

Clearly, this assumption is satisfied by the simple Cournot model we are using as an example. Alternatively, if we consider the Prisoners Dilemma (PD), we have the following payoffs:

$$\Pi_{PD} = \begin{bmatrix} 2 & 0 \\ a & 1 \end{bmatrix}$$

There are two strategies: cooperate C or defect D, with $\pi(C,C)=2$, $\pi(C,D)=0$, $\pi(D,D)=0$ and $\pi(D,C)=a$. For this to be a PD we require $a>2$: it must pay to defect when the other person is cooperating: it also ensures that D is the dominant strategy. However, assumption 1 will only be satisfied if $a\leqslant 4$. To see why, note that if $a>4$, then

$$JPM = \frac{\pi(C,D)+\pi(D,C)}{2} = \frac{a}{2} > SJPM = 2$$

Hence, for the model to apply to the PD we need to assume that $a\leqslant 4$.

When we look at the economy as a whole, we can summarise what it looks like in terms of the competition in each market. One way to do this is to take each pair $\{i,j\}$ and measure the proportion of markets (islands) which have firms playing this pair of strategies,[26] $P(\{i,j\})$. Let $P(S)$ be the proportion of markets where the firms are producing collusive outputs and hence earning the JPM profits.

So, here we have the Duopoly Archipelago. On each island we have a duopoly of firms choosing a strategy pair. We can describe the economy at any time t in terms of the proportions of markets having each possible pair. As a last point, we have to think of the average profits in the whole economy. This is simple to compute: we merely take the combined profits earned with each strategy pair $\{i,j\}$ and then take a weighted average with the population proportions $P(\{i,j\})$ as the weights. The average profits in the economy at time t are then

$$\overline{\Pi}_t = \sum_{\{i,j\}} P_t(\{i,j\}) \cdot \left(\frac{\pi(i,j)+\pi(j,i)}{2} \right)$$

4.2   Aspirations in the Duopoly Archipelago

The concept of an aspiration level has been around for a long time. It has been put forward both as a good model of individual decision-making in the mathematical psychology literature (Lewin, 1936; Siegel, 1957) and as a model of *organisational* decision-making with relevance to the firm (Cyert and March, 1963; Kornai, 1971; Simon, 1947). Although there are variations, the core idea is simple enough. When attempting to solve a problem, agents (let us think of these as firms) formulate a target: if they achieve this target they will probably stop searching. The aspiration level is a target to which the managers aspire and towards which they plan. As such, the aspiration level is a search heuristic a bit like a stopping mechanism, as for example the reservation wage. In the optimal search literature, the unemployed worker (for example) follows the rule: search until you receive an offer greater or equal to the reservation wage. In fact, under various assumptions, one can derive this as an optimal stopping rule. The aspiration level is a target outcome: if the target is attained by a particular solution or action, then this plan is deemed acceptable and the search is stopped. Of course, aspiration levels can be adjusted in response to experience of the decision makers themselves and outside events. The literature on aspirations does not conceive of the aspiration levels coming from some optimising process: rather it is a boundedly rational attempt to find a good solution.

The aspiration level here has two elements. First, there is the aspiration level as representing *external* forces imposed upon the firm or managers from outside (i.e. the capital market). This is represented by the role of average profitability as an external benchmark for 'normal' profits. Second there is the *subjective* element inside the corporate mind, the targets that come up from the interpersonal interaction of managers and others within the firm. In this model, firms at any time adopt a pure strategy.[27] Each firm follows the following simple learning rule. It has an aspiration level $\alpha(t)$. If it is earning less than $\alpha(t)$, then it decides to *experiment* with probability 1; if the firm is earning at least $\alpha(t)$, then it will continue with the existing strategy (this is Hick's '*quiet life*' alluded to in the above quote – if it aint bust, then don't fix it).

For simplicity, we assume that all firms share the same aspiration level,[28] with that level satisfying the condition that in the long run it has to be no less than average profits. This seems a reasonable assumption reflecting the role of capital markets in industrialised economies, and it means that the aspiration level is endogenous (as in Borgers and Sarin, 1997; Karandikar *et al.*, 1998; Palomino and Vega-Redondo, 1999), reflecting the past and the current profitability of the economy, as well as reflecting firm-specific factors and the history of the individual firm. The assumption we make is that whatever other internal or external factors there are, in the long run the capital market must be satisfied. In fact, we do not have to make explicit the mechanism generating aspirations: we merely impose the following conditions on their evolution (if this looks too technical, just jump to the next paragraph):

Assumption: Aspirations

(a) $\underset{t \to \infty}{Lim}\left[\alpha_t - \overline{\overline{\Pi}}_t\right] \geqslant 0$

(b) $\alpha_t \leqslant JPM$

Part (a) says that in the long run (as t tends to infinity), the aspiration level α_t must be at least equal to average profits $\Pi(t)$. Part (b) also says that firms must not be over-optimistic: the highest realistic aspiration for the firms is that they can earn the *JPM* profit.

Well, we can make things *really* simple: this assumption is satisfied if in each period the aspiration level equals the current average profitability,

$$\alpha(t) = \Pi(t)$$

The aspiration level model here gives the mechanism determining the experimentation by firms. *Experimentation* means that the firm tries to alter strategy, and the question we next ask is: what determines the probabilitiy that the firm switches from its existing strategy to another, the *switching probabilities*.

The actual switching probability may be determined by many things: the experience of the firm, what other firms are doing (through *imitation*), or by strategic considerations (as in *best-response* dynamics). There might also be some randomness or 'noise' in the switching process: mistakes are made, or policies improperly implemented, and so on. This might be very complex to model in detail. However, we make the following general assumption about switching probabilities:

> *Assumption*:   switching probabilities
> There exists some $\gamma > 0$ such that all switching probabilities exceed γ.

What this means is that *anything is possible*: there is a small but strictly positive probability γ that the firm will choose any particular strategy. Of course, some strategies might be much more likely to be chosen: however, no strategy is ruled out. This is not as odd as it sounds: firms sometimes do things that seem pretty stupid with hindsight but looked good at the time!

Whilst we have interpreted switching behaviour as the same firm in two periods changing behaviour, the formal model would be exactly the same if we think of a different firm in each period. For example, a firm in a particular market might exit (due to bankruptcy or death). In this case the switching probability would pertain to the 'place' of the firm: the probability that next period the firm taking the place of the existing firm would play a particular strategy.

4.3   The Evolution of Collusion in the Archipelago Duopoly

So, we have set up this archipelago economy, describing the nature of markets (summarised by the payoff matrix) and the behaviour of firms (aspirations and switching probabilities). What happens to it? Well, this is easy to describe. Let us take for simplicity the simplest case where the aspiration level at any time t equals the average profitability, $\alpha(t) = \overline{\Pi}(t)$. Hence, at period t, we can divide market/islands into three categories:

- *Above aspiration*: Both firms are earning at or above the average. If both firms are above aspiration, then they will just keep on doing what they are doing.
- *Below aspiration*: Both firms are earning below average profit. Both will experiment, and under the assumption that switching probabilities are all

strictly positive, if both firms are experimenting then anything can happen! There is a strictly positive probability that any pair of outputs/strategies will be chosen.

- *Mixed, one firm above, one below*: In this case, the firm that is meeting its aspiration keeps on with its existing strategy; the one that isn't experiments.

Now, the exact evolution of this economy will be quite complex and will depend on the exact switching rules used, and so on. However, we can say something *in general* that will hold for *all archipelago economies that satisfy the three assumptions we have made*: namely (a) that the payoff matrix has the property that joint profit is maximised with equal profits for both firms; (b) that aspirations tend to average profit in the long run; and (c) that when experimenting, anything is possible.

First, consider any industry where both firms are choosing the collusive strategy and earning *JPM*. Clearly, it is never possible for average profits to exceed this level: $JPM \geqslant \Pi(t)$. Whilst it is possible for an individual firm to earn in excess of *JPM*, it is not possible for two firms in the same industry, nor for all firms in the economy. Hence, industries that are collusive will necessarily be in the above aspiration category. Furthermore, once an industry arrives at collusion it will stay there forever! In technical terms, this is called an *absorbing state*: once you arrive in this state, you are 'absorbed' and never leave it. It is a bit like the cockroach motel: the roaches check in, but never check out. An astronomical analogy is a black hole: matter goes in but never comes out again.[29] So, over time, we can be sure that *the proportion of industries in the economy which are collusive will never get smaller: it must either grow or at least stay constant*. In the case of Cournot duopoly, the collusive outcome involves both firms producing an output of 0.25 and earning 0.125 each.

Second, let us consider the case of industries where both firms are below aspiration. These will tend to be competitive industries, where both firms are producing a large output and earning low profits. Both firms will be experimenting: hence literally any outcome (i.e. strategy pair) is possible, including the collusive outcome. There is a strictly positive probability that both firms will choose the collusive outcome. Looking at the economy as a whole, we will observe a strictly positive flow from those industries that are below aspiration into the collusive absorbing state.

Let us put these two facts together: once firms become collusive, then they remain collusive; and a proportion of below-aspiration industries become collusive. In the end, if we look at the long run of the economy we can see that the proportion of firms below aspiration must eventually disappear: they will be absorbed by the collusive state that is in the above aspiration category. This means that, in the end, there can only be two categories of firms left: the above aspiration and the mixed.

Third, consider the mixed-aspiration category; this category cannot survive in the long run either. To see why, just note that there is a continual flow of industries from the mixed to either the above aspiration or the below-aspiration categories. To see why, note that under the assumption that all switching probabilities are strictly positive, there is a positive probability that the below-aspiration firm in a mixed industry will choose the same strategy as its competitor. If this happens, then in the next period both firms will be earning the same profit and hence be either both above or both below aspiration. Since the proportion of industries with both firms below aspiration must go to zero in the long run, this flow from mixed industries must in the long run be to above-aspiration industries, with the proportion of mixed industries going to zero.

Finally, consider the above-aspiration category excluding the collusive industries. Since the proportions of firms with one or both firms below aspiration goes to zero over time, it follows that all industries must be above aspiration. However, how can all firms be at or above the average? Well, there are two ways. First, all industries arrive at the situation where they are all in the same payoff symmetric state: that is, all firms choose the same output levels. This could happen at any level of competition. Secondly, if at the start (or at anytime) there are some collusive industries, then the only possible long-run state is for all industries to be colluding. If there are some colluding industries at any time, then they

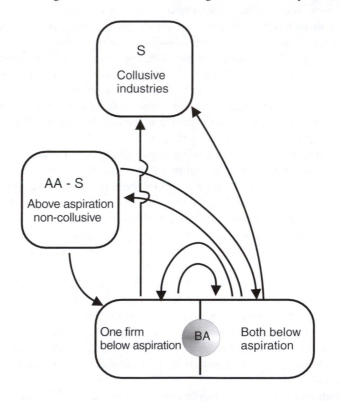

Figure 8.6   *Flows of industries between aspiration states*

will not go away. There is then no possibility that the rest of the economy can persist in a state which earns less than *JPM*.

In Figure 8.6 we depict the flows of markets between the different categories. At the top is the roach motel: the absorbing collusive state. Below that are the other above aspiration industries. On the bottom are the two mixed and below-aspiration industries. Now, clearly, under the switching assumption, there are outflows from the below-aspiration set to all of the others (anything is possible) every period. Likewise, there are flows from the mixed industries: again, they can go to all of the other categories, except that the flows need not be active every period (it depends exactly which pairs are involved). Lastly, there are flows from the above-aspiration group to both the mixed and below-aspiration groups. These flows occur not due to switching, but to changes in the aspiration level: if the aspiration level rises (as average profits rise), then the current profits of firms in these industries may be below the new aspiration level. We can see that there is a continuous flow between the various categories: but in every period, some firms will end up in the absorbing collusive state. There is no way for industries to escape it in the long run!

In essence, the argument is that *in the long-run, all firms need to earn at least the average profit. Assuming that there are some industries (even a very small proportion) colluding at some point, then for all firms to earn average profits means that they must collude and earn JPM.*

> *Theorem*: the inevitability of collusion (Dixon, 2000b)
> Suppose that at some time there are some collusive industries. Then under the assumptions, in the long run all industries will collude.

This is a remarkable result. It shows that the pressure of the capital market on firms will force them to collude: competition cannot survive! Let us just think how this works, the forces involved.

How can collusion persist, how can it be stable? We all know the standard arguments that there is an incentive to deviate from a collusive output: one of the firms can earn higher profits if it deviates by (for example) producing a larger output. Suppose that one firm does this. Then it will increase its own profits, but reduce the other firms' profits (and reduce the combined profits). The other firm will now be below aspiration, and hence it will start to experiment: for example it may produce a larger output. Then both firms will become below aspiration and continue to experiment until both firms are above aspiration: that is, collusive! We can think of the period of experimentation following the defection as analogous to a punishment (as discussed in Chapter 6). Whilst there is no sense in which the punishment is optimal, it will act in a similar fashion. The point is that although aggressive or competitive behaviour might bring a higher payoff in the short run, it cannot survive in the long run. The reason is that it will generate a response from the competitor which will set the industry in motion until it can settle down into a situation where both firms are earning average/normal profits. This is not unrealistic: firms who are very aggressive towards rivals will become involved in price wars and similar episodes. Their shareholders might well prefer them to reap the long-term rewards of a cosier relationship with competitors.

The implications of this result might be taken as quite far-reaching: we should expect the operation of capital market pressures to enforce collusion, not competition. Competition tends to reduces profits, at least in the long run, and hence cannot be sustained in the long run. The model as presented did not include entry. However, entry *per se* need not alter the result. If there is a fixed number of firms in the industry (two or more), then the same arguments will indicate that collusion will be established between them. Now suppose that we impose an entry condition on the economy. One way to do this is to divide the model into two stages: first an entry phase and then the market phase. There is a fixed set-up cost. With free entry, entry will occur to the point where expected profits are zero. If we take expected profits as the long-run steady state profits (that is, *JPM*), then the *JPM* per firm will equal the entry cost. Given the free entry equilibrium number of firms, the equilibrium will be collusive: free entry just drives the average profit to zero. It is perhaps worth looking briefly at an example of how the theorem might work out in a concrete example.

4.5   An example: Cournot Duopoly

Perhaps the simplest economic application of our model is to the Cournot duopoly model with linear demand and without costs which we have considered earlier. Recall that *JPM* is 0.125, and is maximised by the output pair (0.25, 0.25). We[30] allowed for $K = 21$ types of firm (not just the three $\{A, B, C\}$). To do this, we chose a grid of granularity 0.025 over the range[31] 0.1 to 0.6, perturbing it slightly by moving 0.325 to 0.333 (1/3), so that the Cournot–Nash output was included. Hence $K = 21$ and there are 231 possible pairs of output. We assumed that there is random switching: if a firm decides to experiment, it chooses each of the 21 strategies with a probability of 1/21.

The simulations were initiated from the initial position with a uniform distribution over all pairs, and the results are depicted in Figure 8.7. In Figure 8.7b, we see the path of average profits over time; in Figure 8.7a the evolution of population proportions of the JPM market (0.125, 0.125) and the symmetric Cournot market are depicted (note that the proportions are measured on a logarithmic scale). From Figure 8.7b, we see that the average profits converge to the symmetric joint profit maximum of 0.125. However, the time path of profits is non-monotonic: at particular times there appear large drops in profit. The reason for this is quite intuitive. As the average profit level increases, it surpasses that of one or both firms, which start to experiment. The profits of firms at those markets will then on average fall below the population average as the firms disperse over some or all output pairs. The effect of this can be quite dramatic: the discontinuity is particularly large when a symmetric market goes critical, since

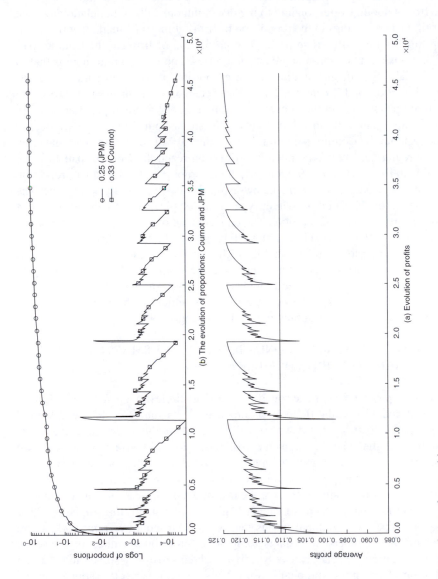

Figure 8.7 *The evolution of competition*

both firms at each such market begin to experiment and spread across all possible output pairs. However, whilst the time-series of profits is non-monotonic and 'discontinuous', there is a clear upward trend and convergence to 0.125.

From Figure 8.7a, the proportion of colluding firms ($P(S)$) is monotonic, but far from smooth. Corresponding to the discontinuous falls in population average profit, there are jumps in the proportion of firms at the JPM market, corresponding to the jumps in average profit. The proportion of firms at the Cournot pair (1/3,1/3) is a highly non-monotonic time series. The first thing to note is that in the initial stages of the simulation, the proportion of Cournot markets exceeds the proportion of JPM markets. This can occur because during this period the Cournot pair is also in the above aspiration set: until average profits reach 1/9, the Cournot pair will 'absorb' markets with one or both firms below aspiration. The fact that the Cournot pair attracts more than JPM is due to the fact that early on more markets with experimenting firms can reach the Cournot pair than the JPM pair. However, after 50 iterations, the Cournot pair has a smaller proportion than the JPM pair, and is in the below-aspiration category most of the time. The time-series of the Cournot market type is not atypical: most pairs except JPM have a similar time-series profile. The convergence of the proportion of markets towards type JPM is steady but slow: this is because the probability of hitting JPM from other locations is small throughout the simulation: from each market in which both firms experiment there is a probability of 1/442 of moving to JPM. Convergence is in general quicker with fewer strategies and non-random switching rules. We explore more specific rules (imitation, best-response etc.) in the Cournot model using simulations in Dixon and Lupi (1997).

5   CONCLUSION: HOW ECONOMISTS CAN GET SMARTER BY MAKING AGENTS DUMBER?

In this chapter we have gone round in historical circles, traversed the surface of a donut and visited the duopoly archipelago. What have we learned? Well, I think that we can see that if we are willing to assume that economic agents are intelligent rather than having some abstract notion of 'perfect rationality', we can learn quite a bit. Agents interact in a social situation and can learn, both from their own experience, and the experience of others (either their neighbours or the general population). If we assume that agents have some ethereal notion of perfect rationality, then we cannot begin to understand this. To assume that agents are perfectly rational means that we have to adopt a framework where they are able to understand what is going on in some significant sense. However, perfectly rational agents can only solve problems we can solve, and we can solve only very simple problems. So, if we stick with perfectly rational agents, we will restrict our vision to simple models.

In this chapter I have outlined the possibility of an alternative approach. Let us assume that agents are boundedly rational: they may even be completely dumb, or just use some rules for updating that are intelligent but not in any sense optimal. In terms of Chapter 6, we are adopting a specific model of reasoning where we specify what the agents think, how they think (I am using 'think' in a broad sense here, since most economic agents are not individuals). We can then model the interaction of agents in some sort of *network*. The networks we have looked at are very simple. However, in principle we can at least imagine the economy as an extremely complicated network: a network possibly as complicated as the neural networks in the human brain or possibly even more complicated. There may have different levels of organisation: for example in the Duopoly Archipelago the capital market worked at the aggregate level, imposing the population average on the individual firms. These levels can then interact and yield interesting and novel outcomes. In the Duopoly Archipelago, if the duopolists were all playing a prisoner's dilemma, then they would (in the long run) be forced to collude. Thus the economy is operating in such a way that individual agents are forced to choose a strategy that is dominated. In a more general context, *an agent's actions in equilibrium may well be far from optimal.* Note that I am using optimal in a private sense: the individual firms are not choosing their best responses to each other (failure of private optimality). The outcome is also not socially optimal: whilst it is true that collusion maximises the joint profits of the firms, the consumers (whose welfare does not appear in the payoff matrix) lose out.

In this sense I think I have answered my own challenge put forward in Chapter 7: there may be strong forces in an economy leading agents away from optimising behaviour in strategic situations. Optimising behaviour can only survive or predominate if it earns higher profits than non-optimal behaviour. In non-strategic situations this need not be true. As we saw in Chapter 6, non-profit maximising managers may in the end earn more than profit maximisers. When ignorance is bliss,' 'tis indeed folly to be wise. *Since most economic interactions are indeed strategic, we should certainly not assume that agents optimise all of the time.*

Economists have tended to ignore these higher level (non-local) interactions and focus on isolated pairs of players, or overlapping networks of neighbourhoods. However, in the information age the economy is becoming explicitly and consciously interconnected: this self-knowledge imperfectly reflects and mirrors the objective interconnectedness of the economy revealed in the story of Infinity in a Pencil (Chapter 1). Higher levels of organisation exist: in particular capital markets and to a lesser extent labour markets bring together different markets and parts of the economy. This is something that economists really need to focus on in some detail in the years ahead. Rather than pondering the deliberations of rational agents interacting alone or in isolated pairs, the focus should be more on intelligent agents interacting in social systems.

Notes

1   For the many examples of systematic and common behaviour that violates conventional axioms, see Thaler (1991, 1992, 1993).

2   And other areas: for example Sargent (1993) for applications to macroeconomics.
3   Nearly all rational agents in game theory papers are female nowadays: they were mainly male before the mid-1980s.
4   Economists are not alone here. Philosophers have tried to do the same thing: for example deriving moral laws from some abstract notion of rationality. It doesn't work there either!
5   I am simplifying things rather a lot here: for a detailed and clear exposition of the process of evolution, you can do no better than reading Dawkins (1986).
6   The biologist Lamark had different ideas. He thought that characteristics acquired during a parent's life could be passed on. In biology this has been shown to be incorrect. However, in terms of social learning it is almost certainly correct.
7   Again, whilst it is clear that Cournot was the first person to introduce the concept of the Nash equilibrium, I follow common usage in naming it after Nash. Economists often used to call the 'Nash' equilibrium a 'Cournot' equilibrium. With the spread of game theory in the early 1980s, this usage dropped out.
8   i is called the 'row' player, because his choice of strategy determines which row we are on: likewise j is the column player.
9   This is a special case of the class of *payoff monotone* selection dynamics in which

$$g_i(t) = g \left[\frac{\Pi_i(t)}{\Pi(t)} \right] \quad \text{with } g' > 0$$

10 Throughout this section, we adopt the simplification that there are only 'pure' strategies and no 'mixed' strategies. Game theorists are much keener on mixed strategies than economists, the whole concept being somewhat problematic. However, for those who want the 'proper' definition, see Weibull (1995) chapter 2.
11 Note that the alien invaders are subject to the same random matching process: they do not arrive by one ship and spread out as in the film version, but arrive as random individuals.
12 Note that if the replicator dynamics has an attractor, it need not be ESS: the attractor of a dynamic system might be a limit cycle or a non-ESS steady state.
13 An alternative concept of stability is *Lyapunov* stability. A steady state is Lyapunov stable if a small deviation does not lead to any further deviation (it need not actually return to the steady state as is required by the asymptotic stability concept).
14 To be accurate, we are assuming that $P = \min[0, 1 - X_i - X_j]$ to secure this result.
15 The analysis here has been brief. For a fuller technical analysis of the relationships between the three concepts, see Weibull (1995, chapters 2 and 3).
16 In fact, the fancy names for all these things come from Graph Theory: the houses are usually called *nodes*, and the paths connecting them *vertices*.
17 The reason it will not work is that to get the donut you need to stretch some parts and compress others. So, if you want to make a donut shape, use a sheet of stretch material. First make a cylinder and then join the ends together.
18 Well, any topologically equivalent shape to a circle, i.e. any line which does not cross itself and has no ends.
19 The two-dimensionality of the earth's surface is reflected in the fact the each point on the surface can be represented by two numbers: its longitude and latitude.
20 I leave out the possibilities of pollution from pesticides, fertilisers and GM crops.
21 The male pronoun does not reflect any presumed irrationality on the part of farmers, although it certainly helps to be crazy if you are a farmer nowadays.
22 We can see the 'imitate your best neighbour' as a heuristic algorithm as discussed in Chapter 7.
23 Remember, since the top and the bottom are connected, there are two borders.

24 There are obvious exceptions here, such as non-profit organisations, or owner-managed firms. However, all commercial organisations are covered by bankruptcy laws and the requirement to be solvent (i.e. a positive cash flow).

25 This needs to be adjusted for risk: the risk-adjusted rate of return needs to be equalised across all industries and firms.

26 In fact, since the identity of the firms is irrelevant, we treat $\{i,j\}$ as identical to $\{j,i\}$: hence without loss of generality we write the pairs as $\{i,j\}$ with $i \leqslant j$.

27 As in the Atkinson and Suppes (1958) 'finite Markov model", where there is a probability that at time $t+1$ the firm will switch from the strategy it plays at t: the key difference with the present chapter is that we use an explicit aspiration-based model.

28 It is straightforward to allow for firm-specific aspirations.

29 In fact, as the British physicist Stephen Hawkins discovered, due to weird quantum effects, black holes do radiate a bit, so matter does escape.

30 I would like to thank Paolo Lupi for implementing this programme in Gauss.

31 We did not allow for a wider grid range (e.g. [0, 1]), because the additional strategies are often ones with very low or zero profits: they slow down the simulation without adding any extra insight

References

Aaronsen, T., Lofgren, K. and Sjogren, T., 1998. 'On wage setting in dynamic general equilibrium under public consumption externalities', *Umeå Economic Studies* 467.

Abreu, D., 1986. 'Extremal equilibria of oligopolistic supergames', *Journal of Economic Theory*, 39(1), 191–225.

Abreu, D. and Rubenstein, A., 1988. 'The structure of Nash-equilibria in repeated games with finite automata', *Econometrica*, 56, 1259–81.

Akerlof, G. and Dickens, W. 1982. 'The economic consequences of cognitive-dissonance', *American Economic Review*, 72(3), pp. 307–19.

Akerlof, G. and Yellen, J., 1985a. 'A near-rational model of the business cycle with wage and price inertia', *Quarterly Journal of Economics*, 100(Supp), 823–38.

Akerlof, G. and Yellen, J., 1985b. 'Can small deviations from rationality make significant differences to economic equilibria?', *American Economic Review*, 75, 708–21.

Alchian, A., 1950. 'Uncertainty, evolution and economic theory', *Journal of Political Economy*, 58, 211–22.

Allen, B. and Hellwig, M., 1986. 'Bertrand–Edgeworth oligopoly in large markets', *Review of Economic Studies*, 53, 175–204.

Aloi, M. and Santoni, M., 1997. 'Decentralised fiscal policy in an imperfectly competitive federal economy', *The Manchester School of Economic and Social Studies*, 45, 353–78.

Andersen, T. M., Rasmussen, B. S. and Sorensen, J. R., 1996. 'Optimal fiscal policy in open economies with labour market distortions', *Journal of Public Economics*, 63, 103–17.

Arrow, K., 1959. 'Towards a theory of price adjustment', in M. Abramowitz (ed.). *The Allocation of Economic Resources*, Stanford: Stanford University Press.

Ascari, G., 1997. 'Optimising agents, staggered wages and persistence in the real effects of money shocks', *Warwick Economic Research Paper*, 486, September.

Ascari, G., 1998. 'Superneutrality of money in staggered wage setting models', *Macro-economic Dynamics*, 2, 383–400.

Ascari, G. and Rankin, N., 1997. 'Staggered wages and disinflation dynamics: what can more microfoundations tell us?', *CEPR Discussion Papers*, 1763.

Atkinson, R. and Suppes, P., 1958. 'An analysis of two-person game situations in terms of statistical learning theory', *Journal of Experimental Psychology*, 55, 369–78.

Axelrod, R., 1984. *The Evolution of Cooperation*, London, Penguin.

Bala, V. and Goyal, S., 1998. 'Learning from neighbours', *Review of Economic Studies*, 65, 595–621.

Ball, L., 1997. 'Efficient rules for monetary policy', Johns Hopkins University, Mimeo.

Ball, R. and Bodkin, R., 1963. 'Income, the price level, and generalised multipliers in a Keynesian economy', *Metroeconomica*, 15, 59–81.

Ball, L., Mankiw, N. G. and Romer, D., 1988. 'The New Keynesian economics and the output–inflation trade-off', *Brookings Papers on Economic Activity*, 1, 1–82.

Ball, L. and Romer, D., 1990. 'Real rigidities and the non-neutrality of money', *Review of Economic Studies*, 57, 179–98.

Barro, R. J., 1977. 'Unanticipated money growth and unemployment in the US', *American Economic Review*, 67, 101–15.

Barro, R. J. and Grossman, H., 1971. 'A general disequilibrium theory of income and employment', *American Economic Review*, 61, 82–92.

Barro, R. J. and Grossman, H., 1976. *Money, Employment, and Inflation*, Cambridge, Cambridge University Press.

Bean, C., 1998. 'The new UK monetary arrangements', *Economic Journal*, 108, 1795–1809.

Bendor, J., Mookherjee, D. and Ray, D., 1994. 'Aspirations, adaptive learning and cooperation in repeated games', *CENTER Discussion Paper*, 9442.

Bénassy, J.-P., 1973. 'Disequilibrium theory', PhD dissertation, Department of Economics, University of California at Berkeley.

Bénassy, J.-P., 1975. 'NeoKeynesian disequilibrium theory in a monetary economy', *Review of Economic Studies*, 42, 503–23.

Bénassy, J.-P., 1976. 'A disequilibrium approach to monopolistic price setting and general monopolistic equilibrium', *Review of Economic Studies*, 43, 69–81.

Bénassy, J.-P., 1978. 'A Neo-Keynesian model of price and quantity determination in disequilibrium', in G. Schwodiauer (ed.), *Equilibrium and Disequilibrium in Economic Theory*, Dordrecht, Reidel.

Bénassy, J.-P., 1989. 'On the role of market size in imperfect competition: a Bertrand–Edgeworth–Chamberlin synthesis', *Review of Economic-Studies*; 56, 217–34.

Bénassy, J., 1995. 'Classical and Keynesian features in macroeconomic models with imperfect competition', in H. D. Dixon and N. Rankin (eds), *The New Macroeconomics*, Cambridge, Cambridge University Press, 15–33.

Bentham, J., 1789. 'Introduction to the principles of morals and legislation', in M. Warnock (ed.), *Utilitarianism*, London, Fontana, 179–214.

Bentley, J. and Saxe, J., 1980. 'An analysis of two heuristics for the Euclidean travelling salesman problem', *Proceedings of the 18th Allerton Conference of Communication, Control and Computing*.

Bertrand, J., 1883. 'Review of Cournot's "*Recherches sur la Théorie Mathémathique de la Richesse*"', *Journal des Savants*, 449–50.

Bhaskar, V., 1990. 'Wage relativities and the natural range of unemployment', *Economic Journal*, 100, 60–6.

Blanchard, O. and Kiyotaki, N., 1987. 'Monopolistic competition and the effects of aggregate demand', *American Economic Review*, 77, 647–66.

Blume, L., 1993. 'The statistical mechanics of strategic interaction', *Games and Economic Behaviour*, 5, 387–424.

Blume, L. and Easley, D., 1992. 'Evolution and market behaviour', *Journal of Economic Theory*, 58, 211–21.

Borgers, T. and Sarin, R., 1997. 'Learning through reinforcement and the replicator dynamics', *Journal of Economic Theory*, 77, 1–14.

Brander, J. and Spencer, B., 1983. 'Strategic commitment with R&D: the symmetric case', *Bell Journal of Economics*, 14, 225–35.

Brander, J., and Spencer, B., 1984. 'Export subsidies and international market share rivalry', *NBER Working Paper*, 1404.

Branson, W., 1980. *Macroeconomic Theory and Policy*, New York, Harper Row.

Brock, W. and Scheinkman, J., 1985. 'Price-setting supergames with capacity constraints', *Review of Economic Studies*, 52, 371–82.

Caplin, A. and Spulber, D., 1987. 'Menu costs and the neutrality of money', *Quarterly Journal of Economics*, 102, 703–26.

Chamberlin, E., 1933. *The Theory of Monopolistic Competition*, Cambridge, MA, Harvard University Press.

Chari, V. V., Kehoe, P. J. and McGrattan, E. R., 2000. 'Sticky price models of the business cycle: can the contract multiplier solve the persistence problem?', *Econometrica*, 68, 1151–80.

Cheng, L., 1985. 'Comparing Bertrand and Cournot equilibria: a geometric approach', *Rand Journal of Economics*, 16, 146–52.

Cho, I., 1987. 'A refinement of sequential equilibria', *Econometrica*, 55, 1367–89.

Clower, R., 1965. 'The Keynesian counter-revolution: a theoretical appraisal', reprinted in R. Clower (ed.), *Monetary Theory*, Harmondsworth, Penguin.

Coleman, J., 1966. *Medical Innovation: A Diffusion Study*. New York, Bobbs-Merrill.

Cooley, T. F. and Hansen, G. D., 1995. 'Money and the business cycle', in T. F. Cooley (ed.), *Frontiers of Business Cycle Research*, Princeton, Princeton University Press.

Cooper, R. and John, A., 1988. 'Coordinating coordination failures in Keynesian models', *Quarterly Journal of Economics*, 103, 441–63.

Cournot, A., 1938. *Recherches sur la Théorie Mathémathique de la Richesse*, trans N. T. Bacon; London, Hafner, 1960.

Cross, R., 1995. *The Natural Rate of Unemployment: Reflections on 25 Years of the Hypothesis*, London, Cambridge University Press.

Cyert, R. M. and De Groot, M., 1970. 'Multiperiod decision models with alternating choices as a solution to the duopoly problem', *Quarterly Journal of Economics*, 84, 410–29.

Cyert, R. M. and March, J. G., 1963. *A Behavioural Theory of the Firm*, Englewood Cliffs, NJ, Prentice-Hall.

Danthine, J. P. and Donaldson, J. B., 1990. 'Efficiency wages and the business cycle puzzle', *European Economic Review*, 34, 1275–1301.

Danthine, J. P. and Donaldson, J. B., 1993. 'Methodological and empirical issues in real business cycle theory', *European Economic Review*, 37, 1–35.

Dasgupta, P. and Maskin, E., 1986a. 'The existence of equilibrium in discontinuous economic games, I: theory', *Review of Economic Studies*, 53, 1–26.

Dasgupta, P. and Maskin, E., 1986b. 'The existence of equilibrium in discontinuous economic games, II: applications', *Review of Economic Studies*, 53, 27–42.

Dawkins, R., 1986. *The Blind Watchmaker*, London, Longman.

Debreu, G., 1952. 'A social equilibrium existence theorem', *Proceedings of the National Academy of Sciences*, 38, 886–93.

Debreu, G., 1959. *Theory of Value*. New York, Wiley.

Denis, A., 1997. 'Collective and Individual Rationality in Economics: The Invisible Hand of God in Adam Smith', City University, London, mimeo.

Diamond, P., 1982. 'Aggregate demand management in search equilibrium', *Journal of Political Economy*, 90, 881–94.

Dixit, A. and Stiglitz, J., 1977. 'Monopolistic competition and optimum product diversity', *American Economic Review*, 67, 297–308.

Dixon, H. D., 1984. 'The existence of mixed-strategy equilibria in a price-setting oligopoly with convex costs', *Economics Letters*, 16, 205–12.

Dixon, H. D., 1985. 'Strategic investment in a competitive industry', *Journal of Industrial Economics*, 33, 205–12.

Dixon, H. D., 1986a. 'Cournot and Bertrand outcomes as equilibria in a strategic metagame', *Economic Journal*, Conference Supplement, 96, 59–70.

Dixon, H. D., 1986b. 'Strategic investment and consistent conjectures', *Oxford Economic Papers*, 38, 111–28.

Dixon, H. D., 1987a. 'Approximate Bertrand equilibria in a replicated industry', *Review of Economic Studies*, 54, 47–62.

Dixon, H. D., 1987b. 'The general theory of household and market contingent demand', *The Manchester School*, 55, 287–304.

Dixon H. D., 1987c. 'A simple model of imperfect competition with Walrasian features', *Oxford Economic Papers*, 39, 134–60.

Dixon, H. D., 1988a. 'Unions, oligopoly and the natural range of unemployment', *Economic Journal*, 88, 1127–47.

Dixon, H. D., 1988b. 'Oligopoly theory made simple', in S. Davies *et al.* (eds), *Economics of Industrial Organisation*, Harlow, Longman, Ch. 6.

Dixon, H. D., 1990. 'Equilibrium and explanation', in J. Creedy (ed.), *The Foundation of Economic Thought*, Oxford, Blackwell, 356–93.

Dixon, H. D., 1991. 'Macroeconomic policy in a large unionised economy', *European Economic Review*, 35, 1427–48.

Dixon, H. D., 1993. 'Bertrand–Edgeworth Equilibria when firms set discrete prices', *Bulletin of Economic Research*, 45, 257–68.

Dixon, H. D., 1995. 'Of coconuts, decomposition, and a jackass: a geneology of the natural rate of unemployment', in R. Cross (ed.), *The Natural Rate 25 Years on*, Cambridge, Cambridge University Press, 57–74.

Dixon, H. D., 1998. 'Reflections on new Keynesian economics; the role of imperfect competition', in H. Vane and B. Snowden (eds), *Reflections on Modern Macroeconomics*, Aldershot, Edward Elgar, 158–203.

Dixon, H. D., 2000a. 'The role of theory and evidence in new Keynesian economics', in R. Backhouse and A. Salanti (eds), *Theory and Evidence in Macroeconomics*, Oxford, Oxford University Press, 203–14.

Dixon, H. D., 2000b. 'Keeping up with the Joneses: competition and the evolution of collusion', *Journal of Economic Behavior and Organization*, 43, 223–38.

Dixon, H. D. and Lawler, P., 1996. 'Imperfect competition and the fiscal multiplier', *Scandinavian Journal of Economics*, 98, 219–31.

Dixon, H. D. and Lupi, P., 1996. 'Learning with a known average: a simulation study of alternative learning rules', presented at the 3rd international conference in computing and finance, Stanford, July 1997.

Dixon, H. D. and Manning, A., 1986. 'Competition and efficiency: an overview', Birkbeck College, mimeo.

Dixon, H. D. and Maskin, E., 1985. 'The existence of equilibrium with price-setting firms', Harvard University, mimeo.

Dixon, H. D. and Rankin, N., 1994. 'Imperfect competition and macroeconomics: a survey', *Oxford Economic Papers*, 46, 171–99.

Dixon, H. D. and Rankin, N., 1995. *The New Macroeconomics: Imperfect Markets and Policy Effectiveness*, Cambridge, Cambridge University Press.

Dubey, P., 1982. 'Price–quantity strategic market games', *Econometrica*, 50, 111–26.

Eaton, J. and Grossman, G., 1984. 'Strategic capacity investment and product market competition', *Woodrow Wilson School Discussion Paper*, 80.

Eaton, J. and Grossman, G., 1986. 'Optimal trade and industrial policy under oligopoly', *Quarterly Journal of Economics*, 43, 383–406.

Edgeworth, F., 1889. 'The pure theory of monopoly', reprinted in F. Edgeworth, *Collected Papers Relating to Political Economy*, 1, London, Macmillan, 1925.

Ekelund, B., Herbert, R., Tollinson, R., Andersen, G. and Davidson, A., 1996. *Sacred Trust: The Medieval Church as an Economic Firm*, Oxford, Oxford University Press.

Ellison, G., 1993. 'Learning, local interaction and coordination', *Econometrica*, 61, 1047–71.

Ellison, M. and Scott, A., 1998. 'Sticky prices and volatile output: or when is a Phillips curve not a Phillips curve', *CEPR Discussion Paper*, 1849.

Erceg, C., 1997. 'Nominal wage rigidities and the propagation of monetary disturbances', Board of Governors of the Federal Reserve System, mimeo.

Fan, K., 1952. 'Fixed point and minimax theories in locally convex topological spaces', *Proceedings of the National Academy of Sciences*, 38, 121–6.

Fershtman, C., 1985. 'Managerial incentives as a strategic variable in a duopolistic environment', *International Journal of Industrial Organisation*, 3, 245–53.

Fischer, F., 1981. 'Stability, disequilibrium awareness, and the perception of new opportunities', *Econometrica*, 49, 279–317.

Fisher, M., 1976. 'The new microeconomics of unemployment', in G. Worswick (ed.), *The Concept and Measurement of Involuntary Unemployment*, London, Allen & Unwin, 35–58.

Fischer, S., 1977. 'Long-term contracts, rational expectations, and the optimal money supply rule', *Journal of Political Economy*, 85, 191–205.

Frank, R., 1997. 'The frame of reference as a public good', *Economic Journal*, 107, 1832–47.

Friedman, J. W., 1978. *Oligopoly and the Theory of Games*, Amsterdam, NHPC.

Friedman, M., 1968. 'The role of monetary policy', *American Economic Review*, 58(1), 1–17.

Friedman, M., 1975. 'Inflation vs unemployment: an evaluation of the Phillips Curve', *Institute of Economic Affairs Occasional Paper*, 44, London, IEA.

Friedman, M., 1977. 'Inflation and unemployment', *Journal of Political Economy*, 85, 451–72.

Fudenberg, D. and Levine, D. K., 1998. *The Theory of Learning in Games*, Cambridge, MA, MIT Press.

Fudenberg, D. and Maskin, E., 1986. 'The Folk theorem for repeated games with discounting and incomplete information', *Econometrica*, 54, 533–44.

Gal-Or, E., 1986. 'First and second mover advantages', *International Economic Review*, 26, 649–53.

Glicksberg, I., 1952. 'A further generalisation of the Kakutani fixed point theorem with application to Nash-equilibrium points', *Proceedings of the National Academy of Sciences*, 38, 170–4.

Hahn, F. and Negishi, T., 1962. 'A theorem on non-tâtonnement stability', *Econometrica*, 30, 463–9.

Hairault, J. O. and Portier, F., 1993. 'Money, new-Keynesian macroeconomics and the business cycle', *European Economic Review*, 37, 1533–68.

Hall, R. L. and Hitch, C. J., 1939. 'Price theory and business behaviour', *Oxford Economic Papers*, 2, 12–45; reprinted in P. Andrews and T. Wilson (eds), *Oxford Studies in the Price Mechanism*, Oxford, Oxford University Press, 1951.

Hansen, G., 1985. 'Indivisible labour and the business cycle', *Journal of Monetary Economics*, 16, 309–27.

Hart, O., 1979. 'Monopolistic competition in a large economy with differential commodities', *Review of Economic Studies*, 46, 1–30.

Hart, O., 1982. 'Perfect competition and optimal product differentiation', in A. Mas Collel (ed.), *The Non-Cooperative Foundations of Perfect Competition*, New York, Academic Press.

Hathaway, N. and Rickard, J., 1979. 'Equilibria of price-setting and quantity setting duopolies', *Economic Letters*, 3, 133–7.

Hicks, J. R., 1935. 'Annual survey of economic theory: the theory of monopoly', *Econometrica*, 3, 1–20.

Hicks, J. R., 1939. *Value and Capital*, Oxford, Oxford University Press.

Hoover, K. D., 1984. 'Two types of monetarism', *Journal of Economic Literature*, 22, 58–76.

Hoover, K. D., 1988. *The New Classical Macroeconomics: A Sceptical Inquiry*, Oxford, Blackwell.

Hume, D., 1750. 'Of money', in D. Hume, *Essays*, Oxford, Oxford University Press.

Ireland, N., 1986. *Product Differentiation and the Non-Price Decisions of Firms*, Oxford, Blackwell.

Jeanne, O., 1997. 'Generating real persistent effects of monetary shocks: how much nominal rigidity do we really need?', *European Economic Review*, 42, 1009–32.

Jones, H., 1975. *Modern Theories of Economic Growth*, London, Nelson.

Kahn, R., 1931. 'The relation of home investment to unemployment', *Economic Journal*, 41, 173–98.

Kalecki, M., 1936, 'Pare uwag o Teirii Keynesa', *Ekonomista* (Poland).

Kalai, E. and Stanford, W., 1988. 'Finite rationality and interpersonal complexity in repeated games', *Econometrica*, 56, 397–410.

Kaldor, N., 1957. 'A model of economic growth', *Economic Journal*, 591–624.

Karandikar, R., Mookherjee, D., Ray, D. and Vega-Redondo, F., 1998. 'Evolving aspirations and cooperation', *Journal of Economic Theory*, 80, 292–331.

Keynes, J. M., 1936. *The General Theory of Employment, Interest, and Money*, London, Macmillan.

Kiley, M. T., 1997. 'Staggered price setting, partial adjustment, real rigidities, and sunspots', Board of Governors of the Federal Reserve System, mimeo.

Klemperer, P. and Meyer, M., 1986. 'Price competition vs quantity competition: the role of uncertainty', *Rand Journal of Economics*, 17(4).

Kotler, R., 1986. *The Principles of Marketing*, 3rd edn, New York, Prentice-Hall.

Kornai, J., 1971. *Anti-Equilibrium*, Amsterdam, North-Holland/Elsevier.

Kreps, D. and Scheinkman, J., 1983. 'Quantity pre-commitment and Bertrand competition yield Cournot outcomes', *Bell Journal of Economics*, 14, 326–37.

Kreps, D. and Wilson, R., 1982a. 'Sequential equilibria', *Econometrica*, 50, 863–94.

Kreps, D. and Wilson, R., 1982b. 'Reputation and imperfect information', *Journal of Economic Theory*, 27, 253–9.

Kreps, D., Milgrom, P. and Wilson, R., 1982. 'Rational cooperation in the finitely repeated prisoner's dilemma', *Journal of Economic Theory*, 27, 245–52.

Lant T., 1992. 'Aspiration level adaptation – an empirical Exploration', *Management Science*, 38, 623–44.

Layard, R. and Nickell, S. J., 1985. 'The causes of British unemployment', *National Institute Economic Review*, 111, 62–85.

Layard, R. and Nickell, S. J., 1986. 'Unemployment in Britain', *Economica*, 53, 121–69.

Leijonhufvud, A., 1968. *On Keynesian Economics and the Economics of Keynes*, Milton Keynes, Open University Press.

Levačić R. and Rebmann, A., 1982. *Macroeconomics: An Introduction to Keynesian-Neoclassical Controversies*, 2nd edn, London, Macmillan.

Lipsey, R. G., 1960. 'The relation between unemployment and the rate of change of money wage rates in the UK, 1862–1957: a further analysis', *Economica*, 27, 1–31.

Lewin, K., 1936. *Principles of Topological Psychology*, New York, McGraw-Hill.

Lockwood, B., 1984. 'Perfect equilibria in repeated games with discounting', *Cambridge University Economic Theory Discussion Paper*, 65.

Lockwood, B., 1987. 'Some recent developments in the theory of non-cooperative games and its economic applications', in Pearce and Rau (eds), *Economic Perspectives*, .

Lucas, R. E. J., 1979. 'An equilibrium model of the business cycle', *Journal of Political Economy*, 83, 1113–44.

Lucas, R. E. J., 1981. *Studies in Business-Cycle Theory*, Cambridge, MA, MIT Press.

Lucas, R. E. J. and Rapping, L., 1969. 'Real wages, employment, and inflation', *Journal of Political Economy*, 77, 721–54.

Luce, R. and Raiffa, H., 1957. *Games and Decisions*, New York, Wiley.

Lyons, B., 1986. 'Mixed-motive duopoly', University of East Anglia, mimeo.

Malinvaud, E., 1977. *The Theory of Unemployment Reconsidered*, Oxford, Blackwell.

Mankiw, N. G., 1985. 'Small menu costs and large business cycles: a macroeconomic model of monopoly', *Quarterly Journal of Economics*, 100, 529–39.

Mankiw, N. G., 1986. 'Issues in Keynesian macroeconomics: a review essay', *Journal of Monetary Economics*, 18, 217–23.

Mankiw N. G., 1988. 'Imperfect competition and the Keynsian cross', *Economics Letters*, 26, 7–13.

Mankiw, N. G. and Romer D., 1991. *New Keynesian Economics*, Cambridge, MA, MIT Press.

Manning, A., 1990. 'Imperfect competition multiple equilibria and unemployment Policy', *Economic Journal*, 100, Supplement, 151–62.

Manning, A., 1992. 'Multiple equilibria in the British labour market: some empirical evidence', *European Economic Review*, 36, 1333–65.

214   *References*

Mansfield, E., 1961. 'Technical change and the rate of innovation', *Econometrica*, 29, 741–66.
Marimon, R., 1987. 'Krep's "Three essays on capital markets". Almost ten years later', *Discussion Paper*, 245, Minnesota University.
Marris, R., 1964. *Managerial Capitalism*, London, Macmillan.
Marris, R., 1991, *Reconstructing Keynesian Economics with Imperfect Competion: A Desk-Top Simulation*, London, Edward Elgar.
Marshall, A., 1890. *Principles of Economics*, London, Macmillan.
Maynard-Smith, J., 1982. *Evolution and the Theory of Games*, Cambridge, Cambridge University Press.
Milgrom, P. and Roberts, J., 1982a. 'Predation, reputation and entry deterrence', *Journal of Economic Theory*, 27, 280–312.
Milgrom, P. and Roberts, J., 1982b. 'Limit pricing and entry under incomplete information: an equilibrium analysis', *Econometrica*, 50, 443–55.
Modigliani, F. and Samuelson, P., 1966. 'The Pasinetti paradox in neoclassical and more general models', *Review of Economic Studies*, 76, 269–301.
Moss, S. and Rae, J., 1992. *Artificial Intelligence and Economic Analysis*, Aldershot, Edward Elgar.
Muellbauer, J. and Portes, R., 1978, 'Macroeconomic models with quantity rationing', *Economic Journal*, 88, 788–821.
Naish, H. F., 1993, 'Real business cycles in a Keynesian macromodel', *Oxford Economic Papers*, 45, 618–38.
Ng, Y., 1997. 'A case for happiness, cardinalism and interpersonal comparability', *Economic Journal*, 107, 1848–58.
Okuguchi, K., 1987. 'Equilibrium prices in the Bertrand and Cournot oligopolies', *Journal of Economic Theory*, 42(1), 128–39.
Oswald, A., 1997a. 'Happiness and economic performance', *Economic Journal*, 107, 1815–31.
Oswald, A., 1997b. 'The missing piece of the unemployment puzzle', Warwick University, mimeo.
Ott, D. J., Ott, A. F. and Yoo, J. H., 1975. *Macroeconomic Theory*, New York, McGraw-Hill.
Palomino, F. and Vega-Redondo, F, 1999. 'Convergence of aspirations and (partial) cooperation in the Prisoner's Dilemma', *International Journal of Game Theory*, 28, 465–88.
Parkin, M., 1986. 'The output–inflation trade-off when prices are costly to change', *Journal of Political Economy*, 94, 200–24.
Patinkin, D., 1965. *Money, Interest and Prices*, 2nd edn, New York, Harper & Row.
Phillips, A. W., 1958. 'The relationship between unemployment and the rate of change of money wage rates in the UK 1861–1957', *Economica*, 25, 283–99.
Pigou, A., 1941. *The Veil of Money*, London, Macmillan.
Polya, G., 1957. *How to Solve It*, Princeton, NJ, Princeton University Press.
Prescott, E., 1986. 'Theory ahead of business cycle measurement', *Federal Reserve Bank of Minneapolis Quarterly Review*, 10, 9–22.
Quandt, R., 1983. 'Computational problems and methods', *Handbook of Econometrics*, 1, 699–764.
Radner, R., 1980. 'Collusive behavior in noncooperative epsilon-equilibria of oligopolies with long but finite lives', *Journal of Economic Theory*, 22, 136–54.
Radner, R., 1986. 'Repeated principal–agent games with discounting', *Econometrica*, 53, 1173–97.
Robinson, J., 1933. *The Economics of Imperfect Competition*, London, Macmillan.
Robinson, J., 1960. *Accumulation of Capital*, London, Macmillan.
Romer, D., 1993. 'The new Keynesian synthesis', *Journal of Economic Perspectives*, 7, 5–22.

Rotemberg, J. J. and Woodford, M., 1995. 'Dynamic general models with imperfectly competitive product markets', *Annales d'économie et de statistique*, 37–38, 357–410.

Rotemberg, J. J. and Woodford, M., 1996. 'Imperfect competition and the effects of energy price increases on economic activity', *Journal of Money, Credit, and Banking*, 28(4), 549–77.

Rubenstein, A., 1979. 'Equilibrium in supergames with the overtaking criterion', *Journal of Economic Theory*, 21, 1–9.

Rubenstein, A., 1986. 'Finite automata play the repeated prisoner's dilemma', *Journal of Economic Theory*, 3, 83–96.

Rudgely, R., 1998. *The Lost Civilisations of the Stone Age*, London, Century.

Ryan, B. and Gross, N., 1943. 'The diffusion of hybrid seed corn in two Iowa communities', *Rural Sociology*, 8, 15–24.

Salop, S., 1979. 'A model of the natural rate of unemployment', *American Economic Review*, 69, 117–25.

Samuelson, L., 1997. *Evolutionary Games and Equilibrium Selection*, Cambridge, MA, MIT Press.

Samuelson, P., 1948. 'The simple mathematics of income determination', in P. Samuelson, *Income, Employment and Policy*, New York, Norton.

Samuelson, P., 1968. 'Classical and neoclassical monetary theory', *Canadian Journal of Economics*, 1, 1–15.

Santoni, M., 1996. 'Union-oligopoly sequential bargaining – trade and industrial policies', *Oxford Economic Papers*, 48, 640–63.

Sargent, T., 1993. *Bounded Rationality in Macroeconomics*, Oxford, Oxford Unviersity Press.

Sargent, T. and Wallis, N., 1976. 'Rational expectations and the theory of economic policy', *Journal of Monetary Economics*, 2, 168–83.

Selten, R., 1965. 'Spieltheoretic Behandlung eines Oligopolmodells mit Nachtrageträgheit', *Zeitschrift für die Gesamte Staatswissenschaft*, 121, 301–24, 667–89.

Selten, R., 1980. 'A note on evolutionary stable strategies in asymmetric animal contests', *Journal of Theoretical Biology*, 84, 93–101.

Shackle, G., 1974. *Keynesian Kaleidics*, Edinburgh: Edinburgh University Press.

Shubik, M., 1959. *Strategy and Market Structure*, New York, John Wiley.

Siegel, S., 1957. 'Level of aspiration and decision making', *Psychological Review*, 64, 253–62.

Silvestre, J., 1993. 'The market power foundations of macroeconomic policy', *Journal of Economic Literature*, 31, 105–41.

Simon, H. A., 1947. *Administrative Behaviour: A Study of Decision-Making Processes in Administrative Organisations*, London, Macmillan.

Simon, H. A., 1981. *The Science of the Artificial*, Cambridge, MA, MIT Press.

Simon, L. K., 1984. 'Bertrand, the Cournot Paradigm and the theory of perfect competition', *Review of Economic Studies*, 51, 209–30.

Singh, N. and Vives, X., 1984. 'Price and quantity competition in a differentiated duopoly', *Rand Journal of Economics*, 15, 540–54.

Skidelsky, R., 1992. *John Maynard Keynes. Volume 2: The Economist as Saviour*, London, Macmillan.

Smith, A., 1759. *The Theory of Moral Sentiments*, Oxford, Oxford University Press.

Smith, A., 1776. *The Wealth of Nations*, London, Penguin.

Spence, M., 1974. *Market Signalling*, Cambridge, MA, Harvard University Press.

Startz, R., 1989. 'Monopolistic competition as a foundation for Keynesian macroeconomic models', *Quarterly Journal of Economics*, 104, 737–52.

Sutherland, A., 1995. 'Menu costs and aggregate price dynamics', Chapter 16 in H. Dixon and N. Rankin, *The New Macroeconomics: Imperfect Markets and Policy Effectiveness*, Cambridge, Cambridge University Press.

Svensson, L., 1997. 'Inflation targeting: implementing and monitoring inflation targets', *European Economic Review*, 41, 1111–46.

Taylor, J., 1979. 'Staggered wage setting in a micro model', *American Economic Review*, 69, 108–13.

Thaler, R., 1991. *Quasi Rational Economics*, New York, Russell Sage.

Thaler, R., 1992. *The Winner's Curse: Paradoxes and Anomalies of Economic Life*, New York, Free Press.

Thaler, R., 1993. *Advances in Behavioral Finance*, New York, Russell Sage.

Tirole, J., 1988. *The Theory of Industrial Organisation*, Cambridge, MA, MIT Press.

Vane, H. and Snowden, B., 1998. *Reflections on Modern Macroeconomics*, Aldershot, Edward Elgar.

Vega-Rodondo, F., 1996. *Evolution, Games and Economic Behaviour*, Oxford, Oxford University Press.

Vega-Redondo, F., 1997. 'The evolution of Walrasian behavior', *Econometrica*, 65, 375–84.

Venables, A., 1985. 'International trade, industrial policy and, imperfect competition', *CEPR Discussion Paper*, 74.

Vickers, J., 1985a. 'Delegation and the theory of the firm', *Economic Journal*, 95 (Supplement), 138–47.

Vickers, J., 1985b. 'Strategic competition among the few – some recent developments', *Oxford Journal of Economic Policy*, .

Vives, X., 1985a. 'On the efficiency of Cournot and Bertrand equilibria with product differentiation', *Journal of Economic Theory*, 36, 166–75.

Vives, X., 1985b. 'Nash equilibrium with monotone best responses', University of Pennsylvania, mimeo.

Vives, X., 1986. 'Commitment, flexibility, and market outcome', *International Journal of Industrial Organisation*, 2, 217–30.

Voltaire, F., 1759. *Candide*, London, Penguin.

von Stackelberg, H., 1934. *Marketform und Gleichgewicht*, Vienna and Berlin.

Weibull, J., 1995. *Evolutionary Game Theory*. Cambridge, MA, MIT Press.

Yarrow, G., 1985. 'Measures of monopoly welfare loss in markets with differentiated products', *Journal of Industrial Economics*, 33, 515–30.

Index